The Lafayette Journal and Courier Presents

MOST MEMORABLE MOMENTS
IN
PURDUE BASKETBALL HISTORY

SPORTS PUBLISHING INC.

CHAMPAIGN, IL

Coordinating Editor: Jim Lefko
Photo Editor: Mike Heinz
Director of Production: Susan M. McKinney
Production Coordinator: Michelle A. Summers
Book Design: Michelle R. Dressen
Dustjacket Design: Terry Hayden

All photographs courtesy of The Lafayette Journal and Courier Library
 and Purdue University

ISBN: 1-57167-256-7

Printed in the United States

804 N. Neil Street
Champaign, IL 61820

www.SportsPublishing.com

CONTENTS

Contents

PURDUE IN FIRST PLACE IN BIG TEN

Fighting Purdue Five Ends Glorious Year

Coffing Plays Brilliant Ball in His Last Game in Purdue Uniform; Scores Five Field Goals; Entire Purdue Quintet Outdoes Itself in Vanquishing Iowa's Comeback Five; Hawkeyes Defense is Stellar One.

March 7, 1921 – Fighting as only a Boilermaker basketball team coached by "Piggy" Lambert can fight and playing spectacular ball throughout the forty minutes of the game, Purdue defeated Iowa in Memorial gymnasium, Saturday night, 21-18. The contest was a glorious climax to a season of ups and downs and reflects a world of credit and commendation upon the coach and the members of the team. Although the Hawkeyes trailed the Boilermakers from the time "Mick" Coffing dropped in a beautiful one from around the center of the floor, the game was filled up with thrills for the spectators, and only when the timer's gun went off, ending the game, was the tension relaxed.

COFFING STARS

To "Mick" Coffing, Purdue's elongated center, goes most of the credit for winning the battle, but due praise must be given every man who got into the game. Don White and Eversman were guarded closer than in any other game this year, but the Hawkeyes failed to realize how dangerous a scoring man Coffing was. It was his long shot after eight minutes of battling out on the floor that gave Purdue a lead which it never relinquished, and it was four other shots made by him during the game that kept Purdue always just ahead of its opponents. The contest was a defensive game from the start and while the Hawkeyes' defensive combination was the best any visiting team has displayed this year, Purdue's was just as good.

PURDUE DEFENSE GOOD

White and Miller made up the keystone of the Boilermakers' defense. Miller at back guard was the old stone wall of old, and but one field goal was put in behind him. White scored nine points in addition to his defensive work. Eversman, Masters and Leverenz gave all they had in every minute of play. Eversman played a wonderful defensive game, and in addition scored a field goal from the floor. The development of this forward has been nothing short of remarkable this year and much should be heard of him during his last two years in college. Masters and Leverenz, who worked the other forward position, were in the thick of the fight throughout. Chaffee and Holwerda, who got into the battle in the closing minutes, played scrappy defensive games.

Kaufman was the main cog in the working of the Iowa machine. His floor work was marvelous and he bolstered up the Hawkeye defense time and time again. He broke up many of Purdue's long passes, and displayed clever dribbling ability.

IOWA ON DEFENSIVE

The game opened fast, with both teams resorting to defensive play, Iowa swinging into their five-man defense. Six minutes of fast playing elapsed before Coffing scored the first points of the game on a field goal from the edge of the foul ring. Coffing again counted, shortly after Iowa had taken time out, when he slipped the ball through from under the basket. Iowa's first point came when Frohwein converted Miller's personal foul into a point. White's two field goals and three free throws completed Purdue's scoring in the first half while Iowa's points came on Shimek's field goal, Lohman's field goal and Frohwein's five free throws.

PURDUE IN LEAD

The half ended shortly after White turned Devin's foul into a point and Purdue held the advantage in the 11-9 score.

Coffing opened the scoring in the second half like he did in the first half by annexing a field goal from the side. Purdue then ran up a comfortable lead of 20-13, but Iowa then clamped down and threatened to even up the score but the final whistle sounded when the score stood 21-18 in Purdue's favor. Iowa scored twice after White had completed Purdue's scoring with a free throw on Shimek's long field goal and Frohwein's five free throws.

Team Captain Don White scored nine points from his guard position in Purdue's 21-18 victory over Iowa.

VICTORY OVER IOWA

Two of Three Teams Can Tie Boilermakers

*Boilermakers' Victory Over Iowa and Illinois'
Unexpected Upset by Chicago Shifts
Standing: Big Ten Season to Close Next
Monday; Deciding Contests Will be Played
Monday and Tuesday of This Week; Two of
Three Teams Have Chance to Tie With
Purdue.*

BIG TEN STANDINGS		Won	Lost	Pct.
	PURDUE	8	4	.667
	Michigan	7	4	.637
	Wisconsin	7	4	.637
	Illinois	7	4	.637
	Indiana	6	4	.600
	Minnesota	5	5	.500
	Iowa	5	5	.500
	Chicago	6	6	.500
	Ohio State	2	9	.182
	Northwestern	1	9	.100

Purdue's victories over Indiana and Iowa and Chicago's unexpected tumbling of Illinois Saturday night furnished material galore for basketball fans over the western conference during the week just finished. The Boilermakers, until Monday night, are undisputed holders of the first position by having defeated Iowa in a thrilling game Saturday night here. The showing of the Purdue team in its last four games, which were played in eight days, three of them on foreign floors, is little short of sensational. But one game was lost, to Michigan, while Northwestern, Indiana and Iowa fell before Purdue's attack.

WHO WILL TIE?

With the Boilermakers firmly entrenched in first, the only question remaining to be decided is just who will share the premier honors with Lambert's heroes. Two of three teams, Michigan, Illinois and Wisconsin, have a chance to crawl up to the top. Either Michigan or Illinois will be in first following the game between those two colleges at Illinois tonight. Michigan is the favorite to win this game, while local sentiment seems to prefer Illinois. Michigan is not particularly popular among Boilermaker fans. The other team, Wisconsin, can make the tie for first place a three-cornered affair by defeating Ohio State. Meanwell's team should certainly come through the Buckeye contest, but dope is rolled too often to make an absolute prediction to that effect. In case the Badgers are defeated, Purdue and the winner of the Michigan-Illinois tilt will be supreme with eight games won and four lost.

Michigan and Wisconsin improved their standing during the week by victories, while Chicago pulled itself into the .500 class by slipping one over on the Suckers. Illinois came near being tripped up by Ohio State earlier in the week, just nosing out the Buckeyes in a hard-fought game.

NEARLY FINISHED

The conference season will be brought to a close this week with the exception of but one game, Iowa-Northwestern, at Iowa, on Monday, March 14. Besides the Michigan-Illinois game, Monday night, another important contest is carded at Bloomington, between Indiana and Minnesota. The tilt will have no bearing on the leaders' positions, but will clear up just who is going to hold up the lower places in the first division. Tuesday night Wisconsin will take on Ohio State at Wisconsin. The Badgers have a chance to tie for first place in this game. Saturday Minnesota and Northwestern clash at Northwestern, and the following Monday the season will close with the Iowa-Northwestern game at Iowa City.

PECULIAR SEASON

The Big Ten basketball season of 1921 has been one of upsets and surprises, and has no parallel for many years back. Purdue, Illinois and Indiana got away to good starts, slipped, came back, slipped again, and only one of the three, Purdue, was able to do the final comeback act which meant the Big Ten title or a tie for it. Michigan and Iowa, with rather poorly arranged schedules, got under way only after having lost a number of games. When these two teams did get to going, however, their performances certainly did raise havoc with the standings. Iowa tumbled the Crimson out of first, took Purdue down in one game, and walloped Northwestern before it was halted by the Boilermakers. No team has been able to stop Michigan, and it looks good to come through against the Suckers Monday night.

Forward A.B. Masters was one of the defensive heroes in Purdue's big win over Iowa, which gave the Boilermakers a share of the Big Ten championship.

PURDUE FACES NYU TONIGHT

Lambert's Fast Quintet to Appear in Feature Contest at Madison Square Garden

Famous Violet Five, Considered Finest in Eastern Basketball History, Favored to Upset Local Outfit; Piggy Plans for Victory Before Crowd of About 17,000

PROBABLE LINEUPS

PURDUE	Position	NEW YORK U.
Kessler (C)	F	Rubenstein (C)
Young	F	Schulman
Elliott	C	Terjesen
Malaska	G	Maidman
Downey	G	Klein

December 28, 1935 – Purdue's basketball squad will dribble-out onto the court at Madison Square Garden, New York City, tonight determined to prove to some 17,000 eastern fans that New York University is not the greatest hardwood combination in the United States. According to eastern reports few games have ever attracted the interest which tonight's Boilermaker-Violet affair is commanding.

Many rate the New York five, coached by the famous Howard Cann, as the greatest quintet in the history of eastern basketball. They declare the Violets can apparently do anything their coach asks of them and accomplish their task with apparent ease. Notre Dame, Pittsburgh, Temple, California and other well known teams have tried to break through the NYU defense during the past two years, but each has been defeated with comparative ease.

LOOK TO PURDUE

Last year Piggy Lambert took a classy Purdue team to Madison Square Garden where it whipped a fast Fordham combination. This favorable impression, along with the great reputation made by Boilermaker teams in the past, has led eastern observers to believe Purdue the only team in the country with a fair chance of winning over Cann's quintet.

Comparative scores against California this year make Lambert's team the underdog. New York whipped the far westerners, 41-26, while Purdue was forced to stage a late rally to come out on top against the Golden Bears, 44-43.

However, Coach Lambert was not allowing this fact to worry him as he prepared to leave for New York Friday noon. Lambert knows his team was off form against the Bears and is sure the Boilermakers will bounce back with a good performance against the Violets.

SMALL COURT

The 80-foot court, which is used by most eastern colleges, is Purdue's real worry. The Boilermaker fast break generally is much more effective on the regulation 90-foot layout. The smaller the floor, the bigger the advantage is for the big men. Purdue leans more toward speed and smaller players.

Lambert's squad left here yesterday noon and was scheduled to arrive in New York this morning at 8 o'clock. A short workout was to be held in the Garden at 10 o'clock in the morning and the big game tonight was carded for 9 o'clock.

New York fans were particularly interested in the prospective battle of the two captains, Bob Kessler and Rubenstein. These two lads are among the country's highest scorers and are expected to lead the way tonight.

Guard Pat Malaska, a dribbling ace, was an integral part of the 1935-36 team that lost to NYU at Madison Square Garden but went on to win one of 11 Big Ten titles under Ward Lambert.

PURDUE LOSES TO NYU, 43-41

Largest Crowd in History of Basketball Witnesses Game

Boilermakers Blow Big 24-14 Advantage as Violets Shoot Sensationally; Young Misses Winning Basket in Last Ten Seconds; Bob Kessler Gains High Point Honors

December 29, 1935 — NEW YORK – (Special) – Over 18,000 persons, the largest crowd in the world ever to see a basketball game, watched New York University's famous Violets nose out a lightning fast Purdue quintet, 43-41, in Madison Square Garden last night. Seldom, if ever, have basketball fans been afforded so many thrills in one game. First, it was Purdue's amazing speed and dribbling and then New York's uncanny shooting which brought deafening roars from the crowd.

FINAL SHOT MISSES

The Violets ran their winning streak to 15 straight last night, but their record was in danger right up until the last ten seconds of the game when Jewell Young missed a comparative setup, which would have given Purdue a victory, 43-42. NYU got the rebound and Malaska fouled one of the Violets as the gun cracked. The free throw was converted to make the final score 43-41.

Purdue dominated the first half's play and looked like a sure winner when it started the second half by increasing its 20-14 advantage to 24-14. Then the New York hurricane struck with sudden force. Piggy Lambert's Boilermakers must have thought they had everything under control, but nothing was further from the truth. One Violet shot after another found the nets. Before Purdue could realize what was taking place, the score was tied at 26-26.

The westerners continued to mill around in bewildered fashion as the rampant Violets went merrily along scoring almost at will. With four minutes left to play, NYU was sailing along in front 42-31.

KESSLER LEADS RALLY

At this point Purdue finally came back to earth. Captain Bob Kessler, All-America forward, led the late Boilermaker assault which all but swept the NYU cagers off the court. Kessler charged under for a basket and then passed to Malaska for another. The Boilermaker star hooked one over his head from the foul line, which landed squarely in the basket. Then Jewell Young, another flashy southpaw, started to work. He hit two free throws and then flipped a one-hander through the net to cut New York's margin to 42-41, with less than a minute to play. The fans howled wildly and players scrambled all over the court during the closing seconds of play. Young took a Purdue pass and dashed under the hoop for what looked like the winning basket for Purdue, but the ball rolled off the hoop and into the New Yorkers' hands and the Violet record was safe.

PURDUE STARTS FAST

The Old Gold and Black netters started out at a dizzy pace, playing the Violets completely off their feet. Young went under to score the first basket of the game and Kessler followed with a long shot which swished through the net. After Kessler made good on a free throw, Jim Seward followed in Young's shot for a basket. Young sniped one from the side and Malaska flashed past two guards for a basket which was not allowed.

With the score standing at 9-0, the Cann-coached quintet rang up three consecutive baskets, but Young hit a free throw and Downey's beautiful pass resulted in another field goal for Kessler. New York staged another rally, but Glen Downey banged away with a long one and followed with a basket from the side. Malaska and Young scored to bring Purdue's advantage to 20-14 at the intermission.

BOILERMAKERS BLOW UP

Lambert's Boilermakers showed no signs of cracking during the first three minutes of the second half, but two long NYU heaves started the Violet machine clicking in baffling fashion and Purdue's defense went all to pieces. Captain Rubenstein and Schulman led the unprecedented New York attack which ran up 28 points in 14 minutes of play.

Captain Bob Kessler and Pat Malaska were the standouts in the Purdue lineup, although Jewell Young and Glen Downey also played some great basketball. Kessler was watched closely, but outscored every man on the floor with five baskets and four free throws. Malaska caught the eye of the fans and critics here with his sensational dribbling and speedy dashes under the basket.

Rubenstein was the star for the winning team, but he received brilliant aid from Klein, Schulman, Terjesen and Witty during the great New York rally.

Purdue to Face Temple Tonight

New York, December 29 – (Special) – Purdue's speedy basketball team remained here today, but was scheduled to leave tomorrow morning for Philadelphia, where it will clash with the strong Temple University quintet in the Philadelphia arena tomorrow night. Lambert's forces were determined to win this tilt in order to gain an even break in the eastern invasion.

PURDUE WINS OPENER, 61-18

New Field House on Display as Lambertmen Pry Lid Off

Johnny Sines Leads Attack Against Indiana State With 23 Points

December 13, 1937 – Purdue's streamlined basketeers, after prying off the 1937-38 hardwood lid in their new fieldhouse Saturday night with a 61-18 victory over Indiana State, will be called upon to face sterner opposition here tonight as they tangle with Xavier University.

Tonight's encounter with Xavier will be in the nature of a homecoming for Clem Crowe, athletic director and coach at the Cincinnati university, a former Lafayette high school star who later gained additional athletic laurels at Notre Dame. Crowe will be the first home town product who has ever brought a collegiate team back to Lafayette against Purdue. The Xavier five is off to a brilliant start this season and hopes to score an upset against the Lambertmen. The game is scheduled for 7:30 and plenty of tickets will be available for late comers.

FIELDHOUSE OPENER

Saturday night Piggy Lambert's new Boilermaker cage edition swarmed all over a hard working Indiana quintet to unofficially open the new sports structure at Purdue. About 6,000 fans were almost as interested in the fieldhouse as in the basketball attraction going on out on the gleaming hardwood.

Wally Marks' Terre Haute giants tried hard and by hitting many long shots were able to keep within firing distance of the Boilermakers, but the visitors were soon so badly outclassed that the contest turned into a rout. Trailing only 30-16 at the half, Indiana State failed to score a single field goal during the last half, two free throws making up the total of Sycamore points in the closing session. In the meantime, Coach Lambert was sending subs into the fray in wholesale lots, one combination looking almost as good as another as far as defensive play was concerned.

SINES GETS 23 POINTS

However, the varsity five, composed largely of veterans, provided most of the offensive thrills. With Johnny Sines leading the way, Piggy's favored cagers turned in one circus play after another to confound their foes. Sines scored 16 points in the first 16 minutes and he was good for 23 during the evening. Young, Anderson, Dickinson, Malaska, Beretta, Zink, Hutt and others were playing fine offensive basketball and it was the clever passing of the combination as a whole which shook Sines loose for many of his 11 field goals.

Practically all Purdue baskets were scored on fast drives under the hoop, with deft ball handling sending the leather zipping from one pair of hands to another.

Indiana State, unable to keep pace with Lambert's fast style of play, and experiencing difficulty working the ball under the hoop, tried for a while to use its height advantage on follow-up shots. However, Marks' cagers soon started shooting from long range whenever they got their hands on the ball in Purdue territory. Watson and Julian bagged a couple but the Sycamores soon lost their shooting eyes and were almost swept off the court by the Old Gold and Black.

PLEASING PICTURE

The fieldhouse presented a pleasing picture to the hungry eyes of Boilermaker basketball fans. Although the cage arena wasn't filled the crowd was the largest ever to see a basketball game in this city.

GRAHAM CRACKERS

By Gordon Graham

Purdue's new fieldhouse has the enthusiastic stamp of approval of 6,000 basketball fans...it's a grand place to watch a basketball game. The floor is a picturesque sight...the lighting is perfect...a large crowd can be handled in quick, business-like fashion...Bob Woodworth, Pop Doan and the many other Purdue officials who have worked hard the past few weeks making final arrangements for fieldhouse basketball, deserve slaps on the back for the fine job they have done.

Piggy Lambert's Boilermakers were determined they should do nothing to detract from the glittering picture...they looked just as good as the fieldhouse.

Those rule changes seem to be right down Purdue's alley...the boys appear in good condition and they certainly keep that basketball moving around the premises.

Of course, it is very likely that Indiana State wasn't strong enough to provide a good warmup test. But Xavier should be able to push the Lambertmen hard enough so that tonight's crowd will be able to get a fair line on the 1937-38 Purdue cage prospects.

Coach Ward "Piggy" Lambert helped start a new era in Purdue basketball with the opening of the fieldhouse in 1937. Earlier in the decade, he worked with Charles "Stretch" Murphy.

BOILERMAKERS FACE INDIANA STATE IN DREAM FIELDHOUSE

Boilermakers Victory Over Iowa and Illinois'
Expect Large Crowd to See First Game in
New Athletic Structure; Lambert Likely to
Start Veterans; Visitors Have Height, But
Lack Experience; Plenty of Tickets

PROBABLE LINEUP

PURDUE	Position	INDIANA STATE
Sines	F	O'Leary
Young	F	Cissna
Anderson	C	Julian
Dickinson	G	Wood
Beretta or Malaska	G	Fick or Watson

OFFICIALS – Referee: Bray, Xavier; Umpire: Chandler, Butler.

December 11, 1937 – Purdue's commodious new fieldhouse will be opened to the basketball public for the first time tonight as the Boilermakers launch the hardwood campaign against the Indiana State Teachers quintet in the first of a trio of home games scheduled within five days. The current Purdue hardwood offering, which will attempt to make up in speed what it lacks in height, will meet Xavier here Monday and Detroit Wednesday before heading on an extended holiday tour that calls for games against DePaul and Loyola in Chicago, Denver at Denver, and Southern California and UCLA at Los Angeles.

EXPECT FAST BREAK

Nosed out of at least a share of the Big Ten title for the first time in four years last season when they finished fourth with eight victories and four losses, the Boilermakers are expected to stick to a typical Lambert fast-break type of offense in their bid for 1937-38 honors.

STARTING PROBABILITIES

Although Lambert was undecided on his starting combination, he is expected to stick to a largely veteran quintet against the Sycamore five here tonight that will make the Boilermakers look like comparative midgets. Jewell Young, All-America forward, who shattered the Big Ten scoring record last season, is expected to team at forward with

John Sines, another senior veteran, with Gene Anderson, sleight-of-hand passer who earned his spurs as a sophomore, at center. Tom Dickinson, fire-horse junior, and either Pat Malaska, speedy dribbling senior, or Fred Beretta, promising sophomore, are expected to be at the guards.

PARKING DOPE

For the convenience of Purdue basketball followers, whenever weather conditions make it permissible, parking facilities on the nights of home basketball games will be available at the northeast corner of the University campus at the intersection of Northwestern and Stadium. It was announced last night by Robert C. Woodworth, acting athletic director.

In addition to the parking area at the northeast corner of the campus, with which all football fans are familiar, there will be a limited amount of parking space on the gravelled area directly north of the new fieldhouse.

Entrance to both parking areas is to be made from Northwestern Avenue.

11

FIELDHOUSE COMES TRUE TO PURDUE'S FANS TOMORROW

December 10, 1937 – Purdue's long awaited fieldhouse will become an actuality as far the basketball public is concerned on Saturday night at 7:30. Coach Ward Lambert's current Boilermaker combination tackles a rangy Indiana State quintet in the opening game of a flurry of home action that calls for additional games with Xavier and Detroit Monday and Wednesday, respectively.

IN DRESS ATTIRE

Providing a seating capacity of approximately 8,500, the commodious new structure, which will be on display to the general public for the first time at Saturday's Indiana State battle, will be in dress attire and in full operation for the opening tilt as the result of concerted overtime action on the part of Purdue's athletic staff.

Judging from early practice drills on the gleaming new portable floor, Coach Lambert will turn loose a quintet that will specialize in a sustained speed attack in the opening trio of home battles. Although still undecided on his eventual starting combination, Lambert indicated last night that the starting choice against Indiana State would be made from Sines, Young, Hutt and Zink, forwards; Anderson and Fisher, centers; and Dickinson, Malaska, Beretta, Yeager and Vernon, guards.

THREE TOUGH FOES

That the Boilermakers will be given strong competition in the home trio of starts that will provide a tuneup for the Chicago and Pacific coast trips is revealed by a study of the rosters of the three teams that will invade the fieldhouse within the next week.

Brief thumbnail sketches of the opening opposition follow:

Indiana State – Coach Wally Marks has developed one of the rangiest combinations on the hardwood. Three lettermen are supplemented by the most promising collection of sophomores and juniors that the Sycamores have boasted in years. Four members of the squad tower at 6 feet 4 inches.

PLENTY OF TICKETS

According to Ticket Manager C. S. Doan, there will be plenty of reserved seats available at the fieldhouse ticket offices for all three games. The tickets are priced at 75 cents each, including tax. In addition to the Purdue ticket office in the new men's gymnasium, tickets are also on sale over the counter at Decker's and Deac's.

Ward "Piggy" Lambert

MIDWEST APPLAUDS PURDUE TEAM AND "PIGGY" LAMBERT

By Paul R. Allerup

March 6, 1940 – CHICAGO — March 5 – Purdue held its 13th undisputed Big Ten basketball championship today, and midwest court fans again are paying tribute to the genius of the Boilermakers' coach, Ward Lambert, dean of Western Conference mentors in years as well as deeds.

The Boilermakers clinched the title in the season final last night by coming from behind with an amazing closing spurt to nip Illinois 34-31.

Indiana, Purdue's arch state rival, grabbed second place in the standings by trimming Ohio State, 52-31. Had Illinois beaten Purdue the Hoosiers would have been co-champions.

Captain Bill Hapac of Illinois almost personally provided his team with a halftime lead of 17-12, and in all tallied 13 points for a season total of 164, which gave him the individual scoring title.

GREAT RECORD

For Coach Lambert, Purdue's championship was another outstanding achievement in a history of personal successes. In the 23 years he has coached Purdue's court teams, Lambert's fives have won or shared 11 Big Ten titles. In only one season, 1919, has Lambert's squad finished out of the conference's first division.

On the basis of games won and lost since 1906, Lambert-coached quintets have a stranglehold on the all-time Big Ten leadership. Throughout his tenure, the Boilermakers have averaged better than seven victories out of ten in conference competition, and three wins out of four against both conference and non-conference foes.

This year the Boilermakers differed somewhat from most Lambert teams in that the squad has boasted no individual high-scoring star. The 1939-40 Purdue team scored with its all-around speed and teamwork on offense and defense. There has been little to choose among the smashing play of Capt. Fred Beretta, one of the Big Ten's best defensive guards, Don Blanken, Forrest Sprowl, Dan Fisher, Bob Igney and Mickey Tierney.

EXCELLENT UNDER FIRE

Lambert's method is to coach each in the fundamentals of the game, make each player as expert as possible in those fundamentals, and then put him on his own. The result has been that Purdue's fives have been noted for their excellence under fire and their ability to solve problems on the floor.

INDIANA CAGERS ACCEPT BID TO NCAA TOURNEY

Hoosier Quintet is One of Four Eastern Teams to Compete; Final at Kansas City on March 30

March 7, 1940 – BLOOMINGTON, IND. — March 6. – The athletic committee of Indiana University today accepted an invitation for the Hoosier basketball team to represent the midwest in the annual National Collegiate Athletic association cage tourney.

The invitation was received yesterday by Z. G. Clevenger, athletic director, who said that selection of the Indiana team was unanimous among the midwestern committeemen.

Eight teams compete in the tourney, four in the east and four in the west. Preliminary games will be played March 22 and 23 at eastern and western sites to be selected while the final series is scheduled March 30 at Kansas City.

Selection of Indiana over Purdue to represent the midwest came as a surprise as the Boilermakers won the Big Ten title while Indiana finished second. Ohio State, last year's Big Ten titleholder, competed in the same tourney.

It was believed that Indiana's two victories over Purdue this season were responsible for the selection. During the entire season Purdue dropped four games, including the two Indiana defeats, while the Hoosiers lost only three, all to Big Ten rivals.

Purdue's legendary coach, Ward "Piggy" Lambert, gave Purdue basketball national prominence.

GRAHAM CRACKERS

By Gordon Graham

March 6, 1940 – If you didn't like the grand climax to Purdue's hardwood season at Illinois Monday night, you probably aren't fully aware of the real reason for Boilermaker basketball success. No Purdue basketball team is ever beaten until the gun fires...minutes or points mean little or nothing to a Lambert-coached team...there's always plenty of time to win.

Like the "myth" of the New York Yankees, Purdue's winning habit is spreading over the midwest. An Illinois gentleman, sitting behind Bob Woodworth, Billy Fox and yours truly, tossed three Hoosiers into a near swoon with an amazing remark at the start of that thrilling Purdue rally...turning to his wife, as Igney and Sprowl hit long ones to cut the Illinois lead to 29-23 with eight minutes left, the gentleman calmly remarked: "Now you will see something – Purdue will beat Illinois by 15 points." The spouse was as shocked as yours truly and started to put up a mild argument, but just then Igney pumped another through the net from far out on the court. The confident gentleman quickly stopped her with: "See there, honey, they do it so easily – they have just been playing with Illinois – our boys have done their best, but Purdue will walk away with them now." When the Boilermakers won by only three points in that riotous finish, we honestly believe that the gentleman was definitely disappointed in Purdue's showing.

We've seen Purdue teams make greater comebacks as far as points and minutes are concerned, but never when so much depended upon the outcome or when things seemed to be breaking so badly. When you consider that four sophomores, playing under terrific college pressure for the first time in their young lives, had a big hand in the affair, the feat seems utterly impossible. Charley Caress, in particular is an example. Charley probably hadn't played 20 minutes of Big Ten basketball before he was thrown into the breach. Red performed as well as any of his mates, and brother that's saying something.

There's little point in going into long praising sprees...Fred Beretta, Frosty Sprowl, Bob Igney, Don Blanken, Mickey Tierney, Dan Fisher, Eli Yeager, and Caress were so good during the season that everybody knows beforehand what should be said about them. They are champions all!

If that Boilermaker rally had fallen short, we would have screamed like a coyote. You've never seen such bad officiating breaks as Purdue received during that gallant surge. Three field goals were taken away from Piggy's battling lads when the conference title might have hinged on every precious point...two of them on the most ridiculous calls ever seen by the eye.

Bill Fox named the officials: Benny Goodman and Ted Lewis. The game was one of the cleanest played this season, yet whistles have seldom blown more often or at more inopportune times. The tip-off of the officiating came early when Clarno fouled the Illinois crowd for raising an ordinary boo. We are glad Purdue missed the technical foul, for no Boilermaker team wants to win any kind of game on such a silly decision.

As a matter of fact, the Illinois crowd, officials and players are to be congratulated for the fine way they conducted themselves during such a hectic encounter.

You can say for us that we practically gave up when the score was 29-19...but you can also say that we abso-

GRAHAM CRACKERS

lutely knew Purdue was going to win when the Sucker lead was cut to 30-27...nothing could have stopped that mad rush...even Illinois seemed to know it.

Purdue was slowly falling to pieces midway in that second period...the Boilermakers were taking silly one-handed shots from long distance...then suddenly Bob Igney decided it was time for him to try one of his specialties...why the Boilermakers hadn't thought of this method of attack before, we will never know, for nothing else was succeeding...Bob dropped that shot...Frosty Sprowl matched it...Purdue got the idea...the ball was passed to Igney again and the Rossville flash whipped another one through...Blanken sniped one from the side...then the rally was halted momentarily while two or three successful drives under the basket were whistled away...the closing splurge was due to clever stealing of the ball in the center of the court by Sprowl, Blanken, Tierney, Caress and Beretta.

The last 50 seconds saw the new hardwood ruling given its most severe test of the year...Purdue went into a stall and in 50 seconds time, Illinois committed seven personal fouls with Purdue refusing them all...Suckers were fouling so

rapidly that three men left the floor in that short space of time.

Indiana? We understand that the Purdue uprising cut short a big Bloomington celebration. Tsk! Tsk! And the Hoosiers beat us twice, too. Ain't it a shame? When those Bloomington boys get used to the big towns like Minneapolis, Columbus, and Chicago, maybe they will be able to cut into the championship pie...some say those Minnesota, Northwestern, and Ohio State defeats can be traced to the tall buildings and the horrible noises made by street cars, elevated trains and the like.

We actually feel sorry for the Hoosiers and we know that if Purdue lost at Illinois we wanted Indiana to be the team which shared the title with Lambert's young netters. But one fact still bumps us in the face...do you realize that Indiana was lucky to finish second? Wasn't Bill Hapac out of uniform the night that Illinois lost 38-36 to Indiana? With Hapac pumping that ball through the net for the Suckers, there is little doubt but that Indiana would have had another loss staring it in the face.

Maybe next time, Indiana...yeah, maybe.

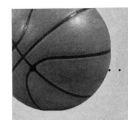

WARD LAMBERT RESIGNS AS HEAD COACH

Melvin Taube Successor to Famous Purdue Net Mentor

Basketball's Great "Piggy" Asks to be Relieved of Strenuous Duties After 29 Brilliant Years; Will Remain on Physical Ed. Staff; Taube Takes Over Immediately

January 23, 1946 – Ward Lewis (Piggy) Lambert, probably the greatest big-time college basketball coach of modern times, resigned his position as head mentor at Purdue University yesterday evening and Melvin H. (Mel) Taube was immediately named as his successor. The fiery, little hardwood genius voluntarily relinquished his head coaching duties after more than 28 years of sensational service in Western conference circles, a period which brought 11 championships to Boilermaker teams.

The nationally known Boilermaker coach served for two years as chairman of the rules committee of the National Basketball Coaches' Association, and also served a two-year term on the board of directors of the organization. He is the author of a textbook, *Practical Basketball*, which has had a wide sale, and has been featured as an instructor in coaching schools all over the country.

PIGGY'S STATEMENT

Lambert in confirming his retirement from basketball said, "I deeply regret giving up my long association with Purdue basketball, but after extended service in a strenuous game, I am anxious to be relieved of the nervous strain and mental punishment that accompanies a head coach-ship."

Lambert's retirement as head basketball coach will be effective immediately, and it was announced that M. H. (Mel) Taube, veteran assistant coach, will take over on an acting basis for the rest of the season, which will find the Boilermakers on the road for five of the seven games which remain on the schedule. Emmett Lowery, who recently returned to the staff after service in the Navy, was designated as assistant coach.

The announcement followed a conference of Lambert with President Frederick L. Hovde and Director of Athletics Guy (Red) Mackey yesterday afternoon. Following the conference, President Hovde and Director Mackey issued the following joint statement:

PURDUE RELUCTANT

"Following nearly 29 years of distinguished service at Purdue university, Professor Ward L. Lambert has requested that he be relieved of his duties as head coach of varsity basketball. The administration has reluctantly agreed with his request to retire from an active and strenuous coaching duty, for his record at Purdue stands second to none. It was only on his insistence that his resignation as varsity basketball coach was finally accepted.

"During the war years, Professor Lambert carried on at the university's request because many of the younger members of the coaching staff were on leave in war service. This situation no longer exists and Professor Lambert's desire to undertake less strenuous duties has been arranged. He will continue as a member of the staff in his capacity as professor of physical education and as head coach of varsity baseball. Additional teaching and coaching duties in other sports will be assigned."

LONG CONSIDERATION

Although Lambert's decision to retire in mid-season came as somewhat of a surprise, it has been known for several years that he was anxious to be relieved of his duties. However, he was prevailed upon to carry on through the war years when the coaching staff was short handed.

In recent years, the 57-year-old veteran has frequently been handicapped by severe midwinter colds that have interfered with his coaching duties. A week ago Saturday, because of illness, he was unable to accompany the squad on its last road trip to Madison and Taube directed the team against Wisconsin.

Lambert's long-time record as Purdue's head basketball coach has been largely responsible for giving the Boilermakers the all-time Big Ten leadership. In 28 years, prior to this season, his Boilermaker squads won or shared in eleven Big Ten titles. In Big Ten competition, Lambert teams have won 288 games while losing only 105, while for all games his squads have won 371 while losing 152. Only one of his 28 teams, back in 1919, has finished below .500 in the conference standing. His basketball combinations have always been noted for their fast-breaking tactics and sustained speed.

TAUBE VERSATILE

Mel Taube, who will take over the direction of the squad for the remainder of the season, is admirably fitted for the assignment. A 1926 Purdue graduate, he is one of the few nine-letter men in Boilermaker athletic history, having won three major letters each in football, basketball, and baseball.

For two years following his graduation, he served as freshman coach in football and basketball at Purdue and then went to Marion, Indiana, high school as athletic director and head coach of football and basketball. From Marion, he went to Massachusetts State College in 1931, where he served as football, basketball, and baseball coach and compiled an outstanding record.

Taube returned to Purdue in the spring of 1936 as assistant football and basketball coach, and with the exception of 1943 and 1944 when he was on leave of absence to serve in the Navy, has been a member of the staff continuously since that time. He was discharged as a lieutenant in the Navy last fall.

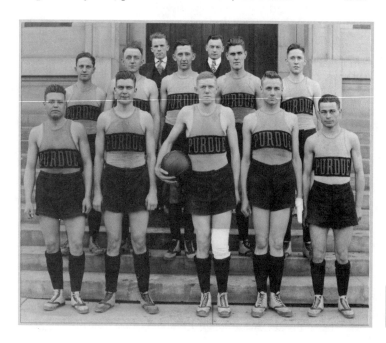

Purdue teams stood tall under Piggy Lambert for over 28 years, winning 11 Big Ten titles.

GRAHAM CRACKERS

By Gordon Graham

This is certainly far from an obituary on one of the greatest figures in college sports. Ward "Piggy" Lambert ...we hope our health is comparable to his at the age of 57...Purdue's Piggy was simply weary of the terrific strain which goes with successful head coaching in a circuit as tough as the Western conference.

No doubt, Lambert hesitated relinquishing his duties at the present time because of a feeling which might prevail in scattered circles that the little net genius was moving out just because his team had lost two straight Big Ten games.

We can guarantee that Piggy had the move he made yesterday in mind some time ago. Lambert told us personally two years ago, after one of his greatest victories, that he really wanted to make that season his last...it was after Purdue had scored a stunning upset over Ohio's champions at Columbus. We are convinced that Piggy stayed on only because of wartime conditions and a shortage of coaches.

Lambert has indicated to us several times in recent years that it was increasingly difficult for him to gear himself to these games so that his enthusiasm and confidence could be reflected in his teams. This season another bad cold gripped him and Piggy probably felt that in all fairness to himself and the fine group of boys he was coaching that it would be better to step out now than to wait until the end of the year.

Just yesterday we were talking with two of Piggy's greatest Purdue stars, Johnny Sines and Jewell Young...both mentioned the numerous times that Lambert's complete confidence, boundless zest for victory, and sympathetic handling practically picked them up by their bootstraps and turned almost certain defeats into blazing triumphs.

We know something about that...our own personal associations with Lambert at practices and on trips almost turned us into a wild person, one who craved Purdue victories and who couldn't anticipate Purdue defeats...he was even able to reflect this competitive spirit into crowds.

Such mental achievement didn't come easily and if Piggy thinks 29 years of that sort of pressure is enough, we should all be happy in the fact he was able to stay on the job that long.

"Look ahead"..."talk on defense"..."you are better than the other man"..."don't be unduly impressed by your opponents' success"..."respect a foe, but never fear him"..."basketball is a mental and condition game"..."don't form bad habits in practice"..."run, don't trot back on defense"..."call out all odd-man fast break situations"..."don't cross-court and avoid passing toward the sidelines"..."meet the ball"..."don't try impossible plays"..."your percentages belong to you in basket shooting"..."be relaxed."

These and hundreds of other pieces of sage basketball advice will be remembered by Campbell, Tilson, Miller, White, Masters, Guillion, Spradling, Kemmer, Murphy, Harmeson, Boots, Kellar, Wooden, Young, Sines, Anderson, Kessler, Shaver, Cottom, Lowery, Blanken, Sprow, Beretta, Ehlers, and the scores of other great basketball players at Purdue who today will regret the retirement of the talented hardwood teacher.

Lambert's 11 championships in 28 years of Big Ten competition roar out in a tremendous voice and assure the fact that the name of Ward "Piggy" Lambert will always be near the top in college basketball.

Now Purdue swings into a new basketball era, with Mel Taube taking over the hardwood reins. Taube was one of Piggy's most apt pupils and has been one of his most trusted assistants for years. Mel not only has our support, but our full confidence in his ability to take up where Lambert left off.

Taube's task is not an easy one, of course, but with strong cooperation and renewed enthusiasm, Mel can lead Boilermakers basketball back to the pinnacle it reached under Ward Lambert.

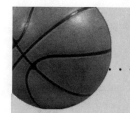

PURDUE PROBES BLEACHER COLLAPSE

Two Killed, Hundreds Injured When Stands at Fieldhouse Collapse

February 25, 1947 — Purdue University Tuesday was counting the toll taken in lives and injuries when the east bleachers in the university fieldhouse collapsed Monday evening during the Purdue and Wisconsin basketball game. The seats were filled with approximately 3,400 students and other spectators, all of whom were dropped to the ground when the stands buckled and fell. An immediate investigation was authorized by President F.L. Hovde.

Two students were killed and at least six others remained in a serious condition Tuesday noon from injuries, as a result of the tragedy. The dead:

Roger R. Gelhausen, 22, a Navy veteran, freshman in physical education, living at 507 Waldron Street, West Lafayette, whose home was at Garrett.

William J. Feldman, 20, a Merchant Marine veteran and sophomore student in aeronautical engineering, residing in Cary Hall Southwest. His home was at 4245 Olcott Avenue, East Chicago.

Hundreds of students were injured, of whom an estimated 166 were taken to hospitals; several

hundred others were treated at the university infirmary and others received only first aid, with their numbers uncounted.

MEETING CALLED

A special meeting of university trustees and President Hovde was called for this afternoon in the university Executive Building to consider steps which may be taken following the fieldhouse tragedy.

HOVDE EXPRESSES UNIVERSITY SORROW

"Monday evening's fieldhouse tragedy has plunged the entire university into inspeakable sorrow," Dr. Frederick L. Hovde, president of the university, declared in a statement commenting upon the bleacher collapse. His statement continues:

"Our deepest sympathy goes especially to the parents of our students who lost their promising young lives and to all those who were injured or suffered from shock.

"The students and others in the stands were magnificent in their conduct throughout the tragic minutes. There was no panic, ho hysteria. Members of the city and state police, fire departments, the university and the hospital staffs should be highly commended for the manner in which they met the crisis, caring for the injured with skill and dispatch.

"The fieldhouse has been closed until careful investigation of the cause of the failure of the stands can be determined. These newly purchased stands were not, according to members of the athletic department, loaded beyond their rated capacity as specified by the manufacturer and approved by the appropriate state officers."

"UNBELIEVABLE"

"It's almost unbelievable," said Guy (Red) Mackey, Purdue athletic director, who was deeply affected by the tragic crash.

"The bleachers, especially designed for the purpose, were purchased new last fall and were erected by an experienced crew," said Mackey. Asked about the continuation of the basketball schedule, Mackey said: "We are concerned now with the victims of the accident. Any decision about the windup of the basketball season will come later."

All physical education classes scheduled in the men's gymnasium and fieldhouse for the day were cancelled.

PURDUE LEADS BEFORE TRAGEDY

Basketball became a minor item just a few seconds after it seemed the most important thing in the world to 11,000 fans in Purdue Fieldhouse last night. The Boilermaker basketball team had just fought its way into a 34-33 lead in one of the most furious hardwood encounters ever seen here when the gun signalled the end of the first half.

As the Purdue five passed through the howling throng on its way to the dressing room the East stand collapsed like an eggshell. Undoubtedly the enthusiasm of the 4,000 students in that section led to the accident. They were standing as one and cheering for their team.

"GREATEST...CROWD"

"There is the greatest basketball crowd in the land," said a veteran basketball writer, pointing his finger to the East section. Then down it went and the bleachers resembled a ruffled straw stack before the Purdue and Wisconsin players reached their locker rooms.

With both the Boilermakers and Badgers turning on the heat from the first whistle the Purdue and Wisconsin teams had staged one of the most thrilling battles possible. It was nip and tuck, with Purdue featuring drives under the hoop and Wisconsin retaliating with deadly shots from medium and long distance.

Paul Hoffman was leading the Boilermakers with 11 points, while Menzel, Selbo and Cook were keeping the hot pace for Bud Foster's invaders.

CANCELLATION?

For Wisconsin the cancellation, which was announced a few minutes after, may prove vital in the Big Nine title race. The Badgers entered the game with an 8-2 record, while Illinois gained an 8-3 standing with last night's victory over Michigan.

Both coaches, Mel Taube and Bud Foster, said after the game that they had no idea whether or not the game would be finished or played over at a later date. That will be left up to the disposition of the Big Nine commissioner, Tug Wilson.

FANS RELATE EXPERIENCE OF TRAGIC TUMBLE WHEN BLEACHERS IN FIELDHOUSE COLLAPSED

By Bud Shelley

Stories of amazing conformity and stories of unselfish praise were woven Monday night and Tuesday by basketball fans who crashed to the Purdue Fieldhouse floor with splintering bleachers at halftime of the Boilermaker-Wisconsin game.

While the only inconsistency in several accounts centered about whether or not the stand gave a whining lurch, all of those who were caught in the tragedy agreed that the fall was forward and that it seemed to take place slowly and end surprisingly softly.

Quite naturally there were a few nearly hysterical mothers, wives and other relatives to be seen milling about in the crowd, but those who went through the ordeal were full only of praise for the generally calm reaction of the others in the audience, as well as others unfortunate enough to tumble.

No Panic

The fans in the west stands, directly across the playing floor from those bleachers that fell, held their positions. No panic developed, and they responded promptly to the orders issued over the public address system.

Philip Deuchler, treated late Monday night in St. Elizabeth hospital, gave this account of the fall:

"I, with some other college students, was sitting about 10 rows from the top of the wooden bleachers. We were standing between halves. Suddenly came the funny feeling of falling forward and downward at the same time...It seemed to take us a long time to get down. I ended up face downward on top of a bunch of people. There was a strange quietness about the whole affair. There were a few people around me with legs caught in the bleachers, and I saw two boys suffering terribly from compound fractures. People seemed to take the whole thing rather quietly. There were a few screams when the stands first collapsed, but then things were quiet. Those caught under the splintered wood merely asked those nearest them to get off the wood so they could extricate themselves. I managed to get up, but couldn't use my left hand."

Deuchler, who is 19 years old and the son of P.G. Deuchler, 580 Detamble Avenue, Highland Park, went on to tell that he was taken to the fieldhouse training room to have his shoulder set, then to the infirmary, and finally to the hospital for X-rays.

Face Injuries

Face injuries were suffered by Wilford Blair, of Kentland, and Walter H. Nelson, advertising manager of the Journal and Courier. Blair, a chemical engineering student, substantiated that the bleachers settled slowly to the floor.

Walter Silvestri of Chicago, electrical engineering junior, was in the same row with Blair, but was not hurt. He said the stand apparently started to give way long before it was noticed in the excitement of the close game.

"A fraternity brother standing next to me asked me, 'Did you feel that?' while the crowd was getting up for the national anthem just before the start of the game," Silvestri said. His companion apparently had felt the seats shift slightly, Silvestri said, but they thought no more about it until the bleacher crunched to the floor.

Nelson, who was attending the game with J. Frank Thompson, manager of Woolworth's, Danville, Illinois, was in the next to the last row of the bleachers at the south end and said he felt no warning shift or cracking of the stands, the first motions being forward. Nelson, too, said the fall was rather cushioned.

Only one member of the Jefferson or West Side basketball teams was reported injured although most of the prep netters were at the game. Fred Mozley, Red Devil forward and center, suffered an arm injury.

Another Athlete Hurt

Another high school athlete, Warren Lull, who sustained a leg fracture at the end of the West Side football season, barely missed having his leg injured a second time. Lull was not able to bend the injured limb sufficiently to place it on one of the foot rails of the bleachers until Monday evening. At all previous Purdue games, Lull had dangled his leg between two rows of the bleachers. Fortunately, it had healed to the stage where he could allow the limb to rest on the row in front of him.

Warren, aged 17, the son of Prof. and Mrs. P.E. Lull, West Lafayette, reported the following interpretation of the incident:

"Some people may say that people were screaming, but I didn't hear anything. I thought we went back slightly at first, and then plunged forward and down." Warren, who was seated "eight or ten" rows from the top, described the crumbling, which is supposed to have

started toward the front of the bleachers, as "like an escalator."

Praises Fans

Local Police Lieut. Joseph M. Clark added praise for the uninjured students by saying, "the students that weren't injured were magnificent. I imagine most of the fellows were ex-GIs and they seemed to know exactly what to do in helping the injured."

Richard Pershing, 19, son of Mr. and Mrs. S.B. Pershing, Lafayette R. 3, was another to feel the "definite jolt" while the huge crowd was listening to the national anthem before the tilt. Pershing said that a similar jolt was experienced only seconds before the collapse. After feeling the second jolt, Pershing and a group of companions looked over the back rail of the last row to see if they could determine the trouble. Facing backwards, the group settled slowly and softly to the fieldhouse floor. Pershing said he held onto the rail until it broke, and then jumped off. During the fall, Pershing saw the back braces slide out, the bases of the vertical timbers clipping east. The sensation was nevertheless a movement toward the playing floor.

Lambert Fieldhouse was the site of a tragedy in 1947 when the bleachers collapsed during a game against Wisconsin.

CHAPTER 7

PURDUE CLIPS HAPLESS INDIANA, 51-49

Howie Williams "Sits Down" to Snipe Winning Field Goal

Riveters' Sophomore Star Tops Off Brilliant Night With Fantastic Shot in Last Five Seconds; First Double Win Over Hoosiers in 10 Years; Finish With 6-6 Rating

March 1, 1948 – BLOOMINGTON — February 29 – Purdue's Boilermakers today owed possession of the old fire bell trophy, a 6-6 record in Big Nine play, and its first double victory over Indiana in 10 years, to forward Howard Williams' ability to shoot from the seat of his pants.

With the Hoosiers leading 49-47, with 56 seconds of play left, Williams, whose 18 points led both teams in scoring, drove under the basket to knot the score.

FANTASTIC HOWIE

Purdue battled back to its basket with time running out. Williams, knocked to the floor in a wild melee under the hoop, stretched out his hands to gather in his own rebound. Sitting squarely on the floor and surrounded by Hoosier players, he

whisked the ball through the net with five seconds to go for a 51-49 Purdue victory, shattering the hopes of a frenzied record Indiana crowd of 11,000.

Indiana's Ward Williams smashed under to give the Crimson its last lead of the evening, a minute and 20 seconds left in the game, to set the stage for Williams' last pair of fantastic field goals.

The victory gave Purdue possession of the fire bell trophy. It also marked the first time a Purdue basketball team has beaten an Indiana team twice in one season since the 1937-38 team turned the trick. In over-all standings between the two schools it set up Purdue's 58th victory in 79 battles.

More notable yet in Purdue's startling triumph was that Ace Guard Bill Berberian, still suffering from a pulled muscle, saw no action. Bill Banks fell back from forward to come through with a more than adequate defensive game, meanwhile contributing four valuable points.

Little Don Ritter, Indiana's top scorer, was held in check for five points the first half and collected only nine the second period to capture Crimson scoring honors with 14 points.

TIED 13 TIMES

Despite a prominent inability of both teams to hit with any consistency – Indiana shot 18 in 91 attempts for a .197 average and Purdue collected on 20 of 90 for a .222 mark – the lead changed hands faster than a short-fused bomb in a game of catch. The score was tied 13 times in the course of the game.

RECORDS FALL AS PURDUE WINS 81-78

McNulty Shatters All Local Markets With 34 Points in Stunning Tilt

Over 9,000 Fans Gasp During Furious Shooting Spectacle; Boilermakers hit 50.7 From Field, Minnesota 40.4; Gophers Threaten In Wild Finish as Riveters Stall.

By Gordon Graham

February 2, 1951 — Purdue's battling Boilermakers, despite their lowly position in the Big Ten standings, shot their way into Old Gold and Black hearts here last night by staging a record-shattering performance against an amazed Minnesota quintet in a sensational game, which ended 81-78 with marks of all descriptions falling down from the rafters.

Records established during the bewildered shooting barrage were:

(1) Purdue—New team record for shooting accuracy in single Big Ten game, 35 of 69 shots from field for 50.7 percent—old record, Ohio State against Indiana 1950, 26 of 53 for 49.1.

(2) Purdue—Tied Boilermaker records for points in single games, 81 against Drake and Denver.

(3) Carl McNulty—New Purdue mark for total points in single game, 34—old record, 29, held by Jewell Young and Andy Butchko.

(4) Carl McNulty—New Purdue record for total points in 20 game schedule, 314—old record, 289, set by Jewell Young in 1938.

There must have been others, but the above records were the only ones immediately visible through the smoke of battle after the skirmish.

Never has there been such a demonstration of basket-shooting on a Western conference court. Nobody can blame Coach Ozzie Cowles and his Gophers for appearing dazed when they discovered they had swished the nets from all distant angles of the floor for a great average of 40.4 only to lose after trailing through most of the encounter. Nineteen of the Minnesota shots were long ones!

Carl McNulty, a 6-3 hardwood genius from little Washington township, set the pattern for the hair-raising spectacle, with a performance which quite likely has never been equaled in the old and powerful Western conference. He did everything in the books, including a tip-in shot for Minnesota.

Consider for a moment an individual performance, which includes the record-breaking mentioned above and in addition a rebounding job that is beyond belief. McNulty took 27 rebounds himself during his 40 minute assignment, while the burly Gophers were getting only 29 in all! Points, 34; rebounds, 27—you beat that kind of night!

Despite errors and a slow start, the tempo of the game began to rise as the Gophers scrambled against Purdue's complete zone arrangement to keep leads of 11-10 and then 15-13. McNulty had been keeping his team in the running up to here with four baskets in six shots. Then came the Neil Schmidt spurt, the one the fans were waiting for.

HERE WE GO!

The game went haywire as Schmidt came up with four, Brewster one, Grenier one, and McNulty another. Suddenly Ray Eddy's club had thrown the Gopher defense into a panic. Under the hoop the Riveters went with one stolen ball after another. The score mounted to 27-17 before the visitors began shooting the nets off the hoop from well out. Skoog, Gelle and Miller battled back against the whizzing Boilermakers and cut the lead to four points before Schmidt went whirling under for two more setups. The half ended, 43-36.

Both teams displayed great mental and physical courage as they refused to crack wide open in the second half. The shooting of either team would have discouraged 90 percent of all college foes. Glenn Bahler and Norm Greiner joined in the scoring for a few short moments at the start of the last stanza before the hot McNulty got under way again. But no matter what Purdue did, Minnesota kept sinking those jump shots from the foul circle and set attempts from the long-side. When Big Pete Brewster fouled out with 17 to go, the score was 54-44, but Purdue seemed badly crippled in the center of its zone defense, where Brewster had been battling the big Gelle, Wallerius, and Johnson.

But John Dermody came in to drop his first two long shots. Skoog, Johnson, and others couldn't miss, but McNulty was always finding the range for Purdue. The score was 65-57 at the 10-minute mark.

HITS 6 OF 7

Purdue tried to slow play down shortly thereafter, but in spite of the great Boilermaker performance it appeared for a while as if a fellow named Richard Means would break Old Gold and Black hearts. Coming here with 11 field goals in 70 shots for a 15.7 percentage and a point production of 1.7 per game, Means hit three long shots in 40 seconds! Not only that, he went on to snipe six of his first seven efforts. The great Whitey Skoog (and we mean great) joined Means, and only the fact that McNulty kept shooting and playing like a maniac

held Purdue's lead at 76-74 with 3:34 to go. The Eddy fighters successfully stalled it out, however, with Schmidt and Greiner sneaking under the hoop for vital lay-ups.

It would be difficult to make any yarn of this type appear as if it weren't an "individual triumph for Carl McNulty," except that isn't the way it was. McNulty has played almost as well in several games this season as he did here Wednesday night.

EDDY "SELLS 'EM"

Rather you can say that Purdue has won four of its last seven and three of its last four, against formidable opposition, because the Boilermakers have been accepting and believing in the type of organization Coach Ray Eddy is installing.

The "Monday Miracle" was fashioned by Eddy's new "six-man regulars," a group he established after several squad failures. Ray stays with them, "foul or not, tired or not," and each night they stay longer with him. The zone defense efforts also are included in the revival, but Eddy and Purdue aren't "married" to any style.

GREINER "PICKS UP"

Glenn Bahler was the acting captain against Minnesota in this record-smashing exhibition. The hottest shooter in the Big Ten for weeks, Bahler, got four points, yet played 40 minutes again. Norm Greiner, often the "fifth wheel" in the newly formed setup, picked up Bahler's "slack" and collected 13. Darrel "Pete" Brewster, who has taken a back seat for two years, is still doing that. The "zone" puts him in unfortunate position time after time, but Pete is sacrificing to help the club and each night doing a better job of it. John Dermody, a sophomore, is the pinch-hitter, who comes in when anybody is overloaded with fouls. He improves regularly, and whenever he completely "loosens up," the aspirin sales will jump all over the conference.

That brings us down to Neil Schmidt, who has been twisting the tails of the best players around the league. His stamina is unsurpassed, and his basketball competitive instinct is fooling one team after another. Neil got 19 points Monday, and eight of them in three hilarious minutes when the Boilermakers were "proving themselves" to Minnesota and the appreciative crowd.

These five unselfish dogged, wonderful men helped Mr. McNulty turn in the most outstanding 40 minutes the Big Ten has seen in our memory.

TAKE NOTES

Statistics can be over-emphasized in almost all games, but more figures should be offered on this particular one. For instance, Purdue outrebounded Ozzie Cowles' well trained Gophers, who possessed height and weight advantages, 50 to 29! We have already mentioned that McNulty got 27 "board retrieves" individually for Purdue. Planning might have had something to do with that.

Purdue lost badly on errors, 14 to 8, but those in attendance know that four of these bobbles came in less than four minutes after the opening tipoff, indicating "jitters."

Even individual accuracy shooting is worth recording on a game like this, so here goes: Purdue—McNulty 15 of 25, Schmidt 8-16, Greiner 6-13, Brewster 3-4, Dermody 2-4, Bahler 1-7. Minnesota—Miller 8-26, Skoog 10-25, Means 6-10, Johnson 6-17, Gille 4-7, Walerius 1-1, Schnobrich 1-3.

These are records which go down for "all-time" in conference competition—clip them, if you wish.

YOU CHECK

However, Purdue deserves more credit for its victory than even yet has been shown. In this story of deadly accuracy, it should be pointed out that Minnesota was even "hotter" than Purdue on field goal shooting. Purdue's short shots were 29 of 51, and long ones 6 of 18; Minnesota, 17 of 44 short, and 19 of 45 long!

Going further, Purdue made 10 "dead" lay-up shots to three for the invaders, and 10 follow or tip-in baskets to five for Minnesota. Thus, the "three of four foot zone" produced 20 clean baskets for Purdue and eight for the Cowles quintet. Maybe that's a new record. And undoubtedly Minnesota's mark of 19 of 45 long shots beats anything seen in the conference.

Before withdrawing from a game of this kind, one would have to point out that Skoog, the Meyer "Whitey" character who has played so many games for Minnesota, is one of the greats Big Ten Basketball should always be proud of. His reactions are so quick that they make you gasp.

A "HOT-HANDER"

Then for the record, this Means person who was mentioned earlier—it turns out that he is "hot-hand Richard" of the circuit—the Big Ten record book shows that Dick Means, of Minnesota, holds the league record for accuracy in one game, "9 of 12" against Wisconsin in 1950—Dick once had his own mark washed ashore when he plunked 6 of 7 here, but fortunately for Purdue, Means missed his last three and finished with a shameful average of 6-10. Don't ask us about these things, we are merely quoting figures.

When somebody breaks Purdue's accuracy record of 50.7 for 69 field goal attempts, we might answer: "Yeah, but Ray Eddy's Boilermakers were so hot on Feb. 19, 1951, that they tipped in two clean baskets for Minnesota and still won." And that is actually true—McNulty batted one in and Brewster another.

If, and when, two Big Ten basketball teams take 158 shots at the draperies, between them hit 45 percent, and finish three points apart, we sincerely hope we are lurking around somewhere in the arena.

BOX SCORE

PURDUE (81)	B	F	P
Bahler, f	1	3	3
Greiner, f	6	1	0
McNulty, c	15	4	4
Brewster, g	8	3	1
Dermody, g	2	0	0
Totals	35	11	13
MINNESOTA (78)	B	F	P
Johnson, f	6	1	3
Miller, f	8	0	3
Gelle, f-c	4	4	4
Means, f	6	0	2
Wallerius, c	1	0	1
Skoog, g	10	0	4
Schnobrich, g	1	1	5
Weiss, g	0	0	0
Totals	36	6	22

Score at half: Purdue, 43; Minnesota, 36.
Free-Throws Missed: Greiner (3), McNulty (4), Brewster (2), Johnson, Miller, Gelle (4), Means, Schnobrich.
Officials: John Tracy, Xavier; Joe Conway, Wisconsin.

SIX-OVERTIME GAME STUNS PURDUE

Heartbreaking Loss Inflicted After Many Chances are Missed

Minnesota Finally Wins Record-Breaking Tussle, 59-56; Boilermakers Freeze Ball Against Zone; Gophers Refuse to Budge; Purdue Holds Winners Without Single Shot in First Four Overtimes, Yet Loses.

By Gordon Graham

Western conference basketball history was made the hard way at Purdue's fieldhouse Saturday night. Minnesota, after being held without a single shot of any kind at the basket during four overtimes, finally came through with a scoring flurry to overcome a 54-51 Purdue lead in the 6th extra session. The Gophers moved into first place on the strength of their freakish 59-56 victory.

SHOOTING DOES IT

The real reason for the Boilermaker setback has been overlooked in the stormy discussion of Saturday's stall. Coach Ray Eddy's shooters were colder than ice, hitting only .317 percent of their shots while Minnesota braced after a frigid start and plunked a dazzling percentage of .462.

Any kind of normal shooting luck would have won for Purdue at a dozen stages of the hectic contest. On five separate occasions, at the end of the regulation period and at the end of the first four overtime sessions, the Boilermakers got a long field goal attempt to none for the league-leading Gophers. All five missed.

The six extra-period smashes all Big Ten records and ties an intercollegiate mark. The fact that there was no action of any kind through 27:27 of playing time probably breaks another record. Purdue froze the ball while the Gophers made no attempt to come after it for 22:37 of this time while Minnesota held on under similar circumstances for 4:50.

Coach Ozzie Cowles' team led 3-2 early in the first half, 29-27 and 31-30 and 41-40 in the second half. On all other occasions Purdue was either in front or tied until the last part of the sixth and final overtime. But the luckless Boilermakers couldn't quite get over the hump and fell into a tie with Ohio State for last in the scrambled Big Ten race.

HAVE GOOD LEADS

Purdue's biggest advantage was 19-9 midway in the first half after the Boilermakers had chiseled ahead 10-3. The locals were on top 27-23 at the half. They led 44-41 with 4:28 left in the regulation game and a few moments later, 47-45 at 1:56. In the fifth overtime Purdue was in front 49-47 and in the sixth the Eddy cagers had a 54-51 edge with 3:26 to play. None of the margins would stand up.

Minnesota stationed the huge Bill Simonovich (6-11 and 275 pounds) directly under the basket and built a tight zone defense around him. Although they were behind, the Gophers refused to come out of this set-up and many now wonder why Purdue didn't start holding the ball and force the visitors into a man to man with the score 19-9.

HOW STALL STARTED

With 2:37 left in the half, and Purdue's lead cut to 27-23, the Boilermakers began the now-famous stall. Denny Blind stood motionless near the center line. The Gopher guards didn't come within 10 feet of him. Purdue mishandled this piece of strategy by not moving in time to get off the last shot, but it still had its four-point lead at the intermission.

For some reason, Purdue junked its stalling strategy between halves and tried to work the ball carefully around the zone. This quickly blew the lead as Dick Garmaker, Simonovich, and Tucker scored six points to go ahead 29-27.

Blind and Joe Sexson finally found the range and the Boilermakers and Gophers began a tense stretch run. The best lead was Purdue's 44-41 affair when Sexson hit a short field goal and Ted Dunn dropped two free throws.

When Garmaker tied the score at 45-45, Dan Thornburg held the ball for 20 seconds to get past the 3:00 mark (when each foul brings two shots). Then Purdue maneuvered until Sexson sank a jumper at 1:56 for a 47-45 lead. At 1:36 Don Beck fouled Simonovich. With a chance to tie up the game, Big Bill missed both shots, but Purdue hearts were chilled when Garmaker stuffed the second miss back into the basket for a 47-47 tie.

Purdue held again and Minnesota refused to budge, being willing for the Boilermakers to take the final shot. Blind again held a little too long and Sexson had to hurry a long shot. Dunn almost tipped the ball in at the buzzer, but both attempts missed.

RUNDOWN ON FREEZE

The overtimes went as follows:

The 6-5 Beck outjumped 6-11 Simonovich and Purdue got the tipoff. Again facing the certainty of the Boilermakers getting one shot to none for Minnesota, the Gophers refused to come out after the ball. In the last couple of seconds Blind's long shot rimmed the hoop.

Beck tipped the ball to Blind and the freeze was on again. This time Purdue missed its best chance to make its strategy pay off. The Boilermakers started their movement a couple of seconds earlier and had time for two quick passes which set Beck up perfectly in front of Simonovich only six or eight feet from the hoop. Don jumped, shot, but missed a heartbreaker.

Beck got the tip once more. For a moment there was a sign that the Gophers might leave their zone and go into a man to man. Purdue carefully tested this possibility by bringing Ted Dunn out near the center line to help hold the ball. Simonovich remained under the basket. Then Beck was brought out to replace Dunn. Simonovich moved four or five feet, but let Beck stand 30 feet away from him. Convinced the zone was still there, Purdue held again until the final seconds. This time Thornburg took the shot, a jumper from the side, but it was short.

Finally the 6-11 Simonovich controlled the tip and Chuck Mencel began holding the ball for Minnesota. The Gophers were even less adept at this "one shot" business than Purdue had been. After a time out at 0:18, the Gophers began to maneuver for their shot. Mencel's pass was deflected by Thornburg and intercepted by Sexson. Joe tore down the court and took another Purdue long shot before the gun, but this one also failed to hit the mark.

GET 49-47 LEAD

Beck outjumped Simonovich, but Garmaker stole the ball for the Gophers. Dunn fouled Garmaker, but Dick missed his shot and Purdue again had control. Sexson found an opening and drove in for a layup and a 49-47 lead at 4:25. Minnesota was called for traveling. With Purdue leading the Gophers came out to press the Boilermaker ball handlers. This finally paid off when Beck and Thornburg mishandled a pass and Lindsley swiped the leather to dribble in for a tying basket (49-49) at 2:45. Purdue began holding and this time Minnesota stayed back in its zone. Sexson took a shot from behind the foul circle in the last three seconds. The giant Simonovich pushed his hand and arm right up through the net and the rim just before the gun fired and while the ball apparently was above the basket. A majority of the customers and players were under the impression that the game was over, that the seeming violation would be called. But Official Paul Sokody came rushing to the scorer's bench yelling that no basket would be allowed on the play. Not only that, he threatened to call a technical foul on Purdue for protesting the play.

Beck tipped the ball to Blind and Garmaker was called for fouling Denny. Blind dropped both free shots and it was 51-49. Minnesota missed a shot and Mencel fouled Blind, Denny making one attempt for 52-49. Simonovich hit two free throws as Dunn fouled out and Bob Bonhomme replaced him. But Thornburg came back with two charity shots when fouled by Tucker and the score was 54-51, Purdue, at 3:26. The Gophers clamped the pressure on and the Boilermakers were forced into damaging errors. Mencel swished one from the foul circle at 3:07. Purdue was stalling with a one-point lead when Sexson threw a bad pass out of bounds. Lindsley got his second basket of the night from the foul circle at 1:50 to put Minnesota ahead, 55-54. When Thornburg was called for traveling, it seemed all over. However, Mencel fell into the

same error and Purdue got the ball back at 1:08. However, the Boilermakers still couldn't find the hoop and Tucker rushed under for two baskets while Beck was getting Purdue's final one.

Thus the Boilermakers lost one of the most controversial games in Big Ten annals, a game which they had many more chances to win than did Minnesota.

EVERYTHING BUT HIT

Purdue did everything better than the Gophers except hit from the field. The Boilermakers had a surprising rebounding margin of 41 to 32, with Beck grabbing no less than 29 off the boards to 12 for the Gopher leader, Simonovich. Purdue made fewer personal fouls, 11 to 15, and more free throws, 16 to 11. But Eddy's gang, which had been shooting 40 per cent through its first five conference games, made only 29 of 63 attempts from the field for .317, while Minnesota was canning out 24 of 52 for .462.

GRAHAM CRACKERS

By Gordon Graham

January 31, 1955 — We've seen many an odd basketball sight in our time, but that affair at Purdue Saturday night cops the prize. While none of the 9,000 fans present want to see another such contest, they treasure the experience of witnessing that one. Twenty years from now they will telling their grandchildren, "I was there the night Purdue and Minnesota held the ball for more than 27 minutes and played six overtimes."

Ward Lambert and Jewell Young were among the Saturday spectators and they remembered almost 20 years back when Purdue held the ball against Illinois in the famous Big Ten stall game of that era. Both Piggy and Jewell say the Boilermakers stood around for 14 minutes unmolested. They had a somewhat larger lead and won by about 12 or 14 points. Illinois was doing the same things, cramping a zone under the basket and forcing Purdue to shoot

from well out on the court. Purdue refused to butt its head into this stone wall and Illinois wouldn't come out, although it was hopelessly beaten if it didn't.

We certainly agree with Ray Eddy on most of his tactics. We would have gone a little farther—we think Purdue should have made Simonovich come out from under that hoop when the Boilermakers had a 19-9 lead. Also, we think the Eddy five should have started off the second half just as it ended the first.

As to the overtime strategy, we think Eddy had it all over Cowles. The Purdue coach couldn't help the boys put the ball in the hoop. Counting the last couple of minutes of the regulation period and the first four overtimes, Purdue had five shots at the basket and one tip-in attempt to absolutely nothing for the Gophers. What's wrong with that percentage, six chances to nothing?

We respect Ozzie Cowles as a basketball coach. He's one of the best in the business, but

GRAHAM CRACKERS

on this occasion we regard Mr. Cowles as plain lucky. His refusal to come out after the ball near the end of the half when his team was trailing put the blame for the stall directly on him. Then later when Purdue was freezing the ball with the score tied, it simply was a question of Cowles not being able to think of a way to give his team an even break.

It's as simple as this: If I would say to you, after I've taken the tipoff at the start of a five-minute overtime: "I'll make a good deal with you. I'm going to get one shot from someplace on the floor and you aren't going to get any. I have one chance to score and you have none." Would you accept such a proposition? Cowles did—and four straight times— once when Purdue had control in the final minutes of the game, and in the first three overtimes.

If Cowles thought Purdue's strategy was wrong, why did he permit his players to try the same thing when Simonovich finally got the tip in the fourth overtime? Conversely, we might ask why Eddy permitted his players to stay away from the ball as Minnesota had done. We think the defenses were wrong on both occasions. Why put yourself in a "sitting duck" position? Sure, you may foul somebody by pressing—but you might get the ball—or force an error or a missed shot—the other way you have no chance at all.

In a national wire story today, Cowles has the gall to imply that Eddy's tactics were wrong. If we go by the old measuring stick of who won, Cowles is right. Otherwise Ozzie is farther off than we have ever seen him.

His most ridiculous statement is, in part: "But we also used the man-to-man. At the start of each overtime we moved into a man-to-man, willing to mix it up." Did any of the 9,000 fans here see Minnesota show any willingness to "mix it up" until the fifth and sixth overtimes?

A couple of times the Gophers did try to lure Purdue into thinking it would use the man-to-man, but Eddy was smart enough to put this to a test. It was no secret that Purdue was trying to take advantage of the slowness of 6-11 Bill Simonovich. It tried to force Minnesota to bring the giant out from under the basket. So when the Gophers made their phony man-to-man gesture, the Boilermakers tested it out. One by one they brought each player out near the center line to see who Simonovich was "guarding." It developed that he wasn't guarding anybody. Big Bill moved a few feet towards Beck when Don went out, but that was all.

Just so nobody will get the idea that Cowles is above using the stall, we might point out that early this very same season Minnesota was leading Northwestern by about five points and with five minutes to play. Cowles tried to freeze the ball and his Gophers lost the game. It all depends on "who is doing it to who."

There is no doubt in our mind as to what player was the most impressive figure of the night—Don Beck! We've had a couple of calls from sports experts over the midwest. "How did Purdue get the ball at the start of so many overtimes?" That is the question that puzzles them since Simonovich figured to do that little job for Minnesota against almost anybody. In the six out of seven tries, including the half-time tipoff, Beck at 6-5 gave his teammates the opportunity to work their "draw them out" tactics. It was an amazing performance against a foe who towers 6-11. There "ain't no justice" sometimes. Beck got the best shot in the overtime battle of the minds. After all of his great clutch jumping (which included 20 rebounds for the night) Beck deserved to be the guy who eventually won the game. Don failed on this one, as his

GRAHAM CRACKERS

teammates did in all of their last-second tries.

Ted Dunn certainly deserves a pat on the back, too. Not many knew that Dunn went into Saturday's game with a sprained ankle. Coach Eddy doubted that Ted would be able to go very long. Dunn was still there until he fouled out in the sixth overtime and Purdue was still leading 53-51 when he left.

Purdue's biggest yelp is directed at Official Paul Sokody, who was so determined to disregard Simonovich's apparent "basket interference" as Sexson fired the final shot of the fifth overtime. Nobody will deny that Big Bill's arm went clear up through the nets and well above the basket. Some say he touched the ball. We didn't see that, but we think the ball was over the basket and that two points should have been allowed.

Not only was Sokody's decision unpopular, but he was a surly, ungracious character in the dressing rooms after the game. We don't believe Coach Ray Eddy ever was able to obtain a satisfactory interpretation of the call. Sokody tried to shoulder on past Eddy, Joe Dienhart, and your agent in the corridor on his way out of the building. Eddy called him on it and again asked for an interpretation of the rule.

"What kind of a place is this?" the official squawked. "Six thousand people were hammering on our dressing room door." Eddy seemed to think that was a lot of people. He asked Bob Shriner, who had been guarding the officials' dressing room door, about it. "Nobody was there that I saw," was Shriner's answer. "Well, they were newspapermen," Sokody declared. We asked the Indianapolis reporters. They hadn't been there. Neither had we. That left only two Minneapolis newspapermen. Maybe they tried to get in. We can't say about that.

The guy must have been expecting "callers." He said he was going to make a report to Bill Haarlow (head of Big Ten officials). Eddy let the upset ref know that he was going to make one, too, and indicated it wouldn't be complimentary.

One Purdue professor has already called us to say that he was sitting just above the basket and that he saw Simonovich's hand hit the ball. Others say the ball was here and there. Most think the penalty should have been called.

We have the rule which applies to such a case. It is from the *National Intercollegiate Basketball Rule Book*, which applies to all NCAA games. Rule 9 of Section 10 says that a penalty must be levied if a player "touch the ball or opponent's basket (the net is part of the basket) while the ball is on or within such basket, or touch the ball while the touching hand or arm is also touching the opponent's basket or is directly above such basket. (Space enclosed by an imaginary cylinder having the ring as its lower base.)"

That leaves it up to your eyesight. If you think the ball was anywhere above the hoop in that "imaginary cylinder," you have a right to think the Boilermakers "wuz robbed."

At any rate, it was quite a game—one which was more of a disappointment to the Purdue players than you realize. Watching them trudge out of the locker room Saturday night, we couldn't help but fear for them against Michigan State Monday night. There have been many games which took more out of the Boilermakers physically, but few which ever drained them so from a mental standpoint. Tremendous tension was built up for each of the numerous key moments. Failure in such a game, when you know you had the advantage and should have won, is hard to shake off.

LUNDY SWEEPS PURDUE'S MVP HONORS

Campbell Named Honorary Captain at Basketball Banquet

The three top scorers on Purdue's basketball squad, which wound up the season with a 15-7 record, the best overall mark of any Big Ten team, shared the special honors awarded at the thirty-fifth annual Lafayette Lions club banquet here last night.

March 13, 1957 — Lamar Lundy, of Richmond, versatile senior center who was the runnerup in point production, was named "most valuable" player.

Joe Campbell, of Anderson, playmaking senior guard, who ranked third in scoring, was named honorary captain for the past season.

Bill Greve, of Waveland, sophomore forward whose 303 points in 22 games was tops for the Boilermakers, was awarded the Ward Lambert Scholarship trophy.

Selection of Lundy, who was named "most valuable" in football as an outstanding end last fall and now has the distinction of being the only athlete in Purdue history to win the same honor on both the gridiron and the hardwood, was a particu-

larly popular choice and brought a standing ovation from a crowd of over 500.

Although Lundy's close-in scoring was an important factor, his brilliant defensive play and rebounding was even more important in Purdue's hardwood successes. The 6-foot-6 inch 226-pound, two-sport star, turned in some of his greatest defensive performances against top competition.

Lundy held Archie Dees, of Indiana, to 15 points while scoring the same total himself and outrebounding the Hoosier pivot man 15-6. He stopped George BonSalle, of Illinois, with nine points, and won rebound honors against the Illini center, 14-7. Lundy scored 19 points against John Green, of Michigan State, while holding the Spartan center to 11 and taking the rebound battle 12-11.

SMALLEST IN BIG 10

Campbell, another senior two-sport star who was voted the honorary captaincy, was the smallest regular in Big Ten play at 5-feet-7 inches. The defending Big Ten golf champion and former national collegiate links king, despite his small stature, averaged 11.8 points per game, in addition to being the key man in the floor game.

SCHOLASTIC CHAMP

Greve, a distinguished student majoring in agricultural economies, had a scholastic index of 5.51 for the spring of 1956 and 5.37 last fall, as compared with a perfect 6.00, to win the scholarship trophy awarded annually to the member of the squad with the highest scholastic index for the two semesters preceding the end of the season.

Four seniors were included among the ten varsity players awarded major letters. In addition to Lundy and Campbell, the senior group included reserves Dan Alvarez, of Gary, and Tom Huber, of Brownstown.

Other awards announced included five minors for the varsity and 16 freshmen numerals.

Dr. R.C.S. Young, of Granville, Ohio, widely known lecturer and educator, was the principle speaker of the evening. Edgar Clain, president of the Lions Club, presided and James Mills, director of Purdue radio station WBBA, acted as toastmaster.

Other speakers included Don R. Mallett, executive dean, representing the University; Guy (Red) Mackey, athletic director; head coach Ray Eddy; freshman coach Paul Hoffman; Earl Ferris, who presented the Lambert award, and Campbell, who made the response for the squad as honorary captain.

Musical entertainment was provided by the Purdue Varsity Glee club under the direction of Albert P. Stewart.

Lamar Lundy excelled in both basketball and football.

PURDUE RALLY NIPS UCLA

Mitchell Hits Final Six in Drive from Late 12-Point Deficit

By Gordon Graham

December 19, 1959 — Johnny Wooden, Purdue's famous all-time All-America basketball star, almost got his wish upon his return to his alma mater last night. When introduced to the crowd of 7,500 by his old teammate and Purdue coach, Ray Eddy, Wooden said: "I wish there was a way for both teams to win."

Purdue's Boilermakers made one of their finest comebacks in recent years to clip Wooden and his UCLA visitors, 75-74.

MITCHELL HERO

Sensational clutch work by junior guard Dick Mitchell, of Elwood, won the game for the young Old Gold and Black squad. Dick came in with a little more than a minute to go and scored Purdue's last six points in an exciting span of 45 seconds.

Officiating, which was unbelievably bad, upset both coaches and both teams. After the wild encounter Wooden said: "It is a shame that I return to my old school and have to say something about the officiating. I don't want to take anything away from Ray and his team. That comeback was terrific. But

everybody in the fieldhouse except the officials knew Winters was supposed to shoot those last two free throws instead of Mitchell. Dischinger is certainly a wonderful sophomore prospect and Ray's team showed possibilities."

Coach Eddy also thought the officiating was far below par, but he naturally thought his team got as many bad breaks as UCLA. The partisan crowd seemed to agree with Eddy.

Purdue had played the clever UCLA squad on even terms for more than 30 minutes when Wooden's outfit got several fast breaks going and combined them with some sizzling outside shooting. The Bruins got eight field goals in the second half from outside the foul circle area. Bob Berry, the little 5-10 guard from Wanamaker, Indiana, took six long shots in the second period and hit all of them.

With the Boilermakers trailing only 45-44 after a 30-30 halftime score, Berry led a brilliant UCLA rally.

LEAD BY 12

In two minutes' time the Bruins shot the count up to 56-44 and it seemed that the Boilermakers were in for their third straight trouncing.

Manzie Winters, Bob Orrill, and Terry Dischinger kept plugging away, but UCLA still led 69-57 with only 3:40 left. Dischinger got four straight free throws and Jerry Berkshire scored underneath to slice the margin to 69-63 with 3:02 remaining, but Purdue's chances still seemed slim.

Forward Terry Dischinger helped Purdue beat UCLA with 27 points and 13 rebounds.

horn was blowing and official Don Elser would not allow the shot. Therefore, Dick was faced with the assignment of making three straight free throws instead of two. The Elwood lad made good and Purdue was on top, 73-72.

But the sharpshooting Berry wasn't through. He got another open shot beyond the foul circle fringe and sank it at 0:20.

Again it was up to Mitchell and he matched Berry's shot at 0:11. UCLA got one more shot but missed it and Purdue was fighting for the ball at the gun.

Except for the shooting, the game was just as close as the score indicates. Purdue was again below its basket sniping form, principally because men such as Orrill and Berkshire couldn't hit. These two performers had only 2 of 18 between them and they are much better than that.

27 FOR "DISH"

Dischinger had another sparkling night despite a slight charley-horse injury. Terry, playing forward this time with Winters at center, got 27 points, on 9 of 18 field goal attempts and 9 of 9 free throws. He pulled down 13 rebounds.

Terry had some help this time from Winters, 6-5 football end, who looks like he will be a valuable addition to Eddy's hardwood squad. Winters played 40 minutes, although he has been practicing regularly only two weeks, and he had 14 points and 14 rebounds.

Mitchell, of course, was a lifesaver with 18 points on 6 of 10 and 6 of 6, although Dick didn't play more than 25 minutes of the contest.

UCLA played good position on the rebounds and worked the ball well until the final four or five minutes. The Bruins made most of their 14 errors in the late stages, having only three in the first half.

The first half was close most of the way. Purdue had one lead of 13-12 when Mitchell, Dischinger, and Winters sparked a 10-point rally. John Green came in for Wooden to put the Bruins back on their feet and UCLA tied the score at 30-30 just before the intermission.

The sniping of Berry from the outside was largely responsible for building the Bruins' final shooting average to .403 on 27 of 67. Purdue had only .361 on 27 of 72. Both clubs did well from the charity stripe, Purdue making 23 of 30 and UCLA 20 of 29.

Winters hit from the corner and Dischinger swished one from the side. Tim McGinley sank another while UCLA's 6-8 John Berberich was making his ninth free throw in 10 tries. The score was 72-69 with a minute left.

Mitchell started his heroics with a set shot from the foul circle at 0:45, and the Boilermakers were in arrears only one point at 72-71.

GOOFY GOINGS-ON

Some goofy things happened in the closing seconds. Bill Ellis was fouled, but claimed an injury, although he was able to walk off the court. This brought Gary Cunningham in to shoot the free throw (or throws—it was a 1 and 1 situation). Cunningham had made three of four, but with the crowd roaring its displeasure, Gary missed this vital shot and Purdue was fouled on the rebound.

It appeared that Winters was the man fouled, but the deadeye Mitchell walked up to the free throw line and made his first shot to tie the score with 0:35 left. Wooden was at the bench protesting and as Mitchell made his second free throw the

DISH'S 52 POINTS TALK OF BIG 10

Michigan State Falls, 85-74

Lucas' 48 Record Gone; Purdue (9-2) At Iowa (8-2) Tonight

By Gordon Graham

February 27, 1961 — What a Dish! All-America Terry Dischinger unleashed scoring streaks, the likes of which Big Ten basketball has never seen, here Saturday night. His sensational splurge of 52 points not only smashed Jerry Lucas' recent conference record of 48, but it beat a fighting Michigan State team, which seemed on the verge of an upset victory in Purdue Fieldhouse. The final score was 85-74, Purdue, as Dischinger dropped 19 of 28 field goal shots and 14 of 15 free throw tries.

Coach Ray Eddy's Boilermakers left yesterday on a happy note as they headed for Iowa City, where the 9-2 Purdue five tangles with 8-2 Iowa in a contest which very likely will decide second place in the Big Ten scramble.

IOWA DEFENSE BEST!

With Iowa miraculously developing into the finest defensive team in top college circles after losing no less than four regulars, Purdue finds itself a distinct underdog tonight, despite the fact that the Boilermakers now boast a 15-5 record on the season and have won six straight conference games.

Iowa continued its amazing work by scoring an easy 61-43 victory over the favored Minnesota Gophers at Minneapolis Saturday night. Don Nelson, the Iowa ace, poured in 30 points and the Hawk defense gave Minnesota only 20 points in the first half.

Tonight's Big Ten feature at Iowa City starts at 8:30, Lafayette time.

A snowy Saturday night in Indiana saw 6,500 rabid fans brave the elements to cheer Purdue's quintet in its last home tilt of the 1960-61 campaign. The hardy customers were well-rewarded. They sat in on one of the great performances of intercollegiate basketball.

PERFECT AT HOME

Purdue wound up its home card with a perfect record, 11 straight in the fieldhouse, but it took all of Dischinger's great talents to turn the trick.

How about this? With 7:58 to go in the nip and tuck battle, Michigan State was leading Purdue 62-61 as Dischinger swished a jump shot from well out to the side to put the Riveters back into a one-point lead.

20 IN 5 MINUTES!

Exactly five minutes later (at 2:58), Purdue had scored 22 points for a clinching margin of 83-69—and "Terrific Terry" had tallied no less than 20 of these! Dish passed off to Steve Rickelman for the only other Purdue score in this blistering streak.

Twenty points in five minutes with victory hanging in the balance! Nothing like it has ever been seen around the conference.

Coach Forddy Anderson and his scrappy Spartan cagers thought they had seen Dischinger in a hot streak early in the first half. With Purdue on top, 14-13, Terry whizzed in seven straight points in two minutes for a 21-13 count. But "The Dish" was just warming up.

MSU fought back and would have pushed well in front but for another Dischinger uprising. From the 9:00 minute mark to 4:00, Terry rolled in 13 consecutive Purdue points!

These torrid spans led up to his 20-point finish to make Dischinger's performance utterly fantastic.

True, Dischinger was not the only cager on the court, but nobody would wish to deny that the night belonged to Terry.

Jerry Berkshire fought like a demon off the boards and all over the court, showing more speed than at any other time in his college career.

SENIORS HELP

Bob Orrill and Dick Mitchell, senior guards playing their last home games at Purdue, were important factors. Orrill thrives on the fast-break style which the Riveters tried against speedy MSU. Mitchell was one of the most important feeders Dischinger had while Dick was in the game. Steve Rickelman staged a second-half comeback on the boards to help Dischinger and Berkshire in this department.

Purdue, generally on the deliberate side, chose to run it out with the Spartans, who play nothing else but the go-go style. The decision might have been a sad one had it not cut Dischinger loose for his most sensational night. Also, there was the fact that the invading Spartans could not hit the hoop from the field with any degree of consistency.

Michigan State blasted away 84 times, but made only 24 for a low percentage of .286. Purdue canned 33 of 71 for a fine .465.

Both teams were hotter than stove lids at the free throw line, Purdue dunking 19 of 23 and MSU

26 of 31. For a time it appeared that free throws might win the contest for the lowly Spartans, but Dischinger took care of that.

Purdue did all right with its fast-break offense, but the usually strong Riveter defense did not hold up well with all of this running back and forth. Despite Dischinger's 20 points, Purdue had to settle for a 44-44 tie at halftime.

GET IN TROUBLE

Eddy's men hit their lone serious cold streak at the outset of the second half. Tim McGinley scored right off the bat and Purdue then went seven minutes before Berkshire dropped the next field goal. The Spartans were also having their troubles and their lead was only 54-51.

The count moved to 57-55, MSU, when Dischinger made his first basket of the half at 10:16 to tie the score at 57-57. Terry then got 24 of the last 28 Purdue points and 20 of the last 22 as previously reported.

Michigan State was handicapped when its top scorer, Dick Hall, fouled out of the contest early in the second period. Hall had 12 points at the time. Dick got himself trapped with a couple of accidental charging fouls. The two little Spartan guards Art Schwarm with 17 and Dave Fahs with 15 led the losers. But it took 33 shots for Schwarm and Fahs to tally 10 field goals between them.

The crippling Hoosier blizzard not only kept newspapers away from Dischinger's record effort, but officials Biebel and Magnussen didn't make it and were never heard from.

SUB REFS OK

With Sectional tourneys tying up most high school officials, the job of finding substitutes was difficult. Purdue finally found Ray Shoemaker, local referee, and Dick Bossung, assistant West Lafayette high school coach. Considering the tough spot they were in, Shoemaker and Bossung did fine jobs. And this game was a blazer right down to the wire.

At 2:58, with the record in his pocket, Dischinger stopped shooting. Purdue worked the ball around to protect its lead. The students didn't like it for a while, but most of them realized it was important for the Boilermakers to protect their margin without taking unnecessary chances since a rough contest at Iowa looms tonight.

GRAHAM CRACKERS

By Gordon Graham

"The Dish" can take it, but better still, he can "dish it out" in gigantic proportions. One of the truly great college basketball performances was seen at Purdue fieldhouse Saturday night. You are already familiar with the fact that Terry Dischinger singed the nets for 52 points, an all-time individual record for a single Big Ten game. But the manner in which they were scored is almost unbelievable.

This was not the soft touch it figured to be. Most scoring records are set in a lopsided game where the player can feel free to go for extra baskets and his teammates join in the fun by feeding him late in the contest. There wasn't a tainted point in the 52 scored by Dischinger against Michigan State.

Purdue couldn't have won without Terry's closing blast. Michigan State had a 44-44 tie at the half, short leads in both periods, and was in front by a point with 7:58 remaining when "The Dish" broke their plate with a rush which never had been equalled here.

Then with 2:58 left and the Spartans finally subdued, there was the big chance for Purdue and Terry to go for the 60 mark, a record which might have held up for years to come. Instead, Dish and the Boilermakers played control ball. Terry never took another shot. It was one of the most legitimate marks ever recorded.

An elated fan grinned and cracked: "Dish was streaky tonight, wasn't he?" Yes, he was...but what streaks they were! Terry didn't score a field goal in the first seven minutes of the game and failed to snag one in the first 9:44 of the second half. That means he swished 19 baskets in the remaining 23:56 of competition.

Dischinger had two first-half splurges of 7 and 13 points. Then he registered 24 of the last 28 points. These fi-ery explosions accounted for 44 of his 52 points.

Close observers were wondering after this exhibition just how many points the sensational Purdue junior would score if the Boilermakers were a fast-breaking team such as Ohio State, Indiana or Michigan State. Saturday marked one of the rare occasions that Purdue has chosen to run it out all the way with an opponent this season.

Terry generally has to hack away steadily but surely for his points. Purdue usually works carefully for shots and takes less than the average team. With the game going pell-mell every outing, Dischinger might easily average over 35 per contest.

His record production put Dischinger well in front of his friendly rival, Jerry Lucas of Ohio State, for Big Ten individual honors. Dish now has 319 points in 11 games for a flat 29.0 average. Lucas has 295 in 12 games for 24.6. If Terry averages only 15 per game in his last three assignments on the road, Lucas would have to score 70 in his two chances to beat the Dish. Possible, but unlikely.

You would have loved the way Terry went over the record...At 4:13 Terry delivered a three-pointer to give Purdue breathing room at 78-68...this gave him 47 points. Seconds later he tied Lucas with a free throw. Then there was the matter of a new mark. Dish drove down the middle, had a fine shot about 10 feet in front of the hoop, but passed off to Steve Rickelman for a short one underneath. Of all things, Steve blew the shot and Terry leaped up to tap it in for 50. Dish banged along one from the side for 52 and then refused to shoot any more.

CHAPTER 13

"DISH" WINS GAME, SCORING TITLE

Purdue 3rd with 9-5

Terry's Last Shot Defeats Michigan

March 12, 1962 — ANN ARBOR, MICHIGAN — Purdue's basketball squad has reached the banquet stage of the 1961-62 season and the Boilermakers are in a happy state of mind. They finished out the campaign with a 77-75 triumph in a blistering battle at Michigan Saturday afternoon. This clinched undisputed third place in the Big Ten on a highly respectable record of 9-5.

Coach Ray Eddy and his Purdue players will be honored at the Purdue Memorial Union building tomorrow night at 6:15 at the Lions club banquet.

All-America Terry Dischinger bowed out as the Big Ten's greatest scorer in sensational fashion Saturday. Terry has taken many a fling at the basket in his three seasons at Purdue, with more than 50 per cent of them hitting the target.

The last of these famed Dischinger shots came with about four seconds remaining and the score tied at 75-75. "Swish"—and the 20-foot archer went in and "The Dish" had won a game for old Purdue with the final shot of his collegiate career.

Despite a sprained ankle, which had kept him from participating in much of the practice for the Michigan finale. Dischinger defended his conference scoring title against the strong threat of thin Jimmy Rayl of Indiana.

Terry wound up with 30 points and 459 for the 14-game Big Ten card. Rayl got 25 against champion Ohio State and checked in with 454. The two rivals had been tied going into the closing Saturday.

MORE RECORDS

Dischinger is wading knee-deep in Big Ten records. He smashed another important one at Michigan. Robin Freeman, the dead-eye shooter from Ohio state, got 455 points in 14 games in 1955 for a 32.5 average. Terry's 30 gave him 459 for 14 games, and a record average of 32.8 for one season. He also tied Don Schlundt's 18-game record of 459 points with that last-second winning shot.

The Purdue ace also extended many records already broken by him. The most important was his career average of 29.71 per game, which tops Freeman's mark of 27.03. Terry set his total points in three seasons at 1,248 as compared to Schlundt's 1,237. And Dish's free throws soared to 179 as against Schlundt's former mark of 157.

Dischinger became only the third man to lead the conference three seasons in a row. The others were Schlundt and John Schommer, who started all of this back in 1907-08-09.

Purdue started out as if it were going to annihilate Michigan. The Boilermaker offense got away brilliantly and led 30-16. Michigan braced strongly. With Tom Cole and Dick Herner leading the way, the Wolverines battled to a 47-47 tie at halftime.

Dischinger had 21 points at the intermission and seemed to have his scoring crown clinched. But Terry was shackled very well in the second half and scored only seven points until he whizzed his winning goal into the hoop.

The Wolverines and Boilermakers scrapped on even terms most of the way during the second half, but coach Bob Strack's home club seemed to have the game on ice when it took a 74-67 margin with only a little over three minutes to go.

STRONG RALLY

Mel Garland, who had a dazzling second half, led the Boilermaker revival. Purdue tied the score with about 1:30 left and then did a sharp job of holding the ball until only 16 seconds remained.

Eddy called time out and set up a pattern designed to bring the winning basket. A "guard around" set saw Garland flip the ball to Dischinger at the foul circle. Terry saw he couldn't drive, so shot from 20 feet out and gave Purdue its 77-75 edge with only four seconds left.

Purdue won its game at the free throw line, hitting 17 of 19, with Dischinger canning 14 of 15. Michigan had 32 baskets to 30 for the Riveters.

Purdue outshot the Wolverines by a slight margin and Michigan nudged in front on rebounds. The Boilermakers hit 30 of 68 from the field for .440, while Michigan canned 32 of 75 for .427. Rebounds were 45 for the losers and 39 for Purdue.

"DISH" TO TRY BASEBALL

"Dish" Will Stay at Purdue Another Year, or Longer

By Gordon Graham

What is Terry Dischinger going to do? This question has been raised hundreds of times in recent months. The greatest scorer in the history of Big Ten basketball finished his Purdue career in a blaze of glory Saturday by firing the winning field goal on his last collegiate shot at Michigan.

Now, what are his plans?

Your reporter talked to Dischinger for a few moments in the Purdue fieldhouse late Saturday night and again Sunday afternoon.

"It appears definite that I will be at Purdue for another full year, possibly longer," said Terry. "I will work toward the completion of my degree (chemical engineering) and the start on my masters. I hope to be able to help Coach Eddy with basketball in some capacity."

WILL LISTEN, BUT—

Dischinger probably has an army hitch to serve some time in 1963, likely to start in either the summer or fall.

So, how about professional basketball?

"I haven't completely shut the door on that," Terry admitted, "but it's hard to see how there would be any way for me to play for at least a year. I will listen to all proposals, but I'm going to finish my schooling."

The Chicago Packers have first draft choice (there are not territorial rights anymore) and they have said they will pick Dischinger if Terry is interested in playing. One report said they would offer $75,000 to be spread over three seasons.

"No offer has ever been made to me or my parents," Dischinger says, "but somebody did try to feel my dad (Donas Dischinger of Terre Haute) out as to whether or not I would play."

TO TRY BASEBALL

Terry is "fair game" now that his basketball days are over—but hold on a minute—he's planning to try out for coach Joe Sexson's baseball team this spring!

"Dish" grinned and said: "Yes, I've decided to try baseball. I may not last very long. I haven't played much for about four years and I will miss the spring trip south because of the Shrine East-West All-Star game in Kansas City."

Dischinger is a first baseman and he played a lot of baseball with strong youth teams in Terre Haute, such as Babe Ruth league and American Legion juniors, in addition to high school ball.

CHAPTER 14

PURDUE WINS IN DOUBLE OVERTIME!

Schellhase had 43

Nips Notre Dame at Ft. Wayne, 112-103

By Bruce Ramey

January 22, 1964 — FORT WAYNE — Purdue and Notre Dame counter-rallied each other into near-exhaustion here Tuesday night, but the Boilermakers held firm through the spectacular battle and earned a 112-103 decision by running off in the second overtime.

Purdue had made a great comeback in regulation time after trailing 88-81 with 3:20 to go. After the 91-91 deadlock, Purdue took a 97-91 margin with 2:00 left in the first overtime. Then Notre Dame made a brilliant rally to tie the score in the final three seconds 99-99.

In the second extra session, the Boilermakers again moved well in front by carefully moving the ball around and breaking for the basket. Their star scorer, Dave Schellhase, scored the first seven Purdue points in this deciding period and 11 of the 13 counted by the winners.

Schellhase, one of the many stars in the wild encounter, was by far the top scorer with 43 points, the high of this sophomore's short career. Schellhase hit 19 of 21 free throws, many of them in clutch situations. The Purdue club as a whole

won the game at the charity stripe with 34 of 43, while Notre Dame was canning 19 of 30.

The cheering crowd saw Purdue take charge at the start, then Notre Dame come strongly to look like a winner. Coach Ray Eddy's gang was on top 28-16 when the Irish began to click. Lead by Ron Reed, Larry Sheffield, and Sam Skarich, Notre Dame wiped out this lead.

IRISH DOMINATE

Despite the fact 6-9 Walter Sahm fouled out in the first two minutes of the second half, Notre Dame continued to dominate play. Sheffield, Reed, and Skarich led the Irish to 66-57 lead before the Riveters began to awaken again.

Bob Purkhiser, Earl Brown, Doug Trudeau, and Mel Garland joined Schellhase in whittling away at the Notre Dame margin. Cutting the edge to 72-70, Purdue fell back again as ND shot in front 80-72 with 5:55 to go.

Jordan's five was still on top 88-81 with 3:20 left. Garland hit two free throws, Rod Hicks sniped a jumper, and Brown tipped one in as Purdue came to within a point 87-88 at 1:51.

The fight had just begun. After two Irish free throws Purkhiser sniped one from the side and Hicks snagged two key free throws to put Purdue ahead 91-90 with 0:42 remaining.

Purdue held the ball, daring Notre Dame to foul but the Irish stayed away. With about six seconds left Garland's pass was intercepted by Skarich. Mel fouled Skarich with three seconds left. Sam made his first attempt and missed the second for the 91-91 count at the end of regulation time.

The Boilermakers moved in front again in the first overtime and Notre Dame made another great rally. Hicks, star pinch-hitter for Purdue in this struggle, got the Riveters well in front, but ND tallied six points in the last 50 seconds for another 99-99 deadlock at the gun.

FOULS HURT ND

Finally the weary rivals came to a decision in the second extra stanza. Notre Dame was handicapped more than Purdue by losing regulars via the foul route. The Irish had to foul often in the extra sessions to get possession of the ball as they were trailing in each session.

Purdue hit 39 of 98 shots from the field to 42 of 106 for Notre Dame. High man for the Irish was Ron Reed with 26.

Notre Dame outrebounded Purdue 76 to 65, but to no avail. The Irish lost their entire starting front line of Sahm, Miller, and Reed plus sub forward Dick Erlenbaugh before the hectic scramble was over.

Purdue's Garland and Purkhiser fed the ball beautifully and the former did a fine defensive job against Sheffield late in the contest, forcing the ND ace in numerous traveling errors.

Dave Schellhase (42) once scored 43 points as a sophomore against Notre Dame.

HICKS BIG HELP

Hicks was probably the key man of all reserves. Rod hit 5 of 10 from the field, copped five rebounds, and dropped four free throws down the stretch.

Purdue used a zone defense much of the time until midway in the second half when it switched to aggressive press. Notre Dame stuck with a man-to-man almost all of the way. The Irish made 20 errors during the 50 minutes of play to 16 for Purdue.

In addition to his whopping 43 points, Schellhase had 21 rebounds for the winners. Brown got 10, Purkhiser 8, Garland 7, Trudeau 5, and Hicks 5. Reed not only topped the losers with 26 points but took in 25 rebounds. Sahm and Skarich each had 10 off the boards.

A crowd of 4,704, composed mostly of Purdue rooters, witnessed the thrilling affair in Allen County Memorial Coliseum.

Notre Dame's all-time edge over Purdue was sliced to 19-18. The Boilermakers now have won two of three since the two schools switched their annual feature to Ft. Wayne. Purdue moved up to 5-8 for the season and ND slipped back to 5-10.

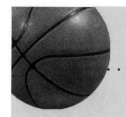

CHAPTER 15

PURDUE UPSETS MICHIGAN, 81-79

Schellhase Second In Scoring Race

March 10, 1964 — ANN ARBOR, MICH. — Purdue's Boilermakers, unable to win a game on the road before last Saturday, pulled one of the nation's top basketball upsets of the season here Monday night, downing the nation's second-ranked team, Michigan, in an 81-79 thriller.

The result allowed Ohio State, which completed its Big Ten season by also losing a surprising upset at home (to Michigan State) last Saturday, to tie Michigan for the loop championship, marking an unprecedented fifth title in a row for the Buckeyes.

Michigan, however, will represent the conference in the NCAA championships, opposing Loyola at the Minneapolis Fieldhouse in the regional on Friday—Ohio State having represented the Big Ten more recently than the Wolverines.

Michigan and Ohio State ended with 11-3 Big Ten marks. The Wolverines lost only once outside the league as they turned in a 20-4 overall record, their best in all history.

Purdue, which defeated host Northwestern Saturday, boosted its league record to 8-6, tying for fourth place with Michigan State in the final standings. Coach Ray Eddy's squad was 12-12 for the full campaign. Only a year ago Purdue finished last in the league, at 2-12, and was only 7-17 over-all.

The decision avenged Purdue's only Big Ten loss at home, a 77-70 game early in January; and it also marked Michigan's only home defeat in all games this season.

The Boilermakers garnered further satisfaction as their sparkling sophomore, Dave Schellhase, clinched runner-up honors in the Big Ten individual scoring race, behind Ohio State's record-setting Gary Bradds. The game here was billed as a duel between Schellhase and smooth Wolverine soph Cazzie Russell, who started the game 15 points behind the Boilermaker star.

GARLAND SPARKLES

Both youngsters were tremendous, with Schellhase finishing with 25 points and Russell with 27. Schellhase closed with 379 in 14 games for a 27-point average, Russell 366 for a 26.1 mark.

While the sophomore stars were living up to their press notices, it was magnificent guard play by Purdue's Mel Garland and Bob Purkhiser which provided the slight difference in the game.

Garland, the only senior in the visitors' lineup, was a ball-handling wizard and contributed 16 points to the attack as he padded his career total which is second in Purdue annals only to the distinguished Terry Dischinger. And it was Garland's two clutch free throws which tied the score at 77-all with 1:50 remaining.

Purkhiser, hitting long efforts from the side throughout the game, topped the winners with 26 points. Several of his baskets were from the 30- to 35-foot range.

Purkhiser snapped the late tie with a short jumper inside the one-minute mark. A moment later, fouled by Wolverine center Bill Buntin, Purkhiser calmly cashed the two free throws which ran the score to 81-77.

Purdue allowed Michigan captain Bobby Cantrell an unopposed basket with 14 seconds remaining, then Garland froze the ball in the final seconds.

The game was a dog-fight all the way, although the Wolverines trailed most of the time— once by 10 points and several times by nine in the first half. It was 43-38, Purdue, at the intermission, by which time Purkhiser had 15 points and Schellhase six baskets and eight rebounds. Buntin, who closed with 19 points for the game, had 14 of these in the first half and also had 8 rebounds.

Purdue held in the front early in the second half, stretching the advantage to eight, at 50-42, and owning a seven-point edge soon after at 54-47.

Then Michigan opened a surge that threatened to salvage the game.

Russell was at his best in the drive, collecting seven points as the hosts went ahead 58-57, sending the appreciative crowd of 7,650 to a frenzy.

SIX PLAY FOR PURDUE

It was nip-and-tuck for the remaining nine minutes with each club building up three-point leads only to lose them again. But Michigan seemed in command, until Garland was fouled inside the two-minute mark.

Michigan's marksmanship and its awesome rebounding faltered in the dying moments, allowing Purdue possession twice after the 77-77 tie, and the Boilermakers made good on both occasions.

Eddy went the entire distance with only six men, spelling big Bill Jones only briefly in the second half after Jones picked up his third personal foul. Jones got his fourth soon after returning, but was around at the finish to help on the bankboards, in addition to contributing 11 points.

Earl Brown converted three free throws for Purdue; and George Grams, the only sub, failed to score.

Oliver Darden was only the third Wolverine in double figures, with 14

FEW FOULS

Purdue's shooting once again was remarkable, especially for a road engagement. The Boilermakers hit 33 of 62 tries for .533. Michigan, tough on the offensive boards, had 81 shots but hit only 35 for .432.

Rebounds were almost even for the game, the Wolverines snatching 45 caroms to Purdue's 43. Schellhase (12) and Jones (9) had almost half of Purdue's total.

The game was cleanly played, with only 13 fouls whistled against each team. At least four of Purdue's were charging violations, denying Michigan free throws, as the Boilermakers actually won at the free throw line, converting 15 of 19 chances to Michigan's 9 of 13.

CHAPTER 16

"SHELL" GETS 57!!

Indiana May Miss Walker Tonight

Michigan, Dave set marks in 128-94 tilt

February 21, 1966 — ANN ARBOR— Big Ten records fell like autumn leaves in a high wind here Saturday afternoon as Michigan's finely-tuned basketball team and Purdue's fantastic Dave Schellhase thrilled 7,200 fans in Yost Fieldhouse. Michigan set a conference high as its offense exploded for a smashing 128-94 victory. Schellhase, in a tight race for national scoring honors, gave his No. 1 standing a lift, with an amazing 57-point effort on 23 of 42 field goal attempts and 11 of 12 free throws.

The game, as a team contest, fell apart early as Michigan's sparkling ball handling, deadly shooting, and fierce rebounding was too much for last-place Purdue. The Boilermakers took Michigan's zone press apart in the early minutes, but the Wolverines went back to a normal man-to-man style and rushed from an 18-16 lead to 30-19.

WATCH DAVE, CAZZIE

It was all downhill after that, but the crowd got its kicks by following the highly advertised Schellhase-Cazzie Russell duel. It was close at the half when Schellhase had 22 and Russell 20, but the Purdue star was not to be denied in the second period. He showed the Michigan defense a variety of shots and moves which it hadn't seen before.

When Coach Dave Strack began removing his regulars late in the game, Russell came out with 28 points and 4:35 left. Schellhase had 47 at the time.

Dave's Purdue mates were now interested in the individual record and they did a fine job of feeding Schellhase down to the wire. However, the Purdue star got many of his own by rebounding strongly on the offensive board.

Schellhase finally topped Tommy Rayl's (Indiana) record of 56 in the closing seconds on a feed from Dennis Brady.

Denny Brady helped Schellhase score 57 points against Michigan.

GRAHAM CRACKERS

By Gordon Graham

Dave "Heinz" Schellhase showed 'em 57 varieties at Michigan Saturday afternoon. Well, perhaps not quite that many, but the Michigan guards admitted that Schellhase made every type of shot they have seen up to now except the "dipper." The Wolverines thought they had the answer to slowing Schellhase, who had never scored heavily against them before, but old "Heinz" was turned loose when the game developed into one of those slam-bang affairs and he gave one of basketball's all-time great performances.

Joe Sexson, who has been around the Big Ten as both a player and a coach, used the right word when he said the Saturday game at Ann Arbor was the greatest basketball "spectacle" he had ever seen. First of all, Michigan had one of those dreamy days when all phases of all departments were in top running order. As Coach George King said, "Not a team in the country could have stayed with Michigan today."

Then there was the drama of Schellhase wearing out the nets for the losers to set a new Big Ten individual record of 57 points. The fans saw the best any Big Ten team had ever done in one game and the best an individual had ever done, all in one afternoon.

"It's something you don't even dream about," Schellhase said yesterday about scoring 57 points against the Wolverines. "When 43 is your high you hardly think of getting 57 against Michigan, which has always been rough on me. It's too bad we couldn't have won, but on that particular day Michigan was the best thing we have seen offensively."

Does a player know he is going for a record in all that din and confusion near the end of a basketball game? Schellhase knew. "The guys on the bench yelled in the last few seconds that I needed one more basket for the record. I don't know how they found out, but they let me know," Dave said.

"There were only about 10 seconds left when Brady and I came down the floor in a 2 on 1 situation," Schellhase explained. "The guard seemed to be concentrating on me, but from about 20 feet out Denny really threaded the needle with a pass and I went under for a layup," the Boilermaker All-America reported happily.

Michigan started out with the 6-8 Jim Myers guarding Schellhase. It didn't work out, so in a surprise move Cazzie Russell was clamped on Dave for the last 10 minutes of the first half and over 15 minutes of the second, until the great Michigan ace went to the bench.

In the past, Larry Tregoning (now graduated) and Oliver Darden worked on Schellhase. Darden is foul prone, but a good defensive man—so Strack gambled with Russell and Myers.

How does a guy get 57 points in one game? First of all, he must have a certain type of game. The ball has to be moving fast from one end to the other. You aren't going to do it in a deliberate offense contest. Then he has to be feeling right.

"I felt especially good before the game, and I thought we were going to beat them like we did up there two years ago," Schellhase told us Sunday. "I told Henry (Ebershoff) that I felt coordinated and confident in my shots—even the ones I missed looked to me like they were going in."

Of all the men on the floor, only Myers outrebounded Schellhase, who picked off 12—Myers had 14.

Jimmy Rayl took 48 shots the game he scored 23 field goals—Schellhase got his 23 down in 42 shots, and many of these were rebounding efforts.

It takes a whale of a game to hoist a scoring average at this late date in a season. Schellhase was leading the nation's scorers last week by only .5 of a point over Dave Wagnon of Idaho State. Purdue's star didn't seem to have much chance of bettering himself when he was headed for Michigan, of all places.

The 57-point splurge raised Dave's average from 31.1 to 32.5. He also moved within one point of Russell in Big Ten scoring. Cazzie had a lead of 30 points going into the fracas at Ann Ar-

bor. Russell scored a tidy 28—you wouldn't think he'd lose much ground on such a production, but he dropped a whopping 29 points. Now Russell has 288 and Schellhase 287. Schellhase won the title from Russell last year, 391 to 340.

Dave Wagnon, current runnerup in the national scoring race, got 40 points Saturday night as Idaho State beat Idaho, 114-96.

Schellhase Named to All-Star Club

National scoring leader Dave Schellhase of Purdue, who set a Big Ten single-game scoring record of 57 points against Michigan Saturday, and Notre Dame's Capt. Bucky McGann were added to the Indiana Collegiate All-Star basketball team that will play Kentucky seniors in April.

Schellhase, 6-4, an All-America both in athletics and scholarship, played high school ball for Evansville North.

McGann, a West Palm Beach, Florida, product, is 6-3.

Indiana University's Gary Grieger of Evansville, Max Walker of Milwaukee and Evansville's Larry Humes and Sam Watkins were signed for the Hoosier squad earlier.

Dave Schellhase scored 57 points against Michigan.

NO. 1 UCLA "SWEEK'S" OUT LAST-SECOND WIN

Boilermaker Cagers Lose, But 73-71 Debut Impressive

By George Bolinger

December 4, 1967 — Purdue's new basketball arena, dedicated in a simple but impressive ceremony Saturday night, may be found wanting in the number of first aid facilities if the opening game there is any criterion of things to come.

Unfortunately for a battling gang of Boilermakers, half of them "new" to the home fans, the dedication contest will go into the record book as a two-point defeat, 73-71. But the opener may never be matched for importance, effort and drama!

It was a heart-throbber all the way, keeping the above-capacity crowd of 14,200 on its feet in a wild finish.

National champion UCLA, coming off an unbeaten season with a roster even stronger than last season's, barely "Sweeked" past the determined Boilermakers.

The deciding shot was a 24-foot effort by Bill Sweek, a sub guard who is one of a very few of the Uclans who hasn't achieved national fame in the past. It was his only score of the game.

In this fashion, then, did Coach George King unveil his sophomore-dominated Purdue crew, voted this past week as co-favorite, along with defending Big Ten champion Indiana, in the upcoming Big Ten race.

GAVE AWAY CORNERS

King's sophomores made a lot of "believers," not the least of which are the defending champion Uclans.

"I was really surprised at Purdue's defense," said Coach John Wooden admiringly. "I rate the Big Ten as a great offensive league, but not particularly adept on defense. But they had a well-conceived plan against us."

King, with a "big" man who almost can match UCLA's splendid Lew Alcindor in height and with a sophomore guard who is favoring an injured foot, used, basically, a "diamond" zone defense.

"Under the basket, we used Chuck Bavis (7-foot) in front of Alcindor (7-foot-1 1/2)," King explained, "with Roger Blalock helping on Alcindor and also taking the baseline and the corners as much as he could. Then, we had two men on the "wings," taking away the side shots, and a man on the point of the diamond, cutting off the middle.

"Actually, we had to give away the corners— you have to give away something. And they got some down the middle, too. But they have a great team with outstanding personnel. And I'm just as proud of our kids as I can be."

The aggressive defense of the lanky Bavis, with Blalock's competent help, of course, limited Alcindor to 17 points—third-low production of his 31-game career. But Lew, who went the full 40 minutes (Bavis played 27, with 6-10 soph Jerry Johnson going 13), was a tower of rebounding strength. He grabbed 19, as compared to Purdue's game-total of 36.

The first 14 minutes of play was mostly Purdue, with fabulous sophomore shooter Rick Mount and veteran Herman Gilliam getting off to fast starts. Purdue led 33-26.

But the Uclans finished the half fast, zooming in front by six, at 45-39, before Mount's 30-footer just before the gun left it at 45-41.

The late Purdue lapse, coupled with the visitors' surge at the start of the second half, indicated that the pre-game "spread" of 15 points, for UCLA, was reasonable.

UCLA LOSES POISE

With Lynn Shackleford, a 1966 fixture but a non-starter here, bombing from those corners, UCLA moved in front by 7, then 9, and finally 12—at 60-48. It appeared all over with 12 minutes remaining.

It stayed that way for several minutes, when Alcindor's lay-up made it 67-55 with nine minutes left.

Then Wooden got another surprise.

"With a lead like that late in the game, we usually win going away," he said. "But we lost our composure, which was both a surprise and a disappointment to me."

Hustling and scrambling all over the floor, Purdue aided the Uclans into several key errors. And, even though encountering free throw difficulties, the Boilermakers crept close. (UCLA made only six points in those final nine minutes.)

Mount, with a Bavis assist, hit a jumper. Gilliam drove for a scoop-up. Jim Nielsen, another unsung Bruin, interrupted with a free throw. It was 68-59.

Blalock connected on a long shot and Bavis contributed one free throw, and Shackleford interrupted with a free throw. It was 69-62.

The remarkable Gilliam hit another long one; and speedy Tyrone Bedford, another soph, roared under for a lay-up. It was 69-66, and the Boilermakers were on the scent of an upset.

Big Alcindor got free for one lay-up at 2:17. But Mount hit a medium-length jumper and Gilliam hooked one home to make it 71-70 at 1:10.

Here, UCLA, violently opposed to the "stall," hung on for dear life—and almost "blew" it.

An error got Purdue the ball at 0:52, but a jump ball was called 11 seconds later. UCLA controlled illegally, and Purdue had the ball out-of-bounds. At 0:29 Mount was fouled—and a technical was assessed when UCLA protested the call too violently.

The free throw trouble continued, as Mount missed the first of the one-on-one, but canned the technical shot to tie it. Purdue had possession out-of-bounds, set up Mount for a shot that missed—and Alcindor swept the board to set up Sweek's winning bucket.

The result extended UCLA's all-winning string to 35, as the nation's No. 1 club seeks the 60-straight record of San Francisco.

Shackleford and starting guard Lucius Allen led the winners with 18 each—and both shone for the visitors. Behind Alcindor's 17, sub Nielsen came up with 9. Edgar Lacey and Mike Lynn, a pair of two-year lettermen who didn't perform for UCLA last season, started here, but made only four points each.

South Bend's Mike Warren, the UCLA playmaker and normally a fine scorer, made but a single free throw, drawing four fouls in the first half, and fouling out after 24 minutes playing time.

MOUNT'S 28 HIGH

Mount, who cooled considerably after making his first four shots, ended with 11 of 27 and 6 for 8 free throws for 28 points, high for the game. Gilliam downed 10 of 17 and added a free throw for 21. Bavis and pesky Bill Keller had 7 each and Blalock 6.

Purdue shot fairly well, downing 29 of 62 (and you don't get easy shots against Alcindor) for .468, but cashed only 13 of 22 free throws. UCLA also canned 13 free ones, in 18 tries, and hit 30 of 78 field shots for a cool .385.

UCLA led in rebounds, 49-36, but made 21 errors to Purdue's mere 11.

Purdue next meets the University of Washington at Seattle on both Friday and Saturday nights.

"The big difference between the Midwest and the Pacific Coast," said Wooden, "is that the man with the ball gets more leeway here. When Purdue gets to the Coast, it will find it gets called for charging more often than in tonight's game."

"I told our boys that if they play this hard and this well they can win their next 23 games," King remarked.

The cage season officially is open!

UCLA (73)	FG	FT	Reb.	PF	TP
Lacey	2-5	0-0	4	1	4
Lynn	2-7	0-0	2	4	4
Alcindor	7-16	3-5	19	1	17
Warren	0-5	1-1	1	5	1
Allen	8-21	2-3	1	4	18
Shackleford	8-16	2-3	9	2	18
Nielsen	2-5	5-6	5	1	9
Sweek	1-3	0-0	0	2	2
Team Rebs.			8		
Totals	30-78	13-18	49	20	73
Purdue (71)	FG	FT	Reb.	PF	TP
Gilliam	10-17	1-3	7	3	21
Blalock	3-4	0-1	7	2	6
Bavis	2-4	3-3	2	4	7
Keller	2-7	3-6	2	3	7
Mount	11-27	6-8	3	3	28
Johnson	0-2	0-0	1	1	0
Bedford	1-1	0-1	3	0	2
Reasoner	0-0	0-0	1	0	0
Team Rebs.			10		
Totals	29-62	13-22	36	16	71

Score by Periods

UCLA	45	28—73	
Purdue	41	30—71	

FG Percentage: UCLA .385; Purdue .468
FT Percentage: UCLA .722; Purdue .591
Officials: Kaefer and Hulet

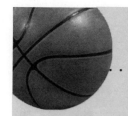

PURDUE REFLECTS BRIEFLY ON SEASON BEFORE GETTING READY FOR MIAMI OF OHIO

By George Bolinger

March 10, 1969 — Having accomplished all of its objectives of recent weeks in remarkable fashion, Purdue's basketball team will start a new—and brief—campaign no later than this afternoon as it starts preparations for NCAA Tourney action.

Coach George King's crew will oppose Miami of Ohio, a team which was highly troublesome on the arena court here in December, in the second game Thursday night (10 o'clock, EST) in the NCAA Mideast Regional at Madison, Wisconsin. (Purdue beat Miami only 78-70 in December.)

The Boilermakers made merry at the expense of Indiana in the regular-season finale Saturday, 120-76, to close out Big Ten play with a glittering 13-1 mark and to post a final regular 20-4 record.

Speaking of records, so many were set by junior All-America guard Rick Mount and by Purdue as a team that it may require a computer to locate all of them.

120 IS ALL-TIME HIGH

Suffice it to say that Mount became the top scorer in both Purdue and Big Ten history; and that Purdue became the top team one-season scorer in conference history.

It was Purdue's best season, scoring-wise, for all games, too—as the Boilermakers led the nation with a 94.8 per-game average (and led the nation in free throw shooting with a .784 accuracy mark, besides being among the top five or six in field goal marksmanship).

It turned out to be that kind of a season—and a list of the more-apparent and more-important marks can be found on page 54.

The 120 total itself established all kinds of highs for Purdue. It was the most ever in one game, most ever in the loop, most ever against Indiana, etc.

Mount went into the Saturday contest needing 12 points for a Riveter mark, 22 for a Big Ten one-season mark, and 39 for a conference two-season mark.

RICK WARMS UP

Despite complete cooperation from his teammates, Mount had shooting trouble for quite a while. But he got his Purdue record before halftime, finishing with 15 points—as the Riveters led by an insurmountable 58-32.

While Mount couldn't find basket range, his teammates were doing a fantastic job on the bankboards. Many of Rick's misfires were followed in for two-pointers.

Eleven more minutes passed before Mount got the Big Ten standard—bringing down the applause of the jammed house and causing a break in the action as Mount was presented with the ball as a permanent keepsake.

"I didn't think I was shooting too badly in the first 30 minutes," Mount said later. "A lot of them went in and out."

There was suspicion that Mount was "pressing" a little while shooting for the record. In any event, he singed the nets for 17 points in the next eight minutes, despite sitting a part of that on the bench.

KELLER HAS BEST GAME

While the afternoon belonged to Mount, individually, and to the remarkable Purdue team—"winningest" ever, in regards to total number of victories—honors and accolades also went to senior guard Bill Keller, winding up his home career with his greatest collegiate game.

Victim of a scoring slump a couple of weeks ago and owning a career high of 26 in the past, Keller continued a recent bombardment of the basket as he notched 31 points—16 in the early going—for a new personal standard.

"That Keller killed us," said losing coach Lou Watson. "Mount wasn't hitting well and we were getting our shots. But we didn't hit either—and Keller really did."

With Mount and Keller almost personally equalling the Hoosiers, the remainder of the Riveters squad was content to fill minor roles. Such as:

Sophomore Larry Weatherford, again supplanting the ailing Herm Gilliam, had 13 points and a fine floor game;

40 OF 49 FREE THROWS

Center Chuck Bavis got the slow-starting Boilermakers rolling in the second half with three quick baskets and an assist for a fourth two-pointer—accounting for all of Purdue's offense for more than four minutes;

Soph forward George Faerber picked off 11 rebounds, second-high for the game, but took only three shots as he set up his mates;

Tyrone Bedford, playing almost half of the game at forward, Jerry Johnson, scrapping Bill

DeHeer toe-to-toe, and Ralph Taylor, another finishing up at home, all played steadily and well.

Purdue wasn't extremely sharp the first half, but ran up a 58-32 lead nevertheless; and the Boilermakers sizzled after Bavis got them started in the final half.

Hitting half of their field shots, 40 of 80, and cashing free throws almost monotonously, 40 of 49, the hosts charged to their all-time high.

Mount had the honor of sending the score above 100 for the sixth time this season (20th time in history); and Rick also had the honor of sending the score to a record-tying 116 and to the new record 118. (Faerber got the final goal, only points of the last 80 seconds.)

"PLAYING THEIR BEST"

Indiana, which had staged a courageous comeback in an earlier one-point loss (95-96) at Bloomington, couldn't find the fire-power and the rebounding strength this time. The Hoosiers were doomed after six or seven minutes, and they couldn't rally.

Ken Johnson and Joe Cooke topped IU with 18 points each and with, respectively, 12 and 9 rebounds. DeHeer, 13, and Rick Atkinson, 12, also reached double figures.

But it was Purdue's game—climaxing a season in which the Boilermakers won their first Big Ten title in 29 years.

The Riveters picked off 64 rebounds to Indiana's 54, again showing fine determination despite the absence of Gilliam, the season-long rebound leader.

"It's all in the attitude of the boys," King noted. "They want to do these things, and they do them. They're working as hard as they have all season, and they're playing their best."

A victory margin that swung from one point to 44 points in only 18 days should cause IU to agree.

Rick Mount secured his place in Purdue history with more than a dozen school and Big Ten Conference records.

RICK MOUNT'S RECORDS AND MILESTONES

(Note: Both team and individual figures from National Collegiate Athletic Association Tourney games will be included in final full-season statistics. Big 10 figures are complete; others are incomplete figures.)

RICK MOUNT

Big Ten Records:

Most points one season: 493
(Old: 474 points by Gary Bradds, Ohio State, 1964)

Highest per-game average, one season: 35.2
(Old: 33.9 by Bradds, 1964)

Most points two seasons: 909
(Old: Bradds, 907, 1963-1964)

Highest per-game average, two seasons: 32.46
(Old: Bradds, 32.39, 1963-1964)

Most field goals, one season: 194
(Old: 184, Cazzie Russell, Michigan, 1966)

Most field goal attempts, one season: 375
(Old: 362, Don Freeman, Illinois, 1966;
and Mount, 1968)

School Records:

Most 40-point games in a row: 3
(Old: 2, Terry Dischinger, 1962—45 & 46)

Most points, one season: 810
(Old: 781, Dave Schellhase, 1966)

Highest per-game average, one season: 33.75
(Old: 32.54, Schellhase, 1966)

Most points, two seasons: 1493
(Old: 1485, Schellhase, 1965, 1966)

Highest per-game average, two seasons: 31.1
(Old: 30.9, Schellhase, 1965-1966)

Most field goals, one season: 317
(Old: 284, Schellhase, 1966)

Most field goals, two seasons: 576
(Old: 533, Schellhase, 1965-1966)

IT'S ON TO LOUISVILLE AFTER WINNING THRILLER

By George Bolinger

March 17, 1969 — Two outstanding basketball teams, Purdue and North Carolina, living on borrowed time after overcoming late deficits in Saturday's NCAA Tourney Regional tests, clash in the first Thursday game of the national finals at Louisville this week.

The two apparently will be seeking the right to face UCLA, champion each of the last two years and in four of the last five years, in Saturday afternoon's title game.

UCLA, awesome in a Regional triumph over Santa Clara, meets Drake in Thursday's second contest at Louisville.

Both North Carolina and Purdue made up late three-point deficits last Saturday to gain Regional crowns—Purdue tying in the last 40 seconds of regulation time and then winning over Marquette, 75-73, in overtime.

ANYTHING CAN HAPPEN

What are Purdue's chances against talented North Carolina; and what are Purdue's chances against the other Thursday winner, should Purdue dump the Tar Heels?

"I just wouldn't bet against this (Purdue) club," Coach George King advised more than a score of sportswriters who surrounded him at courtside at Madison, Wisconsin, Saturday immediately after Rick Mount's shot from the corner finally subdued the hostile Warriors (and their hostile fans).

"After this, I'd say anything can happen."

Next to Mount, who redeemed a mediocre, for him, shooting performance with two last-minute bombs, King may have been the happiest man in the United States. Although he's in the NCAA for the fourth time (the first three with West Virginia), he's in the Finals for the first time.

LONG ON COURAGE

And he saw his injury-ridden club, which faltered after a brilliant start against the Warriors, twice regain life and hope—and eventual victory—after almost hopeless situations.

With senior forward Herm Gilliam apparently set to resume a starting role at Louisville and with North Carolina apparently due to play a "Purdue-type" of game, in which shooting accuracy may provide the difference in the final score, King can look ahead with reasonable hope—maybe even with confidence.

It won't be easy. No game will be easy at this stage of the tourney trail.

But thousands of Purdue fans learned Saturday that their favorites are as long on courage as they are on talent—and the fans may never again be fainthearted.

LONG DRY SPELL

This was a game that was! The Boilermakers, with as many heroes as they had entries in the

Sophomore Larry Weatherford helped Purdue bet Marquette in the 1969 NCAA Tournament with two field goals in the game's final three minutes.

scorebook, alternately took Purdue fans to the heights and plunged them to the depths.

After possibly the most tense 45 minutes of play in Boilermaker basketball history, it was fitting that Mount, the most publicized prepster ever in this basketball-mad state, should fire the shot that sent Purdue into the NCAA Finals for the first time ever.

After a first half which saw Purdue constantly in front, Marquette fought back to a tie at 48-all with 12 minutes left.

From that point it see-sawed until the 5:35 mark, when Al McGuire's Warriors moved into a 60-59 lead.

Unbelievably, Purdue, the nation's top scoring team, didn't score for five full minutes. The Warriors didn't do much better, content to protect their

one-point edge with a fine possession game, until the great George Thompson cashed two free throws at 1:51. It was 62-59, Marquette.

ANOTHER "TEAM" WIN

By this time Co-Capt. Bill Keller, the Riveter floor leader, had fouled out. Co-Capt. Herm Gilliam, making his first playing appearance in 18 days, was limping around on the floor. And Mount, as noted, was off-target.

(Meanwhile, big center Chuck Bavis was watching from the sidelines in street clothes, after suffering a shoulder separation two days earlier.)

Into the breach marched a flock of unheralded heroes. Sophomores George Faerber and Larry Weatherford, junior Jerry Johnson, subbing for the ailing Bavis, somehow fashioned a tie score and the overtime.

Pulling together as they have done all season, the Boilermakers got in front in the extra session and never trailed. But it went down to the final two seconds in a deadlock, before Mount's picture-perfect shot from the corner zipped through the basket.

ALMOST ALL OVER

Pandemonium broke loose in the Purdue section and among the players themselves, while a thoroughly dejected band of Warriors unbelievingly realized that they had lost what appeared to have been a sure thing.

The Warriors, excellent sports after an aggressive, hard-nosed contest, were as low as the Boilermakers were high.

"It was tough for them," King sympathized to the writers. "If they had made the free throw with two seconds left, it was all over. Or the tie-up after the free throw. And they missed a one-on-one free throw a few seconds before that."

King wasn't spelling it out, but the bad luck which has dogged his team physically had been evened out on the playing floor—leading to a thrill-packed victory such as the regular-season road triumphs at Indiana and at Michigan State.

MARQUETTE IS GOOD

King patiently explained Purdue's last-second strategy for one final shot.

"We used a double post, off which either Jerry Johnson or George Faerber could make a 'pick.' Anyone, Herm Gilliam, Larry Weatherford, or Rick Mount, could have taken the last shot. Whoever had the ball with eight seconds to play was to go for the shot.

"Fortunately, Rick got free.

"Marquette did a good job on us. They could play in the Big Ten and easily be one of the top clubs."

King went on answering questions, but only one thing really stood out. Purdue had won its first two NCAA tests in its basketball history, and the Boilermakers were on their way to the Finals.

FT MISSES AT 0:02

Most of the game was wrapped up in the closing seconds of regulation time. On Keller's fifth foul, at 0:59, Dean Meminger missed the first of the one-on-one free throws. Purdue got the rebound and, at 0:36, Faerber slipped in for a lay-up.

Seconds later Faerber lunged for the ball at mid-floor, shook it loose from Thompson, retrieved it, and passed off to Weatherford, who was fouled. At 0:19, Weatherford zeroed in on both free throws, giving Purdue a 63-62 lead.

But the Warriors worked it in close to center Ric Cobb, who attempted a lay-up, but was fouled by Johnson at 0:02.

Cobb made his first attempt, took his time but missed the second try, and Joe Thomas' tip-up rolled off to Johnson, who hugged the ball as time ran out. It was 63-all.

GET FOUR-POINT LEAD

The overtime was a little less nerve-wracking, but only a little.

Just after the tip-off, Purdue launched a fast break on which Gilliam was fouled. It was like money in the bank as Herm cashed both shots.

But sub guard Jack Burke, the only reserve employed by the Warriors, drilled long, and it was knotted again at 4:29.

Purdue then missed three straight shots before Johnson tipped home two points on a back-hand effort. When Gilliam quickly stole the ball and fed Weatherford for a fast-break lay-up, the decision seemed sealed at 69-65 and 2:41 left.

But Thompson drew a foul from Faerber at 2:18, and hit both tries; then, after a Mount attempt was blocked, Meminger drove close and hit a short jumper. It was 69-all at 1:53.

ONLY VICTORY MATTERS

Weatherford popped a beauty from the corner at 1:33. But the irrepressible Meminger, who was moved to forward for a berth on the All-Tourney team, drove under and scored at 1:11 to tie it at 71.

Mount slipped into the left corner and hit a 17-footer at 0:53. But back came Thompson with great moves to snake under for a lay-up at 0:34. That set the stage for Mount's winning heave.

Mount finished with 26 points, but it wasn't a good game even in this low-scoring affair. He connected on only 11 of 32.

But the end result was the only thing on Rick's mind, as well as on the minds of the other Riveters.

Averages and statistics were meaningless. Purdue had defeated a good team and was en route to the NCAA Finals.

Everything else was meaningless.

ALL-TOURNEY TEAM

(As selected by press, radio and television)

George Thompson
Marquette, 6-2 Sr. Forward

Dean Meminger
Marquette, 6-0 Soph. Forward

Dan Issel
Kentucky, 6-8 Jr. Center

Bill Keller
Purdue, 5-10 Sr. Guard

Rick Mount
Purdue, 6-4 Jr. Guard

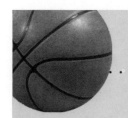

PURDUE PULVERIZES NORTH CAROLINA

Boilers to Battle Bruins in "Big One"

By George Bolinger

March 21, 1969 — LOUISVILLE, KY. — UCLA and Purdue, which opposed each other 113 days ago to open the season in Los Angeles, close against each other here tomorrow afternoon (4:15 EST) with college basketball's biggest goal at stake: the NCAA championship.

Thursday night's action in the 31-year-old meet produced two major surprises. Purdue ran away from slightly favored North Carolina, 92-65; then decided underdog Drake carried UCLA to the final click of the clock before bowing to the mighty Bruins.

UCLA survived by 85-82. But it was only 83-82 nine seconds before the final horn—and one errant UCLA pass at that stage could have sent the Bruins into tomorrow's consolation game (2:10 p.m.).

If things "happen in threes," the only real surprise left for the experts would have to be a Purdue victory tomorrow—a possibility that suddenly has dawned on the experts who saw unbelievably strong guard play by the Boilermakers against the Tar Heels.

UCLA's Johnny Wooden still doesn't "believe"—he still is no disciple of outside shooting. He indicated the Purdue shooting was "fantastic" Thursday night, and he left his audience to draw the inference that it wouldn't happen again.

Seeking his fifth NCAA title in the past six seasons, Wooden still has college basketball's most effective weapon, 7-1 1/2 Lew Alcindor. When Alcindor trots onto the Freedom Hall floor tomorrow, big Lew will be seeking his 90th victory in a 92-game UCLA career.

But the Bruins proved vulnerable to speed and outside shooting against Drake—and they may see more speed and better outside shooting tomorrow.

In any event, what started out as a UCLA romp to a third straight NCAA championship suddenly has developed into a horse race—and it is fitting that Kentucky should provide the site.

Purdue's guards, All-America Rick Mount and senior co-captain Bill Keller, shot North Carolina into complete frustration Thursday. And both men appeared to be at the peak of their game for one final effort which could bring Purdue the top prize in the Boilermakers' first venture into NCAA basketball play.

After Jerry Johnson's fielder opened the night's scoring before 18,435 in the huge goal house, Mount and Keller tallied the next 24 Purdue points—earning a 26-18 lead at that point.

Larry Weatherford replaced Keller and got the next five Purdue points, giving the guards 29 in a row and 29 of the first 31.

North Carolina, which losing Coach Dean Smith almost pleadingly labeled an outstanding team, whittled an 11-point deficit at 31-20, to a mere four by halftime, 39-35.

Purdue's guards had 32 of the first half total. But, the best was yet to come.

After the Tar Heels pulled within three (41-44), Keller and Mount were off again. Within moments it was 52-43; then, with 13 minutes left, 61-44.

Besides his offensive efforts, heading him towards a 36-point night, Mount came up with a startling defensive job on Tar Heel All-America Charlie Scott. Taking Scott head-to-head for more than six minutes, Mount completely shut him out. The combination was too much for the Eastern champs, who came apart at the seams to eventually fall 31 behind, before losing by 27.

"It was a great effort," said Riveter Coach George King later, "much greater than I had anticipated."

King didn't used any starter more than 33 minutes, and he had emptied his bench of all 12 men on the traveling squad with more than three minutes left to play.

"We weren't looking ahead to anyone," King said. "I'm very happy with this kind of an effort."

It was unnecessary for King to single out his guards for praise. At one stage, with Purdue leading 61-44, Mount and Keller between them had matched North Carolina's total. But King had high praise for the others.

"Herm Gilliam," he outlined, "is limited by his bad ankle, but he did everything we expected (8 points, 9 rebounds); Frank Kaufman had a big part in our victory (dueling the Tar Heels' big lineup under the bankboards); Tyrone Bedford had a strong game, as did Larry Weatherford.

"Our club has grown (improved) since our opening game with UCLA. We have great togetherness."

Coach Smith almost was in shock after the game.

"They (Purdue guards) made a shambles of our pressure defense," he noted. "And that's the most fantastic long-range shooting I've ever seen. Nobody shoots like that on the Atlantic Coast from New England to Florida.

"This is the best Big 10 team I've seen since Ohio State of the Jerry Lucas-John Havlicek stage.

"They clog the middle to keep us from getting the ball inside and they caused a record number of turnovers for us.

"We didn't regard Mount as a good defensive player either, but that stretch when he guarded Scott hurt us.

"Purdue was a better defensive team than we expected it to be. It's the best team we have played so far.

"Purdue has the best offense to go against UCLA, although our team might have been better on defense against UCLA because of our height."

While hitting 53 points in the last half, despite a generous use of reserves, Purdue boosted its field goal shooting for the game to .487 on 38 of 78.

Keller finished with 20 points, continuing his fine scoring of recent games, as he and Mount combined for 56. Seven others aided in the scoring.

North Carolina got 55 points from its starting front line of Scott (16), Bill Bunting (19) and Rusty Clark (20). But the Tar Heel guards and a flock of substitutes were ineffective.

BULLDOGS BARK

While the fans were denied the expectant close game in the opener, Drake kept the crowd in its seats until almost midnight before succumbing to the Bruins.

Alcindor, John Vallely and Curtis Row pushed the Uclans out in front, 11-2, and it looked as though a rout was in the making. The Bruins maintained a small lead for more than 15 minutes, but couldn't pull away. It was 37-30 with 4:45 remaining, then Willie McCarter, Gary Zeller and Willie Wise zipped the Bulldogs into a tie at 37-all, and UCLA had to settle for a 41-39 halftime lead.

UCLA normally spurts at the start of the second half of each of its games.

BATTLE BACK

This time, though, it was Drake which started fast. The Bulldogs pulled into brief leads at 43-42 and 45-44 and fashioned a 47-all tie before Rowe, Alcindor and Vallely put the West Coast champs on top at 55-48.

Again Drake battled back, tying at 57 and 59, then fell 12 behind at 78-66.

UCLA led safely into the closing seconds, when McCarter's fast finish with an assist from Dolph Pulliam brought it to 85-82 with nine seconds left. But Drake couldn't get the ball again, and Lynn Shackleford made it 85-82 with two free throws after time had run out.

Better Level With Mount

N. CAR (65)	FG	FT	Reb.	PF	TP
Bunting, f	7-13	5-7	7	2	19
Scott, f	6-19	4-6	6	3	16
Clark, c	7-9	6-10	9	2	20
Fogler, g	1-4	0-0	2	2	2
G. Tuttle, g	2-4	0-1	3	3	4
Delany, g	0-2	0-0	1	4	0
Dedman, c	0-1	0-1	4	2	0
Brown, f	1-4	0-0	1	0	2
Gipple, g	0-3	0-0	1	0	0
Chadwick, f	1-2	0-0	2	0	2
R. Tuttle, g	0-1	0-0	0	0	0
Eggleston, g	0-0	0-0	0	0	0
"Team"			1		
Totals	25-62	15-25	37	18	65

PURDUE (92)	FG	FT	Reb.	PF	TP
Gilliam, f	3-11	0-0	8	0	6
Faerber, f	3-3	2-2	9	3	8
Johnson, c	2-5	1-3	5	4	5
Mount, g	14-28	8-9	4	0	36
Keller, g	9-19	2-32	5	3	20
Kaufman, c	0-1	2-3	6	4	2
Weatherford, g	3-6	1-1	2	1	7
Bedford, f	3-3	0-0	5	4	6
Taylor, f	1-1	0-1	3	0	2
Longfellow, g	0-1	0-0	2	0	0
Reasoner, c	0-0	0-0	0	1	0
Young, g	0-0	0-0	0	0	0
"Team"			2		
Totals	38-78	16-22	51	20	92

North Carolina	35	30	--65
Purdue	39	53	--92

Assists—North Carolina 15 (Scott 6, Delany 2, Dedman 2, Bunting 2, Clark, Fogler, G. Tuttle); Purdue 17 (Gilliam 7, Keller 5, Mount 3, Kaufman, Bedford).
Field goal percentage—North Carolina .403; Purdue .487.
Free throw percentage—North Carolina .600; Purdue .727.
Officials—John Overby and Irv Brown.

LOUISVILLE, KY.—Rick Mount has attained marvelous coordination through hours and hours of practicing pitching a basketball toward a hoop. But his fascinating, fantastic accuracy is due to more than coordination alone.

Purdue's junior All-America basketball player has vision and judgment which are almost unbelievable.

For the second time this campaign, Rick has spotted a basket which was not level. For a second time he has had to debate the matter with "home" officials. And for a second time his tremendous judgment has been proved correct.

Wednesday while working out with the Boilermakers at Freedom Hall here for the NCAA finals, Rick told Purdue Coach George King that one of the baskets was not level. King advised tourney officials, who promised to have the basket "leveled" before Thursday night's games.

Again yesterday, Rick noticed that the basket was not level. Officials argued with Rick, but a subsequent test proved the Lebanon sharpshooter to be correct. The basket was put in proper order.

Earlier this season, Mount went through the same procedures before having a basket at Iowa leveled.

PROBABLE LINEUPS

UCLA (28-1)	Pos.	PURDUE (23-4)
Lynn Shackleford (6-5)	F	George Faerber (6-6)
Curtis Rowe (6-6)	F	Herman Gilliam (6-3)
Lew Alcindor (7-1 1/2)	C	Jerry Johnson (6-10)
Kenny Heitz (6-3)	G	Rick Mount (6-4)
John Vallely (6-2)	G	Bill Keller (5-10)

Tip-off: 4:15 Freedom Hall
Series: UCLA leads 5-3
Score this season: UCLA 94, Purdue 82
Broadcasts: WBAA, WASK; Television: NBC Network

In NCAA National Finals—

Boiler Basketballers Big Bombs Misfire; Team Finishes 2nd

By George Bolinger

MARCH 23, 1969 — LOUISVILLE, KY. — Fairy tales can come true. And dreams can come true.

For Coach Johnny Wooden and his real, live giant, Lew Alcindor, the fairy tale of three consecutive NCAA basketball championships came true here Saturday.

For Coach George King and his band of talented, gritty Boilermakers, the dream, hinged on marvelous shooting, failed to materialize—just as the brand-new, $35,000 electronic marvel, the Freedom Hall scoreboard, refused to function properly.

Lew, the giant, keyed up emotionally and at his physical best, climaxed an amazing collegiate career with something special to remember as he ruled the floor, leading UCLA to a 92-72 victory in the NCAA title game.

That result gave Alcindor and Wooden a 30-1 record this season, a 91-2 record over three seasons, and an unprecedented third straight crown.

It also gave Wooden, the one-time All-American Purdue player, five national titles in six years, likewise unprecedented. But the first two championships were different. They were won on the playing floor-not in the stratospheric heights where the 7-foot-1 ¹/₂ Alcindor performs so effectively.

On this occasion, Purdue "bombs" and the electronic marvel both misfired way up there.

The Purdues don't have, nor do they need, any excuses.

ALL OVER EARLY

The Boilermakers had their chances—92 shots from the field—to destroy the giant and his helpers. Handling the ball very well (only four errors) and rebounding well under the circumstances (48 to UCLA's 61), Purdue did everything except get the ball through the hoop.

This shortcoming was very un-Purdue-like. Ditto the scoreboard, installed for the championships, which faltered just after the game's start—as Purdue did after an early 6-6 tie.

In seven minutes, UCLA bounced that 6-6 to 26-10, and Purdue never got back into it. The Boilermakers once came within nine (38-29), they trailed by a not-hopeless 11 at halftime (42-31), and, with Alcindor on the bench, they closed to within 12 (75-63) after trailing by as many as 20.

When it got down to 12, back came Alcindor. And the most effective man the college game has known finished things in a blaze of glory.

The game boiled down to two simple factors: Alcindor's almost unlawful efficiency and Purdue's inability of the "big three" (figuratively, not physically), Herm Gilliam, Bill Keller and Rick Mount, to hit.

Purdue's classy trio hit a mere 18 for 67 (.268), even below the puny team average of .293 (27 of 92). Mount, one of the very best outside shooters the game has ever known, was 3-for-18 in

Guard Larry Weatherford helped Purdue reach the NCAA title game in 1969.

the first half (.167) and the Boilermaker team only 12-for-51 (.235).

Mount, at one stretch, missed 14 shots in a row.

By the time Purdue found the range more consistently, when it got to 75-63 with six minutes to go, desperation measures were necessary. Purdue fouled repeatedly, although not flagrantly, in the closing minutes, and the Uclans picked up 13 of their final 17 at the free throw line.

The fairy tale came true; the dream didn't.

LEW IS A LULU

Alcindor's great performance and Purdue's mediocre shooting to the contrary, Saturday's super-important contest was decided in large part two days earlier.

On Thursday, Purdue simply had demolished North Carolina and Drake just missed upsetting UCLA.

Both games served as a warning to the Bruins, who came to play their very best in the finale.

Alcindor's effectiveness around the baskets was phenomenal. He had 10 baskets in the first half alone, eight of these on lay-ups (or lay-downs, if that's what you call shots well above the rim). He was a perfect 4-for-4 on free throws and had

grabbed 11 rebounds—besides blocking a couple of shots.

It really was all over after nine minutes, when Alcindor out-scored Purdue 14-10 and UCLA led 24-10.

Alcindor had 24 in the 42-31 half, Mount had only 8.

RICK TALLIES 28

Later, Mount warmed up, but it didn't make the least difference. UCLA once led 67-47. A stout rally cut it to 75-63, still leaving the Boilermakers hopelessly out of it.

Like a fairy tale, it was unreal. Unlike a bad dream, Purdue's plight was real.

It was all Alcindor!

Big Lew went 15-for-20 from the field, 7-for-9 at the free throw line, took 20 rebounds, and blocked several Purdue shots as he notched 37 points in 36 minutes, getting in his best licks when they meant the most.

Three other starters were in double figures: guard John Vallely with 15, Curtis Rowe 12 and Lynn Shackleford 11. But these men weren't overly-impressive in any way.

Mount, displaying All-America class by refusing to fold, eventually got up to 28 points. Keller had 11, as did junior center Jerry Johnson in a good offensive show against Alcindor.

23-5 SEASON!

But UCLA dominated almost everywhere: 32 baskets to 27, 28 free throws to 18, 61 rebounds to 48, etc.

In every way, it was Alcindor's game, his season, his career.

Despite the wide final margin, Purdue really didn't fare badly.

In a year of many, many records, the Boilermakers posted a 23-5 mark, annexed an undisputed Big Ten championship, and placed second in the nation in their first NCAA tourney assignment. Two of the losses were to champion UCLA; only one loss could be classed as an upset.

In most quarters, UCLA was a solid favorite in the finale.

The defeat was disappointing, the margin of defeat was very disappointing. But the over-all season was the best of the modern era.

And there's plenty returning next season!

PURDUE'S "DAY OF FRUSTRATION" ENDS WITH IOWA AS CHAMPS

By Bruce Ramey

March 2, 1970 – Iowa left town early Saturday evening with the Big Ten basketball championship neatly bound and secured with two games yet to play, and left behind them a stunned partisan Purdue crowd that will talk about the game for a long, long time.

When the scoreboard flashed the final score, 108-107, the immediate talk was about the officials and the officiating that resulted in a technical foul called on the crowd for throwing paper on the playing floor. Momentarily forgotten were Rick Mount's record 61 points and 27 field goals.

While that embarrassing, unnecessary crowd incident didn't determine the outcome of the game, it was typical of the frustration the Boilermakers were faced with all afternoon.

This game (for Iowa) meant the title. For Purdue it was a chance to keep its title hopes going, and hoping that either Ohio State, which lost at home to Michigan State, or Northwestern would throw the Hawks and Boilermakers into a playoff.

FOUL WARNINGS

All the pressure was on Purdue. A loss ended the race, while Iowa had two games to use as a cushion.

By the time Mount had hit the first five of his 27 field goals for a 10-6 Purdue lead, the Boilermakers had been whistled for five personals and

Rick Mount scored 61 points in a loss to Iowa.

One of the most honored players in Purdue basketball history, Rick Mount (right) adds to his trophy collection with the MVP award in 1970. Also collecting awards were George Faerber (far left) and Tyrone Bedford, alongside Coach George King.

Iowa two. This set the tempo for the first half, and when the first 20 minutes had ended Purdue had been saddled with 20 personals and Iowa 12.

Four Purdue starters were in foul trouble – Tyrone Bedford had four, Larry Weatherford, Bob Ford and George Faerber had three each.

"It is unfortunate that we had to play a game this important with different players than we normally use," said Purdue coach George King after the game.

"Iowa just played a hell of a game," King said, "and I'd rate it as strong as the club we took to the (NCAA) tourney last year.

"It's just a shame we had to have these kinds of people work a game this important."

King was referring to referee Bob Brodbeck who warned the crowd (via the PA announcer) that a technical would be assessed on the crowd if any more paper or debris was thrown on the playing floor.

SIX-POINT PLAY

Paper was thrown on the floor, and turned the game around at that point. Purdue was leading 70-67 when Chad Calabria drove under and was fouled by Boilermaker Steve Longfellow. Calabria's shot was good, Longfellow was charged with a foul and a wad of paper came from the stands back of the south basket. A technical foul was called. Calabria made his free throw, made the technical shot, Iowa was given the ball out of bounds and Glenn Vidnovic scored seconds later on a layup. The six-point play gave Iowa a three-point lead instead of the three-point deficit.

Purdue went on to take the lead as Weatherford, who was limited to one point the first half, hit stride with Mount and the Boilermakers were in front, 88-80, with just over 8 minutes left.

Purdue still was in front by nine (101-92) with 3:40 to play, and King ordered a 3-2 zone defense.

"Weatherford and Mount each had four fouls, and we couldn't go into a stall as they (Iowa) had only three fouls on them at that stage. They could deliberately foul to get the ball. That dictated our strategy. Iowa generally does a good job against a zone, and our 3-2 upset them a little, but not enough," King said.

Actually Weatherford had only three fouls at the time, as he picked up his fourth, fouling Fred Brown, at 3:33. Brown made both shots to start Iowa's winning drive. Vidnovic scored later on a steal, and Purdue's Ford retaliated with a followup on a missed Purdue shot. Ford was fouled by Vidnovic (his fourth and the team's fourth and last foul of the half), but missed the free throw.

Brown came through with two baskets from in front – one a 12-footer and the other from 20 feet out to bring the count to 103-100. Ford fouled out at 1:32 when he made contact with Calabria, who dropped both free throws. Seven seconds later Bedford left the game as he was charged with his fifth foul while bringing the ball across the center stripe.

Bob Ford had 11 rebounds before fouling out in the dramatic loss to Iowa.

Calabria scored on an 8-footer in front of the hoop to give Iowa a 104-103 lead, but Jerry Johnson put Purdue back on top on a clever feed from Longfellow, then Iowa's John Johnson hit a baseline shot from the right side, and Vidnovic hit a pair of free throws on Faerber's fifth foul with 10 seconds to go, making it 108-105. Mount drove the length of the court for his last two points with two seconds showing and Iowa was the new champ.

Ralph Miller, Iowa coach, praised the poise of his players, and was critical of the crowd conduct.

"The crowd tested the officials, and the officials turned on the crowd. It's ridiculous. Debris thrown on the floor can hurt a player, theirs as well as ours. It was a nice time, for us, for it to happen," the beaming Iowa coach said.

"This has to be one of my biggest wins. At least I don't know of any that has meant more to me," Miller said. "We've had two very peculiar games – this one and the one at Illinois. I was positive we were going to win both. Here we were down by nine with 3:30 to play, and I still thought we could win. The pressure all was on Purdue. We were not tense. We still had two games in which to win it."

For Mount, it was a frustrating day. He set a single game Big Ten record with his 61 points, and a single game record with 27 field goals. "But we lost," he moaned later in the dressing room.

The Big Ten's greatest scorer needed 47 shots to get his 27 field goals, and was given eight free throw attempts and made good on seven.

He now must score 50 points in the remaining two games to break the four-year record of 1,451 points by Indiana's Don Schlundt.

He'll get that chance Tuesday night at Michigan State and this Saturday in the Arena, when Minnesota comes to town.

Mount and Weatherford were the only Boilermakers in double figures with 61 and 21 points. Iowa had four starters above 20 – Johnson with 26, Calabria 25, Brown 23 and Vidnovic 20.

Shooting was almost the same – Purdue going .523 and Iowa .521. Rebounds were identical, 46 each. Johnson had 12 for the Hawks and Ford 11 for Purdue, despite playing only 29 minutes.

Purdue versus Michgian State—Rick Mount, driving against the Spartans, finished his college career with 2,323 points and a 32.3 scoring average, still the best in Purdue history.

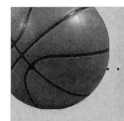

BOILERMAKERS GAIN REVENGE BY WINNING NIT TITLE TILT

By Bruce Ramey

March 25, 1974 – NEW YORK — It wasn't the NCAA title. It was second best.

But don't try to tell that to Purdue. The bubbling Boilermakers won the 37th annual National Invitation Tournament; and they gained a measure of revenge by beating Utah, 87-81.

"In 15 years of college coaching, this is the first time I've ever won the final game of the season," said Boilermaker coach Fred Schaus. "I've been involved in several post-season tourneys, but this is the first time I've coached a team that won one, and I just can't say enough about this bunch of guys."

"This bunch of guys" crowded into the interview room, just off the playing floor of Madison Square Garden, a few minutes after accepting the championship trophy from Scotty Whitelaw, commissioner of the Eastern Collegiate Athletic Conference.

"This bunch of guys" was down by five points (46-41) at the half, and had not been shooting well, but the players kept their poise when personal fouls began to pile up to put the pressure on Utah – Purdue eventually gaining revenge for that 87-85 loss at Salt Lake City back on New Year's night. And "this bunch" at times consisted of a unit made up of two freshmen (Gerald Thomas and Tom Scheffler), two sophomores (Bruce Parkinson and Mike Steele), and senior Frank Kendrick.

Frank Kendrick scored a team high 25 points in the NIT Title game.

Coach Fred Schaus and the Boilermakers celebrate their 1974 NIT Championship over Utah.

Clutch play by Thomas and Steele, with 3:20 to play, gave Purdue the cushion it needed to take complete command in the closing moments.

With Purdue leading only 76-74, Steele missed the front end of a "one-on-one," but Thomas, leaping high, tipped the ball back to Steele, who dropped in a soft shot that gave the Boilermakers a 78-74 lead. Just 17 seconds later Thomas dropped in a pair of free throws to give the Boilermakers a six-point bulge, 80-74.

Five straight times the Boilermaker defense stopped the Utes without a point, while John Garrett, who finished with 24 points, picked up a loose ball and put it in, and Kendrick added a free throw to make it 83-74 with only 44 seconds left.

Utah cut the lead to four with a field goal by the NIT's Most Valuable Player, Mike Sojourner, and a three-pointer by sub Jeff Jonas.

Bruce Parkinson broke loose from the traffic under the Utah basket and took a long feed from Steele and put the ball in for Purdue's last basket with 16 seconds left, and the Boilermakers and their followers began celebrating.

The 22nd victory for Purdue this season (counting the win over Sub-Pac in the Hawaiian Classic) was a fitting climax for the Boilermakers, who have played their best basketball in the last six weeks. And it left the third-place Big Ten finishers with only nine losses.

This last one didn't come easy, as Purdue trailed by nine points early, 26-17, and was down by seven with 1:18 to play in the first half, 46-39. But a field goal by Garrett, a soft lay-in from the side after an assist by Parkinson, cut the deficit to five at halftime (46-41).

"We wanted to go inside more to Sojourner, starting the second half," said Utah coach Bill Foster. "But Purdue's defense cut us off, and we had to go back to our outside game.

"We also got careless with the ball at crucial times – and you can blame their defense for some of that.

"And Schaus got more out of his bench than we did, particularly after Medley (Tyrone) got in foul trouble.

"Purdue is a good club, and tough to beat."

Those errors Foster spoke of? Utah had 23 of them, while Purdue had only 11 – five in the first half and six in the crucial second half.

Plus, Purdue out-shot the Utes in the second half, 52.9 (18 of 34) to 43.7 (14 of 32). Utah had 47 rebounds to Purdue's 34, with Sojourner, alone, taking down 19.

The Utes, a high-scoring club, set a tournament record for scoring with 392 in their four games. (The old record was 354 by St. Bonaventure in 1960.)

Purdue's bench was most obvious in point production. Scheffler (six), Steele (eight) and Thomas (four) contributed 18 points, while Utah's bench scored only nine.

CHAMPIONSHIP

Purdue	41	46 – 87			
Utah	46	35 – 81			

Purdue (87)	FG	FT	A	Reb	TP
Rose	5-10	0-0	0	6	10
Kendrick	9-18	7-10	1	9	25
Garrett	8-18	8-8	2	3	24
Parkinson	4-9	0-0	7	1	8
Luke	1-3	0-0	4	0	2
Scheffler	3-6	0-0	0	5	6
Steele	2-5	4-6	9	4	8
Thomas	1-2	2-2	0	1	4
Team				3	
Totals	33-71	21-26	23	32	87

Utah (81)	FG	FT	A	Reb	TP
Terry	3-8	0-0	0	6	6
Menatti	4-4	2-2	2	3	10
Sojourner	10-15	3-5	9	19	23
Burden	11-15	5-5	2	3	27
Medley	3-6	0-0	7	0	6
Whiting	0-1	0-0	0	5	0
Jones	1-3	0-0	1	1	2
Jonas	2-6	3-4	2	1	7
Bergen	0-11	0-0	0	1	0
Team				6	
Totals	34-69	13-16	23	45	81

Errors Purdue 11 Utah 23
FG Percentage: Purdue .465 Utah .493
FT Percentage: Purdue .692 Utah .813
Fouls (fouled out) – Purdue 18 (none) Utah 25 (Medley)
Officials– Hal Grossman and Mickey Crowley
Attendance – 13,246 estimated

Luther (Ticky) Burden, the tourney's leading scorer with 118 points, got 27 of them against Purdue, and Sojourner had 23. The only other Ute in double figures was Charles Menatti with 10.

Purdue's balance consisted of 25 by Kendrick, Garrett's 24, 10 by Bruce Rose and eight by Parkinson. Purdue's other starter, Dave Luke, had two.

Parkinson, in addition to winning the tourney's assist honors with 30, had seven rebounds to top the Boilermakers – one of which he converted into a key field goal that gave Purdue a 76-72 lead.

Clutching their Accutron watches and the NIT trophy, Schaus and "this bunch" headed for the cold midwest and a rally in Mackey Arena on the Purdue campus last night – with pride, poise, discipline and defense their best allies.

Boston College upset Jacksonville for third place in the tourney, 87-77. BC's Jere Nolan set a single-game assist record in this one with 14.

Discipline and defense paid off with a spot in the final game as the Boilermakers pulled away from Jacksonville in the second half Saturday afternoon.

Not able to shake the Dolphins in the first half after twice taking six-point leads, Purdue pulled away in the second half, getting an eight-point lead at 50-42 when Luke fed Kendrick for a layup. It was one of Luke's seven assists as the Cincinnati senior had one of his better games.

The Boilermaker defense, which allowed the Dolphins to shoot 46.2 percent in the first half, shut them off the final 20 minutes with only 10 field goals in 48 shots, 20.8 percent.

Henry Williams, 6-6 wingman, and Leon Benbow, 6-5 and worker of the other wing, hit 11 of 20 the first half, but when clamped a bit tighter in the second half they hit only six of 30.

Meanwhile, Garrett was doing an outstanding job on Jacksonville's 6-10 Butch Taylor in the inside. Taylor, who had only four points and five rebounds in the first half, got five points and one more rebound in the second half before going to the bench with five fouls with 3:08 to play.

Rose, pushed into a starting assignment after the injury to Jerry Nichols, responded with 12 points and eight big rebounds, and was one of four Boilermakers to hit double figures. Garrett, connecting on nine of 14 shots, finished with a game-high 21, Kendrick and Parkinson had 15 each, with Kendrick taking 11 rebounds and Parkinson holding his tourney lead in assists with seven.

Schaus got fine help from his bench in Steele and Thomas.

"They were a big boost for us," he said, "and it was a fine experience for Gerald (Thomas)."

Thomas, the freshman from Connersville, played errorless ball, his usual good defense and added four key points. Steele, going to the boards on defense, took down seven key second-half rebounds as the Boilermakers blocked out well.

"Purdue just played excellent defense," said former Ohio State Buckeye and now Jacksonville coach Bob Gottlieb. "Their defense was the best we've seen all year. They contested our passing lanes very well and kept us away from the boards.

"Our shot selection was not as good as it has been, and Purdue's pressure caused that.

"I'm tremendously impressed with Bruce Parkinson. You can't overestimate the value of his floor generalship and his ability to hit the open man on the fast break."

The Boilermakers in the second half shot an even 50 percent, hitting 16 of 32 shots, and had 27 of their 51 rebounds in that period. Utah, obviously after Madison Square Garden and NIT scoring records, poured it on undermanned Boston College as coach Bill Foster kept his starting lineup on the floor until the last minute with a 24-point lead.

Sojourner led the Ute scoring with 29 points (13 or 20 from the field) and had 19 rebounds plus numerous blocked shots; Burden, held to only five points in the first half, finished with 28; Medley added 17, and Menatti and Terry had 12 each.

BC's fine sophomore, Bob Carrington, 6-6, had a game-high 33 points, 25 in the first half, but Utah shut him off in the second half.

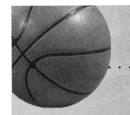

PURDUE FACES BUTLER TONIGHT AFTER THRILLER OVER MINNESOTA

By Bruce Ramey

January 5, 1976 – INDIANAPOLIS – Purdue is tied for first in the Big Ten; and Boilermaker freshman Kyle Macy is the conference's leading scorer.

And all that came about Saturday night as the Boilermakers knocked surprising Minnesota, now 8-1, from the ranks of the nation's undefeated basketball teams with a 111-110 double-overtime thriller.

Coach Fred Schaus called the Big Ten opener "the most exciting game I've ever been involved in during the regular season." And the 14,645 fans in Minnesota's old Williams Arena agreed.

But all that excitement could vanish in a hurry tonight if Purdue can't handle pesky Butler in Market Square Arena. (Tipoff time is 8:05.)

Macy, the 6-3 freshman guard from Peru, showed why he was rightly named Indiana's "Mr. Basketball" of 1975 with an ice man's performance that brought 4-5 Purdue from a 14-point deficit at half time to one of the biggest wins in Boilermaker road history.

All Macy did was score 38 points, drop in his last 12 free throw attempts, and get 11 of Purdue's 19 points in the second and last overtime period – including four clutch free throws for Purdue's final four points.

And he played the entire 50 minutes!

"That was an amazing performance and show of stamina by an 18-year-old," Schaus said. "But, don't forget, it was really a team effort.

"A lot of credit must go to Robbie McCarter," Schaus said, referring to the 6-8 Boilermaker senior who played a total of 27 ½ minutes – more than he played in any game in his previous three years as a member of the Purdue varsity.

"Robbie was the catalyst who got us moving in the second half. He played good defense and did a great job on (Mike) Thompson down the stretch."

McCarter drew a couple of charging fouls on Minnesota's 6-10 sophomore center, who finally fouled out with 2:12 left in the first overtime period.

Thompson got 33 points and 12 rebounds before he left, and blocked eight Boilermaker shots.

McCarter also fouled out with 1:30 left in the first overtime, but the Boilermaker bench was proving superior by that time, a situation pointed out clearly by first-year Gopher coach Jim Dutcher.

"They (Purdue) are the first team that has gotten to our bench," Dutcher said. "At the end, the tallest man we had on the floor was 6-3, and you can't control the boards very well with that kind of height."

By that time the 6-10 Thompson, 6-8 Gary Korkowski and 6-10 Dave Wine, plus guard Phil Saunders, all had gone to the bench with five fouls as the Gophers were whistled for 28 personals. Purdue was tagged with 25, but lost only McCarter and Wayne Walls.

Purdue took that 14-point deficit (50-36) into the dressing room, where Schaus gave them a lecture. ("I won't tell you what I told them, because you can't print it," he said.)

The Boilermakers came out pressuring, and Minnesota went into a zone defense – and stayed with it for a long time. Purdue beat the zone almost at will, out-scoring Minnesota 12-6 to get back into the game at 56-48, then took the lead at 78-76 as Macy dropped in a pair of free throws with 3:59 left.

Walter Jordan, who also had a super game with 21 points and a game-high 16 rebounds, hit a 15-footer with two seconds left to tie the score at 83 and send it into overtime.

Macy got four points and Jordan five in the first extra period, offsetting Gus Johnson's nine for Minnesota. Jordan missed an attempt at the buzzer.

In the second overtime, Macy got 11 of his 38 points, twice taking the ball away from a Gopher without fouling within a span of 20 seconds. The first time he picked the ball from the hands of Phil Saunders in the corner, took two steps and attempted a field goal, which was ruled good on a goal-tending call.

Seconds later, Macy stole the ball at the opposite end of the court and converted a pair of free throws when he was fouled in retaliation with just 22 seconds left. He stepped to the free throw line again with eight seconds left and dropped in his 11th and 12th free throws to give the Boilermakers a 111-108 lead.

Purdue then played it cautiously, pressing only lightly to avoid fouling as Ray Williams drove the lane for Minnesota's last two points with three seconds left. Purdue did not inbound the ball.

"We just stood around too much on defense the second half," Dutcher said, "and they got a lot better shots."

Purdue couldn't match the Gophers' shooting, but did a great job on the boards and at the free throw line in the second half. Minnesota had a 27-11 edge in rebounds the first half, but in the second half the Boilermakers led 20-18 in individual grabs.

Whipping the Gopher game, Purdue shot 53.2 per cent in the second half, with Macy getting down 13 of 20 and Eugene Parker a hot 7 of 10. Jerry Sichting, who spelled Parker briefly, hit both

of his shots, giving the trio of guards a fine 22-for-32.

Against Butler tonight, the Boilermakers will be looking at a team that is 5-5 and coming off a 91-83 Saturday night win over Augustana of South Dakota.

PURDUE—MINNESOTA BOX SCORE

Boilers 111, Gophers 110
Two Overtimes

Purdue	36	47	9	19	– 111
Minnesota	50	33	9	18	– 110

Purdue (111)	FG	FT	RB	PF	TP
Jordan	7-18	7-13	16	3	21
Walls	3-13	5-6	4	2	11
Scheffler	0-0	2-2	1	0	2
Parker	7-10	0-0	2	1	14
Macy	13-20	12-13	2	2	38
Thomas	0-0	1-2	1	2	1
White	1-2	0-0	0	0	2
Sichting	2-2	0-0	1	3	4
Steele	4-6	2-2	4	5	10
McCarter	3-10	2-2	3	0	8
Team			11		
Totals	40-81	31-40	42	18	111

Minnesota (110)	FG	FT	RB	PF	TP
Williams	9-21	7-11	10	5	25
Thompson	14-19	5-8	12	2	33
Korkowski	1-2	1-2	1	0	3
Saunders	4-9	2-4	4	4	10
Lockhart	9-12	2-2	6	7	20
Johnson	5-9	3-3	9	2	13
Winey	1-1	0-0	3	0	2
Jones	1-1	2-2	0	0	4
Kosmoski	0-0	0-0	0	0	0
Team			4		
Totals	44-74	22-32	49	20	110

FG Percentage: Purdue .494; Minnesota .594
FT Percentage: Purdue .775; Minnesota .687
Errors: Purdue 15; Minnesota 28
Fouls (and fouled out): Purdue 25 (McCarter, Walls); Minnesota 28 (Thompson, Korkowski, Winey, Saunders)
Officials: Fouty, Mathis, Rucker
Attendance: 14,645

TV BOILERMAKERS "ROCK-N-ROLL" OVER HOOSIERS

By Jeff Washburn

February 21, 1977 – Purdue and Indiana treated a national television audience and a full-house at Mackey Arena to a perfect example of Indiana basketball Sunday afternoon, and when the shooting circus was over, the Boilermakers had claimed a hard-earned 86-78 victory to remain alive in the race for the Big Ten championship.

Using what junior guard Eugene Parker called "a full-court press that got us rocking-and-rolling," the Boilermakers erased a one-point halftime deficit and turned it into a 43-38 lead with just 53 seconds gone in the second half.

Sparked by that full-court press, Purdue outscored the Hoosiers 30-14 in the first 10 minutes of the second half for a 67-52 advantage – canning 12 of its first 17 field goal attempts – and held off a late I.U. rally for its 11th Big Ten triumph in 14 games.

With Parker hitting from the parking lot, Walter Jordan going one-on-one and Tom Scheffler and Joe Barry Carroll dominating the inside game, Purdue finished the second half with 20 baskets in 29 flings for 69 percent.

But the defending national champions from Bloomington were not about to roll over and play dead. Indiana meshed 20 of 34 fielders after intermission for .588 gunning, led by a sensational individual performance by junior guard Jim Wisman, who scored a career-high 25 points.

Indiana cut the 15-point Purdue lead down to six – 80-74 with 1:27 left in the game – before a slam-dunk by Carroll started a four-point play for the Boilermakers 13 seconds later that put the game out of reach.

Purdue Coach Fred Schaus had inserted his three-guard offense with 2:30 remaining in the game, and 6-1 Jerry Sichting fed Carroll for the dunk at 1:14. I.U.'s Jim Roberson fouled Carroll on the play, and Walter Jordan rebounded the missed charity toss and rammed home his sixth basket of the game at 1:10 for a safe 84-74 advantage.

The classic battle was marred just 24 seconds later when Indiana All-American center Kent Benson and Carroll collided as the Boilermaker freshman went up for a layup. Benson fell hard to the floor (Carroll was called for a charging foul) and was taken to University Hospital for x-rays of his back, which has given Benson trouble all year.

Wayne Radford and Roberson sandwiched baskets around another Carroll dunk in the closing seconds, and Purdue had its first win over Indiana in Lafayette since 1974.

In the first half, Wisman, who entered the game with a 5.5 scoring average, knocked in seven of nine jumpers and a free throw for 15 points. Wisman's bombs came over the sagging 2-3 Purdue zone, which was geared to keep the ball away from 6-11 Benson.

The 2-3 zone limited Benson to just two shots in the first half (he hit both for four points), but the

BENSON SORE, BUT OKAY

Kent Benson, Indiana's 6-11, 245-pound senior All-American center, who left the floor of Mackey Arena in great pain Sunday afternoon after colliding with Purdue's Joe Barry Carroll, probably will play out the season for the Hoosiers.

Word from Bloomington this morning was that Benson is very sore after reinjuring his lower back in the collision.

He was taken to Purdue's University Hospital for x-rays, which according to Dr. Bill Combs, "were negative."

Benson returned to the Bloomington campus with his parents after the game.

Wisconsin plays at Indiana Thursday, and chances are that Benson, who has been bothered by back problems for two years, will be able to play.

Eugene Parker paced Purdue with 18 points in a big nationally-televised victory over Indiana in 1977.

rest of the Hoosiers, primarily Wisman and freshman forward Mike Woodson, peppered the nets with jump shots, as Indiana hit 18 of 34 field goal attempts for .529.

Purdue led 31-25 with 3:50 left in the first half, but Indiana outscored the hosts 13-6 the rest of the way for a 38-37 margin after 20 minutes. Purdue hit only .406 from the floor (13 of 32), but knocked in 11 of 13 free throws to just two of five for Indiana.

Then, like a flash of lightning, Purdue turned the game around in the first minute of the last half. Jordan hit a jumper, and then two straight Hoosier turnovers against the press resulted in four more Boilermaker points.

After committing only five errors in the entire first half, Indiana turned the ball over 13 times in the second half, and did not shoot a single free throw while Purdue meshed nine of 12.

For the game, Indiana converted 38 buckets in 68 attempts for 55.9 percent, while Purdue canned 33 of 61 for 54.1 percent. But the Boilermakers stepped to the foul line 25 times, hit 20, as the Hoosiers ended with just two of five free ones.

Wisman led all scorers with his 25 points on 12 of 18 from the floor, and the 6-2 guard dished out nine assists – also tops for the game. Woodson, who fouled out with 2:39 left in the game, tossed in 16, Billy Cunningham had 14 coming off the bench and Benson added 12 on six-of-seven firing, but pulled down only five rebounds.

Parker paced the Boilermaker cause with 18, but five other Purdue players scored in double figures.

Purdue outrebounded Indiana 38-28, led by Wayne Walls' nine caroms.

CARROLL IMPRESSES WOODEN; MICHIGAN TEST ON TV, TOO?

by Bruce Ramey

February 21, 1977 – "He's a tremendous young talent," John Wooden said Sunday afternoon of Purdue's 7-2 freshman center, Joe Barry Carroll.

Still seated at the announcer's table at the end of the official scorer's bench following Purdue's 86-78 win over Indiana, Wooden paused from signing autographs to evaluate the young Boilermaker.

Carroll, who came off the bench to spell Tommy Scheffler at center, played 20 minutes, scored 12 points on six-of-seven shooting, took down six rebounds, had three blocked shots, one steal, one assist and one error.

"Yes, he has great talent and obviously a great future. For one so young he has great poise," said Wooden, who coached some great ones himself at UCLA – like Kareem Abdul-Jabbar (Lew Alcindor) and Bill Walton.

"Fred (Schaus) is doing the right thing, too, in bringing him along slowly, not putting great pressure on him. Yes, he's a fine young player."

Asked what instant replay of the Carroll-Kent Benson collision under the basket with 46 seconds left showed, Wooden said, "I don't think Carroll charged him. I think the officials missed that one."

The main concern at game's end yesterday in both dressing rooms was the condition of Benson, who was taken to the University Hospital for x-rays.

Bobby Knight, understandably, was shaken by the injury to his big center, the guy who has been Indiana's strong man for three years.

Knight is down to a squad of 10 players now that Rick Valavicius has left the squad, and if Benson can't continue the season he won't have enough players with which to scrimmage.

Knight declined to elaborate on the departure of Valavicius, answering questions in this field with, "Ask him. He was not in school Friday, and my main concern is that he get back in school and finish the semester."

The Indiana coach did leave the interview room on a humorous note. Asked if he'd like to take his Hoosiers to the NIT, Knight quipped, "I'll play anywhere. Hell, I'd even go to the CCA tourney." He bitterly complained after he was forced to take his Hoosiers to the CCA in 1974 – and won it.

When a major network moves in to do a telecast, as NBC did of yesterday's Purdue-Indiana game, the logistics are almost bureaucratic. Two or three cameras are not enough. You got to have six or seven. Enough cable and wire was draped and stretched in and through Mackey Arena to fence in half of the cattle country in Texas. And credentials were issued to 30 people – including Dick Enberg and Wooden.

Sunday's TV experience was in effect, a shakedown for next year's NCAA Mideast Regional, which has been tentatively assigned to Purdue.

Also, word from the Big Ten office today is expected to designate the Michigan-at-Purdue game on March 5 as the Big Ten TV Game-of-the-Week. That has been a wild-card date.

CHAPTER 26

OH, SO CLOSE

North Carolina Ends Purdue's NCAA Hopes

by Bruce Ramey

March 13, 1977 – RALEIGH, N.C. – Purdue lost the scoring formula in the final 2:08 last night and fell 69-66 to the University of North Carolina in the Eastern Regionals of the NCAA basketball tourney.

When Walter Jordan hit a layup for a 66-63 Purdue lead with 2:08 left, the Boilermakers were through scoring, but there was a lot of basketball left, as there were thrills, in steaming Reynolds Coliseum.

That scoring drought was not confined to field goals, as the Boilermakers, after hitting 14-of-15 free throws in the first half, didn't get to the free throw line once in the second half, a fact that was disturbing to Coach Fred Schaus.

"They (North Carolina) didn't play it any different in the second half, yet we don't go to the line once, and that's darn difficult to understand," Schaus said.

"And I didn't see the official give a warning signal before he counted five and slapped us with a technical for not coming out to the ball," Schaus said.

The score was tied at 62-62 when that call was made, and the Tar Heels' great guard, Phil Ford, dropped in the free throw for a 63-62 lead, and that left 4:36 on the clock.

Eugene Parker, who hit 12 points for the Boilermakers, gave Purdue a 64-63 lead on a six-footer, and the Boilermakers went into a delay until Jordan's layup at 2:08 for the 66-63 lead.

Mike O'Koren cut the lead to 66-65 with a pair of free throws, then Carolina's winning points came on a 19-footer over a Boilermaker zone with 1:17 left.

The Boilermakers had two more possessions, but lost the ball against a scrambling Tar Heel defense. Bruce Parkinson, playing his final game, was whistled for traveling when O'Koren positioned him on an in-bounds play with 13 seconds left.

Ford, who finished with a game-high 27 points, got UNC's final two points on free throws when fouled by Parker with 10 seconds left.

Purdue shot a fine 49.1 percent, but got only 11 field goals (in 23 shots) in the second half. UNC finished at 47.5, and converted seven of 10 free throws in the second half.

North Carolina now goes to College Park, Md., to play Notre Dame in the Eastern semifinals Thursday, while VMI, which defeated Duquesne, 73-66, plays Kentucky.

The second half was a low-scoring affair after a first half which saw Purdue take a 44-42 lead.

Both teams scored only 49 points in the second half.

For the game, the score was tied six times and the lead changed hands 14 times.

"I would say that Purdue is the best non-conference team we've seen all year," said Dean Smith, after his Tar Heels defeated the Boilermakers for the first time in three tries.

"They handled our offense better than any team we've played all year."

Both coaches used every defense in the book – man, zone, zone trap, zone press, and man press – and the heat hurt both clubs in the second half.

The first half saw both coaches running players in and out to keep them fresh in the heat and humidity, and the players needed the rest as the pace was hot as the weather and tension matched the humidity.

The Tar Heels meted out to a four-point lead at 10-6 as O'Koren and Ford supplied the offense and Ford led the defense.

Purdue tied it at 10-10 on Walls' second field goal, then went ahead on Sichting's 15-footer. The Tar Heels again took the lead on Kuester's jumper over the Boilermakers' 2-3 zone, and upped the score to 22-19 as Ford, who got 16 points in the first half, hit twice more.

Tom Scheffler, with two fouls, came off the bench to give Purdue the lead at 23-22 on a fine rebound basket with 7:54 left. Purdue increased its lead to three points (27-24) as Walls hit on a great feed by Parker, then went up by four on a three-pointer by Carroll with 4:48 left in the half. Jordan's fielder made it a six-point lead, and it stayed that way when Parker hit a 15-footer with 3:41 to play.

O'Koren hit a free throw on Jordan's second foul, Ford hit a driving layup, and then came out of a mad scramble under the Purdue basket for another driving layup, and was fouled by Parker with :05. Ford tied it at 42-42, but Parker hit a 25-footer just ahead of the buzzer to give Purdue a 44-42 halftime lead.

The Boilermakers hit 15-of-30 shots (50 percent) to North Carolina's 28 of 39 (46.2 percent), but had six fewer rebounds than Carolina.

Ford led the Heels with his 16 points and Parker had 10 for Purdue.

Two UNC starters, Kuester and Buckley, had three fouls each, and Scheffler three for Purdue.

Tom Scheffler, who lettered from 1974 to 1977, got into foul trouble early in Purdue's dramatic NCAA tournament loss to North Carolina.

CHAPTER 27

BLIZZARD, GOPHERS FAIL TO STOP PURDUE

by Dick Ham

January 29, 1978 – Minnesota and Purdue have a history of playing long games, but Thursday's game Saturday in Mackey Arena has to be a record.

This one took three days to get in the books because of the blizzard and when it was over Purdue was still challenging for the Big Ten championship with a 72-64 victory that left Coach Fred Schaus' Boilermakers tied for second place with Michigan which defeated Indiana, 92-73, with 5-2 records.

Purdue had no trouble filling the arena to capacity as the faithful turned out in unexpected numbers and left only about 2,000 seats empty. These were quickly snapped up by students who patiently waited for the game to start and the doors to be thrown open.

With the 14,123 cheering every move, Purdue nailed Schaus his 99th Boilermaker victory and set up a real showdown with the Wolverines at Michigan Monday.

Actually, there was only one weather-related casualty connected to the game and that was an official who was unable to make it because of road conditions. That was quickly rectified, however, as Lafayette official Joe Smelcer was called in to fill the vacancy. Smelcer, who has worked Indiana state high school championships, did a creditable job teaming with Big Ten official Verie Sell in keeping the game running smoothly.

Until the final 4:10 of the contest, the struggle was as tight as the paper on the wall. But for the last 10 minutes it was the Boilermakers who were taking command.

The game was tied 17 times and there were a total of 28 one-point margins with the last one coming at 10:00 with Purdue in front 52-51.

After the Boilermakers had battled to a 34-33 halftime advantage, Coach Jim Dutcher's Gophers gained the edge four times before Purdue's Joe Barry Carroll sparked the Boilers with a driving "stuff" shot at 13:38.

That seemed to ignite Purdue both offensively and defensively and it proceeded to outscore Minnesota 20-13 down the stretch.

Carroll, who was having a game of his own under the basket with the Gophers' heralded Mychal Thompson, also merits mention for the defensive job he did on the Big Ten's leading scorer. Carroll stopped Thompson cold with only 11 points – far below his 21.7 average.

However, Dutcher refused to put any blame on Thompson. "He has played so well, so long for us I guess anyone is entitled to a bad game. He's our offense, though, and when he goes five for 19 shooting, we are going to get beat," Dutcher said.

While Carroll did do the bulk of the work he had help from the active Purdue zone defense and Walter Jordan during his 12 minutes of bench rest. The only player able to keep the Gophers, who had been "holed up" at the Holiday Inn North since

Joe Barry Carroll was held to 12 points in Purdue's blizzard-delayed victory over Minnesota.

Wednesday afternoon, in the game was Kevin McHale.

Another high point in the Boilermaker win was a 20-point performance by guard Eugene Parker, who teamed with Jerry Sichting to hit 15 of 21 from the outside. Parker's career total swelled to 1,270 points and put him fifth on Purdue's all-time scoring list, displacing Frank Kendrick.

Following Carroll's dunk the Boilers raced to a 66-59 lead with 4:19 to play and then the only bad spot in the game for them popped up as they missed three straight free throw attempts, two of them in the one-and-one situation.

Thompson then got his second basket in 11 second-half shots to close it to 66-61 with 1:23 to go. Sichting got those back from the foul line to administer the coup and Parker scored the final four points of the contest for his spot in the record book.

Purdue worked its four-corner offense effectively in protecting its advantage and forced the Gophers into the clinching free throws as the Boilers outshot Minnesota from the stripe, hitting 12 of 18 to the Gophers' two of seven.

Parker's 20 topped the Boilermakers with super support coming from Sichting's 16, Jordan's 14 and Carroll's 12 while McHale's 18 carried the brunt of the Minnesota offense as Thompson finished with 11 and Osborne Lockhart with 10.

Both teams played very well considering the long postponement with Minnesota committing only 12 turnovers to Purdue's 13.

The decision ended a string of four straight overtime games between the old rivals and gave Purdue its 53rd victory in the 108-game series.

CHAPTER 28

ROSE HOPES FOR BEST, HITS RECRUITING TRAIL

By Bruce Ramey

April 8, 1978 – Does Lee Rose, Purdue's new basketball coach, have any specific goals in mind as he takes over the Boilermaker basketball program?

"A few years ago I was being interviewed for a job. I was much younger then, and it came down to that basic question – 'What are your ambitions?' My goals then and now are to do the best I possibly can," Rose said.

Are there any particular records Rose is interested in?

"Basketball has been very important in my life, and I don't think that when I die I'll go to that big gymnasium in the sky," he said. "I try to keep that perspective.

"As far as I am concerned there are only two records in basketball that mean anything. Johnny Wooden has one of them. How many national titles has he won? Ten, and that's not a bad coach to look at. And Coach (Adolph) Rupp has won the most games. You can't win more games than Coach Rupp. You can't live that long.

"Yes, the game is for the kids, it's for the student-athletes," Rose said.

One of the more important points in his introductory talk before the media was recruiting.

Rose, who was an assistant at the University of Cincinnati for three years (1965-67), is familiar with the Midwest and aware of the talent normally produced in Indiana, and other Midwest states.

"Even while at Charlotte I knew who the good players were in this part of the country, and we tried to get some of them to visit us, but we knew it was difficult to get them out of Big Ten territory," he said.

He also indicated he would be looking hard at the recruiting list put together by Fred Schaus, and assistant coaches George Faerber and Roger Blalock.

"It could be worse…if my arrival here was after the national signing date," Rose said. He said he had not been an advocate of using junior college players, but possibly would "for a basic need."

He also does not think playing freshmen is entirely a good thing.

"In the long run it has a very difficult effect on coaches. You have to be alert for dissatisfaction and dissension."

Athletic Director George King is obviously pleased to land a man of Rose's background – 41 years old, 253 wins and 85 losses, NIT runner-up in 1976, and an NCAA finalist in 1977.

King said C. M. Newton, head coach at Alabama, for whom Rose played at Transylvania, was very complimentary when he found out Purdue was interested in Rose.

"I also got a call from Al McGuire, and he gave him a fine recommendation," King said. "I don't know if it was because the two of them went head-on a year ago, or not." McGuire's Marquette team defeated UNCC, 51-49, in the semifinal game of the NCAA tourney last year.

Rose admitted that breaking loose from UNCC was difficult – he was both head basketball coach and athletic director.

"I was here (West Lafayette) for a visit last Sunday, and George King finally offered me the position last (Thursday) night. There were many loose ends to be tied together back in Charlotte. While we are here, at this moment, a letter is being read to my players announcing my decision. My assistant, Mike Pratt, is being announced as the new head coach."

King said Rose was on the original list of 10 coaches in the running for the Purdue job – 16th head coach in history. Blalock and Faerber were on the list, too.

Rose introduced his family, which accompanied him to West Lafayette and was present in King's home.

His wife, Eleanor, was seated beside their two sons, Mike, 16, and Mark, 14.

"Mike, the oldest, is a starting linebacker in football and a starter on his high school basketball team,"Rose said.

"Mark is a quarterback on his junior high team, plays point guard in basketball, pitches in baseball and is president of his class," he said.

It doesn't appear that working with two former head coaches, Schaus and King, will be a problem for Rose.

"I look forward to working with Schaus, and I've told him he can have as much input in our program as he desires, and can even sit on our bench if he likes," Rose said.

Asked who he admired most in the coaching profession, Rose became the perfect diplomat.

"George King and Fred Schaus," he said.

Less than 30 minutes after the press conference ended, Lee Rose was talking to his first Purdue recruit, who "just happened to be on campus this weekend."

He said he would be in Lexington, Kentucky, to see Joe Barry Carroll play with the U. S. All Stars against Russia on Sunday night and then probably would be in New York talking to another recruit on Monday.

PLAY LOSES, LAST-SECOND SHOT WINS

By Jeff Washburn

January 14, 1979 – Ten seconds to go. Game tied 50-50. Your team has the ball. What would you do?

Well, Purdue basketball Coach Lee Rose faced that very situation Saturday afternoon in Mackey Arena as the Boilermakers battled No. 1-ranked and defending Big Ten champion Michigan State.

With the game on the line, Rose called back-to-back timeouts, and using all of his knowledge and coaching know-how, devised a play that would win the game.

There was just one problem. The play never developed. But junior forward Arnette Hallman made Rose look like a genius as he calmly swished a 25-foot, off-balance jumper to give Purdue a classic 52-50 upset win.

"Gentlemen, that was the worst play ever devised in the history of basketball," Rose told reporters after the game. "His (MSU Coach Jud Heathcote) defense on the play was great, and my coaching was terrible.

"We wanted to get the ball to Jerry (Sichting) or Joe Barry (Carroll), but our play failed when Michigan State denied both those players the ball. Arnette couldn't pass and time was running out, so he just put it up." In a Mackey Arena first, Rose took his team back onto the floor a few minutes after the conclusion for a victory lap to a standing ovation.

"You don't beat the No. 1 team in the nation very often," sophomore guard Brian Walker said. "So, I guess the victory lap was appropriate. It was fun."

Hallman, who scored only four points in the game, said of his heroic shot, "I can remember winning a game like this when I was in high school, but the circumstances were entirely different. There was a missed free throw in that game and I got the rebound and hit a shot at the buzzer.

"The shot today felt good when it left my hand, but 25 feet out is a long way. But as I watched it, I thought it was in.

"As we had it set up, the shot was supposed to be Jerry's, but when I got the ball, Brian Walker, our point guard, was covered, so I couldn't get the pass away for him to reverse the floor to Jerry."

(In basketball strategy, reversing the floor is passing the ball around the top of the free-throw circle to a player on the opposite side of the floor.)

"I remember turning and seeing five seconds on the clock and then I heard Brian saying 'shoot, shoot,' so I did," Hallman said.

"I played with my back to the basket a lot as a center in high school, so I was accustomed to shooting a turn-around jumper. But since I've been in college, most of my shots have been stand-still jumpers. I guess the experience paid off.

"I saw the last-second shot on TV the other night when Illinois beat MSU, 57-55, and I know how tough it must be for the Spartans to lose two straight almost the exact same way."

Brian Walker explained why he told Hallman to shoot: "I finally got open with about five seconds left, but I yelled to Arnette because time was running out, and if he had passed to me, I don't know if I could have gotten off a shot in time.

"I thought it was better for him to take a long shot than no shot at all."

Sichting said, "Yes, I was supposed to get a shot, but I was covered." Then with a smile, he said, "We've got to take turns at being the hero."

Heathcote walked into the interview room and said, "I don't know whether to answer your questions or vomit.

"If Hallman would shoot that same shot 20 times in practice, he might make three or four at most.

"We thought they would try and go to Sichting or Carroll, so we set up our defense accordingly. We were in a zone defense, and we thought we made the right guy (Hallman) take the shot.

"Terry Donnelly (6-2 guard) was on Hallman (6-7 forward) with his hand in his face. When Hallman shot, I thought there was no way it would go in. Then it looked on target and it went in.

"This has been a rough week for the Spartans. We haven't lost two straight games in the last two years. We will just have to regroup."

Donnelly said, "I didn't think Hallman would take the shot, but the whole afternoon was strange, so I guess we could expect as much.

"I had my hand in his face, and he looked off-balance. I did all I could without fouling him,

but the ball still went in. That's basketball.

"Losing two straight by two points on last-second shots is really tough to take as a player, because you know had you done one more thing in the game, you might have won.

"If we've got to lose, I'd rather it be by eight or 10 points. Those don't hurt as bad."

Arnette Hallman (45) lettered for Purdue in 1979 and 1980 and played in 11 post-season games. His biggest shot was the game-winner versus Michigan State.

SWISH! BOILERS TOPPLE MSU ON LAST-SECOND SHOT

By Bruce Ramey

January 14, 1979 - "It was the worst play ever devised," Coach Lee Rose joked of Arnette Hallman's twisting jump shot at the buzzer that gave Purdue a 52-50 Big Ten win Saturday evening over No. 1-ranked Michigan State.

Rose had planned on getting the ball to Jerry Sichting for a shot off a pick, or lobbing the ball in to Joe Barry Carroll for the final shot.

It didn't turn out that way, as Hallman ended up with the ball as the clock ran down in the tie game.

"I heard somebody say 'Shoot it' and I knew we didn't have much time left. I turned, jumped and got my body facing the basket. I didn't think it was going to be very good at first, but the closer it got to the hoop the better it looked," Hallman said.

It was only his second field goal of the tense, tight battle that gave the Boilermakers a 2-2 record in the Big Ten, and pulled the Spartans, defending conference champs, down to the same level. For all games Purdue is 12-4 and MSU 9-3.

Tense? Tight?

The Boilermakers lost a seven-point halftime lead, went behind 48-46 with 3:24 left to play, then won the cat-and-mouse game by forcing a turnover with 10 seconds left. That set the stage for Hallman's winning field goal.

Hallman, the 6-7 leaping junior college transfer from Joliet, Illinois, also had a hand in forcing the turnover.

Michigan State's Earvin Johnson, the "Mr. Magic" to Spartan fans, was controlling the ball in the backcourt and passed along the side to 6-7 David Charles. Hallman pressured Charles, forcing him to throw high back to Johnson and the ball went back over the center line, giving Purdue possession out of bounds in front of the Purdue bench with 10 seconds left.

Rose called two time outs before putting the team back on the floor. Michigan State Coach Jud Heathcote had the Spartans in a zone, guessing that Purdue would go to Sichting or Carroll. But Hallman ended up with the ball paired against the 6-2 Terry Donnelly across the floor, over 20 feet away from the hoop as the clock ran down. His shot beat the horn and the crowd of 14,123 partisan fans erupted in delight.

Carroll, who finished with 27 points, had tied the score at 50-50 at the 2:00 mark by stuffing in a basket off a lob pass from Brian Walker.

Donnelly, MSU's top free throw shooter (86.4 percent), was fouled by Brian Walker at 1:20 and missed the front end of the one-and-one, Carroll getting the rebound.

Seven seconds later Rose called Purdue's first time out and the Boilermakers went into their four-corner delay, hoping for an easy shot.

Johnson and another Spartan trapped Brian Walker against the sideline and forced a turnover with 29 seconds left.

Now it was the Spartans' turn to go for the last shot, after Heathcote used his last time out. Hallman forced the turnover on Charles' pass and nine seconds later got the winning basket.

Purdue took control of the game at the start when Sichting hit an 18-foot baseline shot for a 2-0 lead – and Heathcote called a time out immediately.

"We had two guys playing one defense, and three guys another," he said. Purdue still kept command, going up 18-10, then 22-15 before Rose ordered a stall with 5:54 to go in the first half in an effort to bring MSU out of its zone defense.

Sichting drove the middle for an easy layup, then Johnson got that one back with a 12-foot bank shot at 5:27, and with a 24-17 lead Purdue worked the ball in backcourt as time ran down. Freshman Keith Edmonson turned the ball over with seconds to go, but Carroll preserved the lead when he blocked Johnson's last-second shot along the baseline.

Heathcote got the message from that first-half Purdue stall and had the Spartans in a man-to-man defense starting the second half. The Spartans also picked up the offensive tempo, chipping away at the Purdue lead.

Donnelly hit three 18-footers over Purdue's 3-2 zone and Rose put the Boilermakers back to a man defense.

Greg Kelser, MSU's leading scorer (19.3 avg.), got a great tip-in and after Johnson's 14-footer from the circle, Kelser had a chance to tie the score at 40-40 on a three-pointer, but his free throw missed everything and Purdue had life with the ball out of bounds and 7:48 to play.

Michigan State took the lead 47-46 for the first time on Charles' two free throws after he was fouled by Carroll (his third) with 4:31 left. Johnson gave MSU a two-point lead by hitting the first of a one-and-one with 3:24 left, but Carroll tied it at 48-48 on a driving reverse layup at 3:03.

Johnson, who missed what would have been the winning MSU field goal in the final minute Thursday night at Illinois, gave the Spartans their last lead at 50-48 on a 12-footer from the right side at 2:36.

Carroll matched that at 2:00 on the lob from Brian Walker.

Then Hallman pulled his magic, forcing the turnover to set up his winning field goal.

Carroll, with his mother sitting at courtside, finished the game with 27 of Purdue's 52 points, plus taking down a game-high 11 rebounds and blocking one shot. The big guy hit 10 of 13 shots from the field and seven of 10 free throws and played 39 minutes.

Sichting, Purdue's No. 2 scorer all season (14.8 ave.), had nine points, freshman Mike Scearce six, Hallman and Drake Morris four each and Brian Walker two.

Charles led the sagging Spartans with 14 and Kelser had 12.

The tense battle was officiated by two officials, instead of the three-man crew normally used by the Big Ten. Fred Jaspers was snowbound in his home state of Iowa, leaving Bob Burson and Tom Rucker to handle the game.

Things went smoothly for the two, except for one technical foul on Johnson for "unsportsmanlike conduct" – laying the ball on the floor instead of handing it to an official after a turnover.

Purdue dominated the shooting, hitting 21 of 38 for 55.3 percent to MSU's 20 of 41 for 48.8. And the Boilermakers controlled the boards with 33 rebounds to the Spartans' 18.

A disappointed Heathcote, still looking for his first win in Mackey Arena, now takes his Spartans home to play Indiana on Thursday night.

Iowa is at Purdue Thursday night.

PURDUE–MICHIGAN STATE BOX SCORE

Purdue 52, Michigan State 50

Mich. State	FG	FT	R	F	P
Charles	4-5	6-6	2	1	14
Kelser	5-11	2-6	6	4	12
Vcent	2-5	1-2	2	5	5
Donnelly	4-8	0-1	1	0	8
Johnson	4-11	1-2	3	3	9
Brkovich	1-1	0-0	1	1	2
Busby	0-0	0-0	0	0	0
Gonzalez	0-0	0-0	0	0	0
Team			4		
Totals	20-41	10-17	18	14	50

Purdue	FG	FT	R	F	P
Hallman	2-3	0-0	3	4	4
Morris	2-4	0-2	5	4	4
Carroll	10-13	7-10	11	3	27
B. Walker	0-1	2-2	1	3	2
Sichting	4-11	1-1	1	1	9
S. Walker	0-0	0-1	3	2	0
Edmonson	0-0	0-0	0	0	0
Scearce	3-5	0-0	2	0	6
Bemenderfer	0-1	0-0	0	1	0
Team			7		
Totals	21-38	10-16	33	18	52

Halftime score: Purdue 24; Michigan State 17
FG Percentage: Michigan State .488; Purdue .553
FT Percentage: Michigan State .588; Purdue .625
Errors: Michigan State 12; Purdue 18
Technical foul: Johnson
Officials: Burson and Rucker
Attendance: 14,123

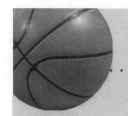

IU HITS, BOILERMAKERS MISS IN LAST SHOT NIT TITLE BATTLE

By Bob Scott

March 22, 1979 – NEW YORK – Even Camelot ended, eventually.

In a typical Purdue-Indiana basketball game, the Hoosiers beat the Boilermakers in Madison Square Garden in the final five seconds Wednesday night, 53-52, to claim the National Invitation Tournament title before 14,889 fans.

Both Big Ten teams slugged it out for 39:55 before Indiana's Butch Carter hit an off-balance jumper from the top of the keyhole for the Hoosiers.

There was several minutes of strategy remaining, however.

Purdue quickly called time out. Then Indiana countered with a timeout as the Boilermakers came out onto the floor to set an offense. Purdue then inbounded from under Indiana's basket to guard Brian Walker, who immediately called a timeout at midcourt – the third one in a total playing time of one second.

Four seconds remained.

Senior guard Jerry Sichting wound up with the final shot – a left corner jumper, his specialty, from 18 feet.

It hit the far rim, however, and bounced off at the buzzer.

Purdue thus ended its season at 27-8, while the Hoosiers finished at 22-12.

For the first time in NIT history, two teams from one conference – the Big Ten – were 1-2.

It was an unusual tactic, however, that aided Indiana's cause.

Trailing 52-51 with 4:26 remaining, Indiana had the ball after Purdue center Joe Barry Carroll missed the front end of a one-and-one bonus free throw.

Instead of attacking on offense to try to gain the lead, Coach Bob Knight's Hoosiers went into a delay attack.

Indiana worked the ball around until 1:05 remained when a Carter pass was intercepted under the basket by freshman forward Mike Scearce. Purdue called a timeout with 1:02 remaining and put starter Drake Morris in for Scearce. The Hoosiers then called a timeout to offset the expected Purdue "four-corners" offense.

The Boilermakers cleverly dribbled and passed as Indiana frantically tried for the steal.

With 21 seconds remaining, freshman Landon Turner fouled Carroll.

The Big Ten's leading scorer went to the foul line for a one-and-one bonus. He missed the first shot, however, and Indiana rebounded. Purdue forward Arnette Hallman then fouled, his team's sixth, and the Hoosiers retained possession.

There were 16 seconds remaining as Indiana used three straight timeouts to set up a last shot.

The ball came in to Carter who hit Mike Woodson underneath. The junior forward quickly was surrounded by Purdue defenders. He tried to get a shot off, was unsuccessful, then whipped the

Brian Walker maneuvers around Indiana's Isiah Thomas.

per game before the finals, but the Hoosiers' sagging zone-man combination allowed him only 10.

Purdue never scored down the stretch, due in large part to the Indiana stall. The Boilermakers had a 52-47 lead with 8:49 remaining, and never scored again.

For Indiana, its first NIT title was the climax to an impassioned season that began with turmoil and uncertainty and finished on a high note. The Hoosiers were only 10-8 in the Big Ten, and three players were kicked off the team early in the year.

Purdue also wound up with a champion's grace. Picked as an also-ran by Big Ten writers in a preseason poll, the Boilermakers became tri-champions in what many believe this year to have been the nation's toughest conference.

The pill is bitter for Purdue. Enduring a 35-game season only to lose by one point to arch-rival Indiana was heartbreaking.

But both teams are champions – first, last and always.

Alabama, decisively beaten by Purdue, 87-68 in Monday's semifinal game, beat Ohio State, the third Big Ten team in the final four, 96-86 to take third place in the tourney.

Boiler Briefs – Carroll finished with 126 NIT points. Alabama's Reggie King edged him with 132 total points for five games. It's an NIT record since the format was expanded to the new 24-team field.

Purdue was the only other Indiana team to get into the NIT finals before Wednesday's game. The Boilermakers won the 1974 NIT over Utah.

The finals Wednesday in Madison Square Garden was the first time Indiana and Purdue had ever met anywhere other than their home state.

ball to a wide-open Carter, who hit the jumper as Indiana won the rubber match of the season's three-game series.

Turner led the Hoosiers with 13 points, while Ray Tolbert and Carter finished with 12 each. Woodson had 10.

Carroll had 14 points, nine below his season's average. The 7-1 Denver native had been hitting at a 28-point clip in four previous NIT games. Hallman chipped in with 12.

Indiana's defense was effective denying Carroll the ball. He had been taking about 18 shots

Arnette Hallman shows his dunking form. He scored 12 points in the NIT championship game.

ROSES FOR MAMA BRING THE HOUSE DOWN

Carroll Displays Skills, Emotion in Farewell

By Jeff Washburn

March 2, 1980 – Sometimes actions speak louder than words.

With 49 seconds left in Purdue's 91-73 basketball victory over Michigan State Saturday afternoon in Mackey Arena, All-American center Joe Barry Carroll left the playing floor for the last time to a standing ovation – or so the 14,123 fans thought.

But Carroll, the 7-foot-1 "franchise" and Purdue's No. 3 all-time scorer, who has shown little or no outward emotion in his four years as Boilermaker, was not ready to sit down.

Instead, he ran to the bench amidst a thunderous chorus of roars and picked up a long white box.

He ran across the floor to greet his teary-eyed, smiling mother with a big hug and handed her the box which contained one dozen long-stemmed red roses. Carroll waved his long arms which have propelled many basketballs through many iron hoops from New York City to Hawaii in the last four seasons, asking the crowd to stand and cheer. The crowd responded with more roars and the NBC cameras focused in on the tall young man from Colorado.

"Today was a fitting climax for a great athlete," Purdue Coach Lee Rose said of Carroll in the post-game interview. Carroll scored 26 points, had 13 rebounds, five blocked shots, two assists and only one turnover in 39 minutes of playing time Saturday as the Boilers locked up third place in the Big Ten.

"He (Carroll) ordered the roses this morning to give to his mother," Rose said, "It was his idea."

Another graduating senior, 6-7 jumping-jack forward Arnette Hallman reflected on his two years as a Boilermaker after transferring here from a junior college.

"I'll miss this place," Hallman said. "The fans have been great, and everybody associated with the university has been great. I just wish I had had four years here instead of two. It would be nice to have two more years left.

"I think the thing that has carried us has been our defense. You look at the Big Ten stats, and we're near the bottom in free throw percentage, field goal percentage and rebounding, yet we've hung in there all the way.

"Some nights the offense isn't there, but the defense will always keep you in a game. We're playing team ball right now, and I think our execution is as good as it's been all year. I think we'll do well in the tournament."

Getting back to Saturday's game, Rose said, "We've had a lot of emotional games, but this was a great one for us.

"We won on the upbeat, and we had a very good shooting afternoon. It might be justice for last year, but we should go to the NCAA tournament now. We have to go. We finished alone in third place, and we needed this one today.

"I thought Michigan State played a good game, and they didn't die after losing the game at Minnesota Thursday night. Scooby (Mike Scearce) had a great shooting game, and when he hits, we're a different club. That gives us the outside threat to open things up inside."

"I had my shots today, and I took them," Scearce said after the game. "When I came in, I felt good, and the shots just went in.

"Even though we lost a tough game to Ohio State Thursday night, we didn't have any trouble getting up for this one, because we knew it was a must game for us to get into the tournament. It seems like we've been playing nothing but must games all season long, so this was nothing different. We just did what we had to do."

Scearce hit on seven-of-10 shots from the floor and grabbed four rebounds in 14 minutes of playing time.

Michigan State Coach Jud Heathcote said, "We got beat in a lot of different ways today. We have trouble playing against dominating centers, and Joe Barry was awesome today. We let down on defense and rebounding, and that killed us.

"We have a lot of guys who have played for a lot (national championship last year), and when we saw we were having a frustrating season, we had some letdowns, which made us not concentrate defensively. We missed some big shots early in the game, and then when we would cut the lead to 10

points, we just couldn't get over the hump and we'd have a defensive breakdown.

"I think Purdue will do well in the NCAA, especially if Carroll plays well. Their defense is excellent, and if Carroll does more than go through the motions, they can be tough.

"I see no reason for not keeping the title in the conference," said Heathcote.

"I think anything can happen in the tournament," Rose said, "and I don't care who we play as long as it isn't another Big Ten team.

"I think it would be great if two Big Ten teams could meet for the championship, and I think they ought to take four of our teams. After all, we (Big Ten) won 82 percent of our non-conference games.

"It's going to be great. This is what we play for."

BIG TEN STANDINGS

	League		Overall	
	W	L	W	L
Ohio State	12	5	20	6
Indiana	12	5	19	7
Purdue	11	7	18	9
Iowa	10	8	19	8
Minnesota	10	8	17	10
Illinois	8	10	18	12
Michigan	8	10	15	12
Wisconsin	7	11	15	14
Michigan State	6	12	11	16
Northwestern	5	13	10	17

CARROLL'S CAREER

Joe Barry Carroll, who scored 26 points in Purdue's 91-73 win over Michigan State Saturday afternoon, became the 32nd player in NCAA history to score over 2,000 points and take down over 1,000 rebounds.

The Boilermakers' 7-1 All-American center, closed the regular season with 2,017 career points, and 1,089 rebounds with his Saturday performance.

Additional highlights of his career:
- Big Ten scoring champion as a junior.
- Third team All-American (AP) and honorable mention (UPI) as a junior.
- Consensus All-Big Ten as a junior.
- Double-figure scoring streak of 59 consecutive games.
- Purdue's all-time career rebounder (1,089).
- Purdue's No. 3 all-time scorer (2,017).
- Career scoring high of 42 points vs. Alabama in 1979 NIT.
- Member of U.S. team in 1978, World Invitational tourney.
- Member of U.S. team in Soviet Union's Spartakiade last summer.
- First-team choice All-American in Basketball Weekly this season.
- One of this year's 10 All-Americans picked by U.S. Basketball Writers.
- Career shooting percentage of 54 percent (812 of 1504).
- Never missed a game, playing in 89 straight.

NCAA PHONING TODAY?

Fans Hoping for Best after Big Boiler Win

by Bruce Ramey

March 2, 1980 – "It's time to bring in the harvest isn't it?" said Purdue Coach Lee Rose after his Boilermakers had defeated Michigan State 91-73 Saturday afternoon to wrap up third place in the Big Ten basketball race.

The Boilermakers had just closed their regular season on the upbeat, closing out 88 days of the toughest college basketball in the country (a Big Ten schedule). The finish brought them undisputed third place in the conference and almost assuredly a bid to the NCAA tourney.

The 48-team NCAA field will be announced starting at 3 p.m. this afternoon, and the first round games will be played either Thursday here in Purdue's Mackey Arena; at Greensboro, North Carolina; at Lincoln, Nebraska; or Ogden, Utah. Friday's schedule is at Providence, Rhode Island; Bowling Green, Kentucky; Denton, Texas, or Tempe, Arizona.

"We'll play anybody, anywhere, and anytime," said Rose as he was asked about a possible preference as to site or opponent.

"I would prefer not to play a team we've already played twice," he said, meaning another Big Ten team. "They'd have a stack of film on us, have us well-scouted, but we'd have the same information on them, too."

Last year, Purdue finished in a tie with Iowa and eventual NCAA champion Michigan State, and was denied a spot because of the NCAA rule limiting a conference to two teams.

That rule has been changed, and an unlimited number of teams from a conference can be bid into the expanded 48-team NCAA field.

Last year, the Boilermakers settled for the National Invitation Tournament and finished runnerup (by two points) to Indiana, which is shooting for the Big Ten championship with Ohio State at 1 p.m. (NBC-TV) today.

The Michigan State team Purdue played before the packed house (and regional TV cameras) in Mackey Arena was only 60 percent of the same club which won last year's NCAA title. Gone were Earvin "Magic" Johnson and Gregory Kelser. But back were 6-foot-8 junior Jay Vincent and 6-8 senior Ron Charles, plus 6-2 guard Terry Donnelly.

That trio accounted for 59 of the Spartans' 73 points (81 percent). MSU finished 6-12 in the Big Ten and 12-15 for all games.

Also gone was Coach Jud Heathcote's fine zone defense of last year.

"Our zone this year is like a sieve," said Heathcote, "so we tried to slow Purdue down with a man defense, which we felt was our best bet."

The Boilermakers ripped MSU's defense for their second-highest point total of the season. The

Joe Barry Carroll

It was a fitting climax to a game that saw the big guy take down 13 rebounds, block five shots, and get one steal in addition to his 26 points. The partisan crowd loved it.

Michigan State, which solved Purdue's defense for 34 field goals in 61 shots (55.7 percent), was in command only one time. The Spartans took a lead 16-11 on a fastbreak basket by Mike Brkovich, but Drake Morris, who finished with 16 points, put the Boilermakers ahead on a rebound basket at 22-21, and Purdue stretched the lead to 46-34 at the half. An old nemesis, missed free throws, kept the lead from being larger as Purdue made only six of 15 the first half.

Carroll hit his first six shots starting the second half and the Boilermakers quickly went up 54-44. The lead stayed mostly at 10 points, as Mike Scearce, off the bench, popped from long range for 14 points to shut off any Spartan ideas of a comeback.

Scearce, the pleasant 6-7 sophomore from Lexington, Kentucky, came off the bench to hit seven of 10 shots, including one from the 30-foot range just ahead of the halftime buzzer.

Morris, who ignited several fastbreak baskets for Purdue with his quick hands, got six of his points from the free-throw line after it appeared Purdue would die with missed free throws. The Boilermakers, in keeping with their ninth place in free throw accuracy in the Big Ten, hit only 13 of 25 for the game.

That 13 of 25 is 52 percent – below the team field goal average of 52.7 (39 or 74) for the 40 minutes.

On the other side of the coin, Purdue had more steals (12) than it did errors (nine). The nine turnovers is a low for the season, with only four coming in the first half.

That's part of what Rose was talking about when he said the Boilermakers finished on "the upbeat."

Rose said he had talked to Morris prior to the game about picking up early fouls in going for the ball. The conversation paid off as Morris didn't get his first personal until 13:40 was left in the game. He did finish with two steals and three assists – and three fouls.

Rose used 12 players, with 10 scoring. He answered the pleadings of the crowd by inserting Anthrop into the lineup with 1:21 to play, and Purdue leading 85-70.

91 points were surpassed only by the 105 against Southeastern Louisiana in Game No. 3 on the schedule last December.

And the 91 points is 17 better than the Boilermakers' previous best in the conference this year – the 74 vs. MSU (73) in the conference opener Jan. 3 at East Lansing, and the 74 vs. Ilinois (66) here Jan 10.

Four Boilermakers, paced by Joe Barry Carroll's 26 points, scored in double figures in the emotion-packed game that saw seniors Carroll, Arnette Hallman, Steve Walker, and John Anthrop bow out before the home fans.

And Carroll, the silent 7-1 center, stole the show when he raced across the floor after being taken out with 49 seconds to play, to embrace his mother and present her with a dozen roses.

PURDUE PUTTING UP ITS DUKES

By Bruce Ramey

March 14, 1980 – LEXINGTON, KY. – Purdue's biggest-ever basketball win over Indiana was indeed a shocker.

The Boilermakers, an at-large entry from the Big Ten into the NCAA Mideast Regional, upset Big Ten champion Indiana 76-69 Thursday night by leading for all but 36 seconds – and how the Boilermakers did lead. They led by 19 points with 8:01 to play.

Purdue did it with defense that nine times stole the ball. And the 21-9 Boilers did it with scoring ace Joe Barry Carroll again limited to well below his average.

That Boilermaker defense and intensity put them into the championship game against Duke at 3:57 p.m. Saturday. Channel 13 will televise the game.

Duke? Yes, Duke. Lightning did strike twice in Rupp Arena Thursday night at the Atlantic Coast Conference's No. 3 team (same as Purdue in the Big Ten) upset host Kentucky 56-54 as Kyle Macy's last-second shot bounded off the rim, silencing the 23,000 partisan fans.

Purdue Coach Lee Rose, who had made a point of officials calling fouls on Indiana's big men who were assigned to shut off Carroll in sessions with the media this week, also saw his pleadings backfire.

Carroll picked up three first-half fouls and was limited to 27 minutes of playing time.

His teammates, primarily Texas sophomore Keith Edmonson and East Chicago junior Drake Morris, took up the scoring slack. Edmonson, given the defensive assignment on Indiana's great Mike Woodson, with Purdue in a man defense, threw in 20 points, by hitting five of nine shots and missing only two of 12 free throws.

Morris, assuming more of a leadership role on the floor, also had 20 points (seven of 14 from the floor and six of eight from the free-throw line) to go with two very important steals.

Arnette Hallman, picking up the defense and rebounding when Carroll was on the bench, added nine points and had nine rebounds.

Brian Walker, who has had to live with some bad raps this year, had three of Purdue's nine steals, plus five assists and five points. Carroll finished with 11 points (same as in the game at Bloomington).

But the difference was that Indiana won that game, 69-58.

It wasn't scoring for Purdue as much as it was defense that made all but Indiana's super freshman Isiah Thomas impotent.

Thomas, the "Big Ten Freshman of the Year," knocked in 13 of 20 shots and successfully converted all four free throws he tried. But, it was Thomas who was charged with six turnovers, several of them steals by Brian Walker. And Isiah Thomas was the only player on either team to put in 40 minutes on the floor. In addition to his 30 points, he had five assists, matching Brian Walker.

The Boilermakers, continuing to play the game they uncovered against Illinois back on Feb. 23, were almost flawless in the first half.

After Ray Tolbert gave Indiana a 2-0 lead with 36 seconds gone, Morris hit an 18-foot jumper to tie it and Hallman's free throw with two minutes gone gave the Boilermakers a 3-2 lead – and Indiana never again could tie the score or lead.

The Boilermakers took an 11-4 lead and at 13:18 Carroll picked up his second foul, putting Woodson on the free-throw line. The big guy went to the bench with 10:27 left in the half and Purdue leading 17-8 when he got his third foul on a charging call.

Purdue stretched the lead to 37-26 at the half as Brian Walker twice got steals and solo layups; Mike Scearce hit two free throws and a 10-footer; and Edmonson and Morris, carrying the offensive load, added eight points.

Indiana Coach Bobby Knight, quiet for much of the first half, got deeply involved with the officials as the half ended and was whistled for a technical foul for "unsportsmanlike conduct."

The Boilermakers went up by 13 points when Edmonson opened the second half by making the technical free throws, and Carroll hit a layup after Purdue got the ball out of bounds.

In that first half, Purdue turned the ball over only twice – and one of the turnovers was Carroll's third foul, the charging call. The Boilermakers also had five steals to go with their five assists.

Still, Indiana had shot 52.2 percent, but had been to the free throw line only three times (making two). Purdue was 12 of 26 (46.2) and had converted 13 of 16 free throws.

Purdue's biggest lead, 19 points, came when Edmonson's free throws made it 57-38.

Indiana's 38th point came on a layup by Isiah Thomas at 9:43, and Purdue's defense held the Hoosiers scoreless until the 6:07 mark, when Woodson made a pair of free throws. The Hoosier ace, held to six points the first half, broke loose for eight more in a brief flurry at this point as Indiana made its best move of the evening. He fouled out at 4:01 and Purdue leading 64-50.

Rose began calling time outs when IU cut the lead to 11 at 66-55, and despite a later flurry of turnovers, the Boilermakers didn't lose their poise, although the lead dropped to six with 40 seconds left.

Morris dropped in clutch free throws with 22 seconds to go, Scearce made one at :11 and Edmonson two more at :05 for a nine-point lead. Isiah Thomas beat the buzzer with a driving layup to cut Purdue's lead to seven – 76-69.

Indiana finished the year at 21-8.

Duke used the Purdue format for most of the 40 minutes of the second game to beat Kentucky for the second time this season. The Blue Devils defeated Kentucky in their season opener, 82-76 in overtime at Springfield, Massachusetts.

Duke jumped in front Thursday night, after leading from the opening tip, to go ahead 37-23 at the half. Kentucky didn't catch up until 27 seconds were left. The Blue Devils went up by one on junior Gene Banks' free throw with 22 seconds left.

After a Kentucky time out with nine seconds left, Macy got the final shot and missed. The Wildcats closed their season with a 29-6 record.

The Blue Devils are 23-8.

PURDUE—INDIANA BOX SCORE

Purdue 76, Indiana 69

Purdue	FG	FT	R	F	P
Morris	7-14	6-8	3	4	20
Hallman	2-4	5-7	9	5	9
Carroll	5-11	1-4	8	3	11
Edmonson	5-9	10-12	4	3	20
B. Walker	2-5	1-3	1	3	5
S. Walker	0-0	0-0	0	1	0
Scearce	1-2	9-11	1	0	11
Stallings	0-0	0-0	0	0	0
Benson	0-1	0-0	0	1	0
Kitchel	0-0	0-0	0	0	0
Barnes	0-0	0-0	0	0	0
Team			3		
Totals	22-46	32-44	32	20	76

Indiana	FG	FT	R	F	P
Turner	0-2	0-0	3	5	0
Woodson	5-12	4-5	6	5	14
Tolbert	3-7	0-2	11	5	6
I. Thomas	13-20	4-4	2	4	30
Carter	2-6	1-2	5	4	5
J. Thomas	0-2	4-4	2	1	4
Franz	0-0	0-0	0	2	0
T. Kitchel	1-2	0-0	1	1	2
Brown	1-1	0-0	0	0	2
Risley	0-0	0-0	0	1	0
Grunwald	1-2	0-0	1	2	2
Isenberger	2-4	0-0	2	3	4
Team			4		
Totals	28-58	13-17	38	33	69

Score at half: Purdue 37, Indiana 26
FG Percentage: Purdue .478, Indiana .483
FT Percentage: Purdue .727, Indiana .765
Assists: Purdue 11, Indiana 14
Officials: Woolridge, Sylvester, Moser

KNIGHT CREDITS PURDUE'S TEMPO AND INTENSITY

By Bruce Ramey

March 14, 1980 – LEXINGTON, KY. – Lightning did strike twice in Rupp Arena Thursday night. First Purdue knocked off Indiana, and then Duke knocked off Kentucky. That's putting upsets back-to-back in any situation.

For Purdue it was one of the biggest basketball wins in a long time. Invited to the NCAA tourney as an also-ran (at large, if you please), the Boilermakers were paired against no-less than the Big Ten champions – Indiana – the team that had beaten them a year ago in the final game of the National Invitation Tournament, and the team that at the start of the season had been voted No. 1 in the nation.

Sure, the Hoosiers lost Mike Woodson to back surgery in December, but they came on to win the Big Ten, after Woodson returned. And they had the celebrated Bobby Knight on the bench, didn't they? This was the Bobby Knight who was featured on CBS "60 Minutes" last Sunday night. Knight apparently came through "60 Minutes" without scarring his reputation – but 40 minutes - or to be exact two minutes – for that's how long his Hoosier's actually were in the game against Purdue – was enough for Indiana.

For Purdue Coach Lee Rose, it was a tremendous win. The man who grew up right here in Lexington, and coached at Transylvania College before moving on to the University of North Carolina–Charlotte before coming to Purdue two years ago, it was one of his brightest moments.

Rose declined to put the win in his "biggest" category, even though he took UNCC to the Final Four in 1973.

Instead, he said, "When was the last time Purdue beat Indiana in the NCAA?"

Never, coach! And certainly never under these circumstances!

The Boilermakers did it without their major weapon for 13 of the 40 minutes as Joe Barry Carroll was benched with personal fouls for that long.

"I told them to go out and have fun," said Rose. And for a Purdue fan, there's not any more fun than beating Indiana in any sport – let alone football or basketball – and on national television.

Purdue now has beaten Indiana 83 times in basketball and lost 53 times.

Not even if they play twice a year for the rest of the 20th century – and Purdue loses – can Indiana even the series.

Knight admitted Purdue took Indiana out of its game plan early.

"Purdue had a strong tempo, which we lacked early, and decided the game in the first half. They had better intensity, and we were never able to recapture it after we closed to 25-22.

"After they got the lead at the half (37-26) it was tough for us to catch up," he said.

Knight didn't make it any easier for his Hoosiers to catch up, after he was tagged with a technical foul shortly after the first half ended while calling the officials' attention to what he felt was a poor job of officiating.

Purdue stretched that 11-point lead to 15 points as Keith Edmonson made the two free throws and Joe Barry Carroll hit a layup after Purdue got the ball in play.

"That had no bearing on the game," Knight offered.

"I asked the official (Blaine Sylvester) why there wasn't a foul called when (Isiah) Thomas was knocked to the floor on a drive to the hoop just before the half ended," Knight said.

"He told me he wasn't the 'under official' and it wasn't his responsibility to call the foul.

"I asked him 'Why the hell can't you call it,' and got the technical from the other official."

The other official was Louis Moser of the Atlantic Coast Conference, a man who, according to NBC's Billy Packer, "will take no guff off anyone."

"It (the situation) was poorly handled," said Knight.

In any verdict, the resulting four points looked very big to Purdue in the stretch when Indiana whittled the Boilers' 19-point lead to just six with 40 seconds left.

Meanwhile, over on the Purdue bench, Lee Rose, the "Mr. Cool," was having a ball of his own.

While Knight was in midcourt laying it on the officials, Rose was standing as close as he could get to make sure of what was going on – and no doubt quietly rooting for the technical foul.

"This certainly was a great win for our players. They played with a lot of commitment and heart. Indiana has a lot of talent," said Rose.

The coach has said twice this week that Indiana "was voted No. 1 in the world by no less than John Wooden at the start of the season, and I certainly won't argue with that."

Still, this is not the same team that Wooden voted "all world." But it has enough of the same players to qualify.

Brian Walker, the guy charged with running the Purdue offense most of the time, was the last man into the showers following the big win. He was besieged because of his steals and assists.

Twice he mugged IU freshman Isiah Thomas at midcourt and got away with two layups.

"Are you kidding?" he replied to the question "Does this make up for the loss in the NIT last year?"

Now Purdue gets to play Duke, the team that upset Kentucky on its home court. And that team does not at all resemble the team that struggled for 30 minutes against undermanned Pennsylvania last week in Mackey Arena.

END OF THE LINE

Boilers Hit Crook in the Road to NCAA Title

By Bruce Ramey

March 23, 1980 – INDIANAPOLIS – The glass slipper was too tight Saturday afternoon for the Purdue Boilermakers, but it fit firmly for the UCLA Bruins.

That puts UCLA, 10-time NCAA basketball champion, against Louisville in the 1980 championship game in Market Square Arena at 9:15 Monday night, and puts Purdue and Iowa into a consolation battle for third place, starting at 6:07 p.m. Monday.

Purdue, losing 67-62 to the young Bruins, dug itself a big 10-point hole midway through the second half and just couldn't get over the hump.

Louisville, behind the scintillating shooting of 6-4 All-American guard Darrell Griffith (34 points), took an early lead and, like UCLA, wouldn't let the game get out of hand in beating Iowa 80-72.

"UCLA did a good job on Joe Barry Carroll, and we didn't hit our outside shots," said Coach Lee Rose.

"You just can't have a bad game at this (championship) level, and we played a marginal game here. We just didn't execute well."

UCLA senior Kiki Vandeweghe, playing under his third head coach in four years, ripped the Boil-ermakers early as Purdue's weak side defense broke down to set the early tempo.

Vandeweghe, who finished with 24 points, had 16 in the first half as the Bruins took a 33-25 lead. He had four breakaway slam dunks by beating the Purdue defense.

Vandeweghe, 6-7, 205, also had a rebound basket and threw in a couple of 15-footers as the Bruins showed they belonged in the Final Four.

Purdue contained the UCLA quickness quite well after Vandeweghe cooled off midway of the first half, yet UCLA took an eight-point lead just before the half as both clubs floundered through a five-minute period that resembled sawmill basketball.

The Boilers, their record dropping to 22-10, made one of their better runs at the Bruins at the mid-point of the second half and cut a 10-point lead to one as Keith Edmonson and Drake Morris joined Carroll in the scoring surge.

Carroll, who scored 17 points, was having as much trouble with the sagging Bruins as he did halfway through the season with Big Ten defense. He finished the evening with eight field goals in 14 shots, but six turnovers – traveling or the ball knocked loose from his hands – were more damaging.

After UCLA had extended the lead to 55-47, Carroll got two free throws; Roosevelt Barnes got a field goal after Arnette Hallman rebounded Carroll's missed free throw, and six more free throws by Keith Edmonson (two) and Brian Walker

Joe Barry Carroll left Purdue as the second leading scorer all-time, first in dunks and first in blocked shots.

(four) cut the Bruin lead to a point (57-56) with 3:40 to play.

It appeared the Boilermakers, who had played extremely well in their four previous tourney games, just might pull out another one.

UCLA's 6-6 sophomore center Mike Sanders knocked in a pair of free throws, and Carroll came back with a field goal to keep it at a one-point game (59-58). Sanders again made a pair of free throws to give the Bruins a three-point lead (61-58), and Carroll scored again on a goal-tending call on Sanders to keep it at one point, 61-60 with 1:31 to play.

Coach Larry Brown put the Bruins into a delay game and freshman guard Michael Holton hit a pair of free throws with 53 seconds left, then it was Vandeweghe's turn to come back into the picture.

Twice the big guy went to the free throw line in the final 41 seconds to shut off Purdue hopes, and each time he produced points to put the Boilermakers into the consolation game.

Purdue pressed the Bruins nearly the entire game, used man and zone defenses, but couldn't shut off UCLA shooting which produced a 50 percent night – 23 field goals in 46 shots.

Still, it was UCLA free throws which made the difference. Purdue put the Bruins on the line 25 times, and 21 times UCLA converted to offset Purdue's 25 field goals in 58 shots (43.1 percent). Purdue hit 12 of 17 free throws and had a slim rebounding edge, 33-32.

"We talked at halftime about our lack of concentration in the first half," said Rose. "The emotion was there to play, but we didn't concentrate well early."

Monday night the Boilermakers will play Iowa, making the consolation game an all-Big Ten affair, while Louisville and UCLA – both of whom shot extremely well Saturday – battle for the NCAA crown won by Michigan State last year.

Louisville, behind Griffith's torrid start – the smooth 6-4 leaper had 16 of the Cardinals' first 18 points – got a break when Iowa's Ronnie Lester left the game with only 12 minutes played when he reinjured his right knee.

Lester, the guy Coach Lute Olson calls "our glue," had kept the tense Hawkeyes in contention by scoring Iowa's first 10 points.

Kenny Arnold took over the point guard spot for Iowa and the Hawkeyes got to within a point at 28-27 with 4:05 left in the first half. Rod McCray, Louisville's 6-7 freshman center, gave the Cards breathing room with four quick points, and Iowa was down by five at the half, 34-29.

Arnold pulled Iowa into a 40-40 tie on a driving layup, but Roger Burkman, off the bench, helped spark Louisville to an eight-point lead at 48-40. The Cardinals kept the advantage, going up by 11 at 66-55, and the best Iowa could do was whittle it to five points at 72-67 on a rebound basket by Steve Krafcisin.

Louisville, shooting 53.6 (15 of 28) in the first half, had no problems with Iowa's man defense in the second half and hit an even better 59.6 (13 of 19).

Olson said the loss of Lester was a factor, and the fact Iowa was too tense at the start – wary of Louisville's shot-blocking ability – contributed to the Hawkeyes' demise.

"Griffith is a great player. The tighter we played him the better he shot," said Olson.

Griffith took 21 shots and hit 14, missing the semifinal record of 16, set by Indiana State's Larry Bird last year.

Griffith got good help from teammates McCray (14) and Smith (13).

Arnold paced Iowa with 20 points. Vince Brookins had 14 and Krafcisin 12. Kevin Boyle, a two-year starter, even though he's a sophomore, went 0-for-8.

Iowa, like Purdue, shot poorly. The Hawkeyes were 43.9 percent for the 80 minutes, hitting only 29 of 66 shots.

BOILERS SNUB IOWA

By Bruce Ramey

March 25, 1980 – INDIANAPOLIS – And the band played "My Old Kentucky Home," again and again and again Monday night.

It wasn't for the University of Kentucky Wildcats either, but for the Louisville Cardinals who won the 1980 NCAA basketball championship with a come-from-behind 59-54 win over upstart UCLA in Market Square Arena.

Earlier, Purdue had taken third place with an impressive 75-58 win over Iowa in the all-Big Ten consolation game.

The Boilermakers, finishing their season with a 23-10 record, blistered the nets for 16 field goals in 23 shots — that's 69.6 percent — the second half in the Iowa rout.

Joe Barry Carroll, Purdue's 7-1 All-American, was awesome as he scored 35 points – 20 in the first half – then set a record with 158 points in the six-game tourney format. The old mark was 142 points by Tony Price of Pennsylvania last year.

Carroll also was named to the all-tourney team, along with Griffith, Louisville's Rod McCray and UCLA's Vandeweghe and Rod Foster.

Carroll hit 14 of 17 shots from the field, converted seven of 11 free throws and had 12 rebounds, four blocked shots and two assists. He also was charged with seven turnovers. And he sent two of Iowa's big guys to the bench with five fouls. Three other Hawkeyes each had four fouls.

Iowa took a three-point lead over the Boilermakers at 25-22 near the end of the first half, but Carroll tied it on a three-point play with two minutes to play, then came back 23 seconds later for another three-pointer to give Purdue a 28-25 lead and capped that with a slam dunk for a 30-25 lead. Purdue took a 32-27 advantage into the locker room.

In the first half, only three Boilermakers scored – Carroll getting 20, Keith Edmonson 10 and Arnette Hallman two. Purdue hit 13 of 26 shots in the first half, and in the second half blew the Hawkeyes out with those 16 baskets in 23 shots.

Iowa, which had knocked off Purdue by 15 points in February at Iowa City, was tagged with 26 fouls by a trio of non-Big Ten officials who appeared to be awed at times by the physical contact on the floor.

Kenny Arnold, who ran the Hawkeyes as ace Ronnie Lester was held out of action with a knee injury, led Iowa with 19 points and got 10-point help from freshman sub guard Bob Hansen – the only two Hawkeyes in double figures.

Joining Carroll in scoring were Edmonson with 17 points, Hallman with eight and Drake Morris with seven – all in the second half.

Iowa, which finished fourth in the Big Ten (behind Purdue in third), closed its season 23-10.

Joe Barry Carroll was an unstoppable force inside, shooting, rebounding or blocking shots.

CONSOLATION BOX SCORE

Purdue 75, Iowa 58

Iowa	FG	FT	R	F	P
Brookins	2-6	0-1	6	5	4
Waite	3-5	2-5	7	4	8
Krafcisin	2-8	2-2	6	5	6
Arnold	8-14	3-5	2	2	19
Boyle	3-8	3-4	7	4	9
Hansen	4-13	2-2	4	4	10
Gannon	1-8	0-0	3	0	2
Heller	0-2	0-0	1	1	0
Henry	0-1	0-0	1	1	0
Grogan	0-0	0-0	0	0	0
Arens	0-0	0-0	0	0	0
Darsee	0-0	0-0	0	0	0
Team			3		
Totals	23-65	12-19	43	26	58

Purdue	FG	FT	R	F	P
Morris	3-3	1-1	1	3	7
Hallman	4-9	0-3	3	3	8
Carroll	14-17	7-11	12	3	35
Edmonson	6-11	5-8	4	2	17
B. Walker	0-1	0-0	5	3	0
Stallings	1-3	2-2	1	1	4
Scearce	0-0	0-0	0	1	0
S. Walker	1-3	2-3	4	2	4
Benson	0-0	0-0	0	1	0
Barnes	0-2	0-0	1	0	0
Anthrop	0-0	0-0	0	1	0
Kitchel	0-0	0-0	1	0	0
Team			5		
Totals	29-49	17-28	37	20	75

Score at half: Purdue, 32, Iowa 27
FG Percentage: Iowa .354, Purdue .592
FT Percentage: Iowa .632, Purdue .607
Errors: Iowa 20, Purdue 23
Assists (leaders): Iowa 12 (Arnold, Hansen 3),
Purdue 22 (B. Walker 4, Morris, Edmonson 3)
Technical foul: Edmonson (grabbing rim)
Officials: Rhodes (SWAC), Herrold (Pac-10),
Turner (Pac-10)
Attendance: 16,637

CARROLL SCORES IN ONE-ON-ONE SESSION WITH MEDIA QUESTIONS

By Bob Scott

March 25, 1980 — INDIANAPOLIS — "JBC, JBC, JBC" the Purdue fans chanted at Market Square Arena, and Joe Barry Carroll didn't disappoint them.

Purdue's 75-58 win over Iowa Monday night in the NCAA tourney was a perfect "swan song" for Carroll.

His final appearance as a Boilermaker basketball player was a dilly – 35 points, 12 rebounds and four blocked shots. Carroll, an all-tourney pick, also shot an astounding 82 percent from the field on 14-of-17.

Carroll, who had no trouble getting up for the Big Ten alley-fighters from Iowa City, also shared the post-game podium with Purdue Coach Lee Rose.

"We won tonight. When you're in a tournament, you want to stay in the win column. Personal glory is not important. It's how you play as a team," said Carroll.

The 7-foot-1 Denver native showed that "handling" the media wasn't such a big deal after all.

Carroll answered numerous questions.

On his future: "We'll be going back tonight and I'll get up in the morning and go to class. I'll become a full-time student again. I'm in line to graduate (management major) on time at this point and that's the next thing in line for me. It's tough to maintain consistency in the classroom during the season, so that's what I'll be concentrating on now."

On the "non-shake" with Iowa's coach: "It's customary for me as a senior this year to shake the opposing coach's hand. We would exchange compliments. I gestured (toward Coach Lute Olson), but he declined. I have nothing but praise for Coach Olson and his team."

On the game: "None of our games have been meaningless for me. We want to put out our best effort all the time. We were disappointed in our play Saturday and the fact we didn't win. But we're one of four teams here out of hundreds in the country. This tournament is the Mecca of college basketball. You get in it and you want to do well."

About all-star games: "As I said, my plans now are to pursue my degree. I'm not sure about all-star games at this point because of the conflicts with my classwork. It's possible right now I may not go to any. Right now, I'm a little behind in my classwork, as many of us probably are."

According to a release from the Pizza Hut Classic, Carroll will not participate in that all-star game, although he was one of the top five vote-getters.

Carroll also burned his name into the NCAA record book with 158 points (26.3 average) to break the six-game record of 142 set last year by Tony Price of Penn.

Lee Rose only coached Purdue for two seasons, but he won a Big Ten title, finished second in the NIT and third in the NCAA tournament.

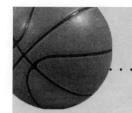

KEADY READY TO START RECRUITING PURDUE

By Jeff Washburn

April 11, 1980 – "I've always said the best basketball players in the world are from Indiana and Illinois, and I'll be recruiting those states heavily," said 43-year-old Gene Keady, who formally was announced as Purdue's 17th basketball coach this morning in a Mackey Arena press conference.

Keady, who guided Western Kentucky to a 38-19 record in his two years at that school, signed a four-year contract with Purdue, calling for a salary of $41,000 per year. The contract will be reviewed after two years, according to Purdue Athletic Director George King.

"I was shocked when Purdue called," Keady said. "It is hard for me to imagine that I went from coaching a high school of 400 students (Beloit, Kansas) in 1958 to the head job at a Big Ten university.

"I met with the players (Purdue) this morning, and I feel we have a good nucleus coming back. Right now, I'm planning on meeting with Billy Keller in hopes of retaining him as one of my assistant coaches.

"Then I'll start recruiting this afternoon. I feel we need outside shooting and rebounding help for next year, and I'll go after Joe Gampfer (Cincinnati), Greg Eifert (Fort Wayne Dwenger) and Russell Cross (Chicago Manley).

"I'm flying to Kansas tonight to speak at a banquet, and there is a player there who can rebound and shoot that I'll be going after.

"I want to recruit Indiana players. I feel if a young man can drive three hours and get home, he'll be happy at a university.

"I won't be recruiting any of the players for Purdue that I was recruiting for Western Kentucky."

Keady was asked questions ranging from his opinion of Bobby Knight to technical fouls to how well he handles cold winters.

"Who?" Keady responded when asked about Knight, but then said, "I hope this doesn't bother anyone, but Knight is one of my best friends."

On technical fouls, he said, "I'm not from the same mold as Lee (former Purdue coach Rose). A technical foul once in a while may help your team."

And on winters, he said, "I'm from Kansas. I can handle winters."

Keady hopes to name Clem Haskins, a former standout for the Chicago Bulls of the National Basketball Association, as another of his assistant coaches. Haskins was Keady's assistant for two years at Western Kentucky.

"I hope to get Clem," Keady said, "but he's the guy I recommended to take my post at Western Kentucky."

After coaching high school ball from 1958-1965, Keady was an assistant coach for one season at Hutchinson (Kansas) Junior College and then took over as the head coach at Hutchinson. He was the head coach there from 1966 through 1974.

His record at Hutchinson was 184-47 (.797).

He left Hutchinson in 1974 to join Eddie Sutton at Arkansas, where he had great success recruiting in Indiana.

He spent four years at Arkansas, and in that time, the Razorbacks won 89 and lost 24 (.788) and went to the NCAA finals in 1978 with Sidney Moncrief, Marvin Delph and Jim Brewer.

Keady then took the head job at Western Kentucky, and went 17-11 in 1978-79 and 21-8 this past season.

"I thrive on pressure," Keady said, "and I'm looking forward to coaching in the greatest basketball conference in the country (Big Ten)."

Keady is married (Diane) and has a 21-year-old daughter Beverly and a 16-year-old son Danny.

Keady is a graduate of Kansas State University, where he played football and basketball, and played one season with the Pittsburgh Steelers in the National Football League. His hobbies include jogging, tennis, golf, fishing and hunting.

The Keady family will wait until the end of the current school year to move from Bowling Green, Ky. Keady's wife is a teacher and will complete her contract.

KEADY (SAID LIKE "KATY") CHARMS PRESS

Tales of Two Cities

By Robert Kriebel

April 11, 1980 – Say "Katy."

Now say "Keady" so that it rhymes with "Katy."

And now you are off to a good start with 43-year-old Gene Keady, introduced to our two cities this morning as the new head basketball coach at Purdue University.

All the statistical details and the pertinent quotes about the new coach appear on Page One and in the sports section; but there are impressions of the man worth sharing.

They held the press conference in a basement-level suite in Mackey Arena called the "VIP Room," used at various times for John Purdue Club functions, or football team film-study meetings, or, when appropriate, for games of "Meet the Press," which was today's ball game.

It would have been cool, one might say with respect to ingenious public relations, to have staged the press conference out in the middle of the floor of Mackey Arena, there by the center circle with the painting of Boilermaker Pete.

But there were between 300 and 400 football coaches up on the arena's main floor, attending a clinic, and the basketball arena was dark so the football coaches could see a film of the 1979 season highlights, including Mark Herrmann, the Golden Girl, the All-American Marching Band, and even a filmed flash or two of Thor, the Wonder Dog, chasing Frisbees across the Ross-Ade Stadium grass.

So anyway, downstairs about 75 basketball-oriented types jammed the paneled, floor-tiled VIP Room lit by ovals of fluorescent ceiling units. A rostrum was set up appropriately foregrounded by the third-place NCAA tourney trophy won by the team coached by Mr. Keady's immediate predecessor, Lee Rose.

Four television cameras on tripods, and eight microphones with cords vanishing off into the crowd, greeted Athletic Director George King and Coach Keady – remember, it's "Katy."

It was the kind of event where everyone was happy and smiling, and the marvelous sense of humor common to people in athletics kept bubbling to the surface.

Interestingly, too, it was the kind of crowd in which the president of the university, Dr. Arthur G. Hansen, and the vice president and treasurer, Frederick R. Ford, and the director of the Alumni Association, Joe Rudolph, were anonymous spectators in the back of the room — mere faces in the crowd.

George King smiled and looked relaxed after admitting things had been hectic in finding the new coach. King introduced Coach Keady's wife, Diane, and daughter, Beverly, who looked most friendly but rather ill-at-ease in this strange city, on this gray Friday morning, in front of all those blazing lights and rows of people sitting in chairs taking notes.

The coach himself, though, is accustomed to all this. After his introduction Gene Keady put his palms on the rostrum, relaxed, bright-eyed, and seemed to enjoy the attention and the answering of questions.

After seeing pictures of Lee Rose, then meeting him, one might have been surprised at his shortness of stature, the calmness in his eyes, and the clearness of his skin.

After seeing pictures of Gene Keady, then meeting him, you are impressed by a man who works hard, stays in perfect condition, never overeats, gets little sleep, brushes his absolutely perfect-looking teeth, and is always thinking, thinking, thinking.

The new coach is a good public speaker, a man who smiles and makes you feel good. His is a personality that would impress moms and dads of giant high school basketball players, to get more to the point.

And so Coach Keady, rhymes with Katy, charmed that miscellaneous crowd that included the tense, fast-working, neck-wiping, shirtsleeves TV newsman Tom Maxedon from Channel 18; the stout, graying, relaxed John Bansch of the *Indianapolis Star*; the several familiar voices of WASK radio – Mike Piggott, Larry Clisby, Harry Bradway; the pale blond features of Joe Pat, the play-by-play voice of the Boilermaker football and basketball networks; *Journal and Courier* sports writers Bruce Ramey and Jeff Washburn and Managing Editor Angelyn Rizzo; Bob Mitchell, a Purdue National Bank vice president; Gil Buck, a Purdue University police detective; and nameless others, men and women, who were either "working press" or "interested bystanders."

And through it all there was that great sense of humor.

"What is your attitude toward cold winters?" the new coach was asked, a witty reference to Coach Rose leaving for sunnier, warmer Tampa, Florida.

"I'm used to them," said Coach Keady, whose name rhymes with Katy. "I can handle them."

And that, too, is a good start, wouldn't you say?

KEADY "TRADITION" MEANS WIN

King: He was our first choice

By Bruce Ramey

April 11, 1980 – "Tradition, tradition," sang Tevye in "Fiddler on the Roof," as he made the song one of the all-time classics in show business.

And "tradition" is what the official search committee looked for in selecting Purdue's new basketball coach. However, Athletic Director George King calls it "progression."

King believes the committee found "progression-tradition" in Gene Keady, who spent the last two years at Western Kentucky University in Bowling Green.

"The important guidelines we looked for in a new basketball coach were that he has shown progression and been successful in his previous years," said King as he introduced Keady this morning at a Mackey Arena news conference

"We found that when we picked Jim Young as our football coach (three years ago). And we found that in Lee Rose, when he was hired two years ago." Rose left Purdue for South Florida one week ago.

"The mold of the man is 'was he making progress in his field?' We see these positive things in Young and Keady. The committee and I made the decision that Keady was our choice – our first choice – as our new basketball coach.

"He has shown successful progression as a high school coach, as a junior college coach, as an assistant coach at Arkansas, where he was head recruiter, and then on his own at Western Kentucky.

"He has the background we were looking for, in the mold of Young and Rose," said King.

Keady, 43, went 100-46 at Beloit (Kan.) High in seven years, taking Beloit to the state tourney three times, finishing as high as third.

He went 184-47 at Hutchinson (Kan.) Junior College and was named "Coach of the Year" three times in Region Six.

He joined Eddie Sutton's staff at Arkansas and in four years the Razorbacks were 89-24.

"He's without question the primary reason for our success at Arkansas," said Sutton in a press release. "I consider him the finest recruiter in our profession and very intelligent about the way the game is played today. He's a winner in all areas."

Keady takes over a program at Purdue that is the most successful in the long history of the Big Ten.

Purdue has the best won-lost record of any school in the Big Ten – 545 wins and 414 losses for 56.8 percent.

That's the Purdue tradition.

Western Kentucky, where Keady was 38-19 in two years, has tradition as well.

Starting the 1979-80 season, the Hilltoppers were No. 1 in the nation in wins per season – 1,034 wins in 60 years for an average of 17.23 per season. Second was North Carolina (17.09), followed by UCLA (16.72) and Kentucky (16.22).

In seasons with 20 or more wins, Western Kentucky ranks second with 23, behind Kentucky with 28. In winning percentage over the years, Western Kentucky was fourth (70.1), behind Kentucky (76.0), North Carolina (71.8), St. John's (N.Y.) (71.2).

Recruiting appears to be a Keady strong point, and he says he's not a stranger to recruiting in Indiana, Ohio, and Illinois.

"I spent most of my time – about 80 percent – recruiting in Indiana when I was at Arkansas," Keady said following the press conference.

"I feel it is absolutely necessary to have good connections with Indiana high school coaches, and this I plan to continue."

Keady said he already had met with the Purdue basketball squad this morning.

He found one very familiar face in Purdue guard Keith Edmonson. He tried to recruit Edmonson two years ago for Western Kentucky.

"I'll have the squad on a weight training program starting Monday," he said.

Tradition? Purdue University has won more football and basketball games than any other school in NCAA Division I in the past two years. In second place? Arkansas, where Keady was first introduced to big-time college basketball.

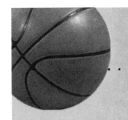

BOILERS' 75.5 FIRING SETS BIG TEN MARK

By Dick Ham

January 6, 1981 – Purdue Coach Gene Keady was extremely pleased with the way his Boilermakers performed in the Big Ten opener Monday night, but Michigan's Bill Frieder wasn't too carried away with his Wolverines.

The conference's two rookie coaches hooked up in an unbelievable Mackey Arena shootout that had 12,647 onlookers shaking their heads and wondering when it would end as the Boilermakers set a Big Ten record of 75.5 percent firing from the floor.

And it didn't end until the Boilers knocked off the Big Ten's only unbeaten team, 81-74, and cut short its bid to join Ohio State as the only team to best the Boilers in the 13-plus years of the arena's existence.

"The kids were really ready to play tonight," Keady said. "We had the intensity from start to finish and it was obviously our best game of the year.

"I thought we did a super job of taking care of the ball and I'm very happy. Being at home helped a lot, of course, but I believed that if we could win this one we have a chance to have a respectable record. But we still have a lot of things to work on yet.

"It seemed that our defense made them a little bit shaky early and thank God for Russell Cross.

"We couldn't get the ball in to him early because they were two-timing him, but the players are smart enough to know that you can't win if you don't get it into the middle. Then, Cross took his man outside and we broke someone else loose. Michigan gave us a lot of layups.

"The whole team played well the entire game and I knew we had it when we got those two or three layups while we controlled the ball late," Keady explained.

Asked about his sparse use of substitutions in the second half, only two, Keady replied. "Well, we rotated players quite a bit in the first half and kept them rested, so I thought they could go all the way. Besides, when they were playing so well I hated to take them out and maybe break it up. We didn't need a rest in the second half."

Keady also spoke fondly of Cross's play. "The way he handles his temperament and his composure make him play as a junior instead of a freshman," Keady said.

Both coaches took time to marvel at the shooting – the Boilermakers hit a Big Ten record .755 from the field, while Michigan banged in .478 from the floor and .833 from the line – but that didn't interest them as much as other phases of the game.

In assessing the Wolverines' first defeat Frieder said, "We did not work a good offense in the first half and we did not execute well. But I was more disappointed in our rebounding. Purdue sure made us pay for our mistakes.

"I know there in the middle of the second half it was a hell of a game, but they never gave us a chance to catch up. Credit Purdue's defense for that and it did a great job on offense as it worked for the good shot. That's what we needed – to work for better shots, especially in the first half.

"We have had rebounding problems in the nonconference season and we aren't a domineering ball club. For us to win we have to run and when you have a team like that it's tough to slow them down.

"Purdue is a good team and I don't care what you guys think of the Gator Bowl tourney, Purdue won it. Do you realize Michigan has never won a tourney out of the state of Michigan?"

In a more light-hearted vein Frieder was asked about vet guard Marty Bodnar's unerring marksmanship from long range and responded,

"He really put on a clinic there in the second half, didn't he? But then all the Purdue guys were putting on a clinic."

Brian Walker, the ramrod of the Boilermaker floor game, admitted it was his job to keep the team together at both ends of the floor. He also felt that the intensity all coaches look for was there for the whole game while Cross handled the Big Ten press herd equally as well as he did himself on the playing floor.

"It was a great game for me. Maybe the Big Ten is a little more physical than I thought it would be, but I've had guys hanging all over me ever since high school. My coach always told me not to let the other team intimidate me," Cross said.

Gene Keady succeeded Lee Rose as head coach in April of 1980.

PURDUE UPSETS HAWKEYES

Palombizio Hits Free Throw at :00

By Bob Scott

March 7, 1982 – Now it's time to sit and wait. Purdue will know tonight if it has landed a berth in the National Invitation Tournament.

Purdue certainly made the NIT selection committee sit up and take notice after Saturday's breathtaking, 66-65 win over Iowa's Hawkeyes.

Michigan City freshman Dan Palombizio coolly shot a free throw with no time showing on the clock. The ball bounced straight up and through the net to set off a jubilant celebration among the sellout Mackey Arena crowd of 14,123.

Coach Gene Keady's Boilermakers finished the regular season at 14-13 overall, and 11-7 in the Big Ten. The Boilers' Big Ten record surpassed last season's league mark of 10-8 when Purdue finished third in the NIT.

The loss kept the dazed Iowa Hawkeyes in a tailspin. It was Iowa's third-straight defeat, and its fourth in the last five games. Last season, the Hawks lost their last two Big Ten games as Indiana slipped past them into first.

Coach Lute Olson's Hawkeyes finished the regular season at 20-7 overall and 12-6 in the Big

Ten. The Hawks will probably receive an NCAA tourney bid.

Saturday's hectic finish in Mackey Arena found Purdue battling back from a nine-point deficit, 54-45, with 10:29 left in the game.

Then Keith Edmonson and Michael Scearce went to work. Scearce, who led all scorers with 19 points, scored six of his points down the stretch, while Edmonson, who finished with 17, popped in seven points.

Edmonson won the Big Ten scoring title over Indiana's Ted Kitchel with a 20.5 average. Kitchel also had 17 Saturday to finish with a 20.1 average.

Edmonson's jumper tied the game at 65-65 with 1:04 showing as the momentum stayed with the Boilermakers.

Iowa went to a four-corners offensive spread to eat up time and get the game's last shot. Olson called a timeout with 27 seconds remaining.

Hawkeye guard Kenny Arnold drove the left side, but Scearce, playing with four fouls, moved over to block Arnold's layup attempt out of bounds.

Iowa again called timeout, with nine seconds left. When time resumed, Arnold fired up a 23-footer, but missed, and Palombizio grabbed the rebound.

It looked like overtime, but referee Jim Bain blew the whistle and called a foul on an incredulous Hawkeye, Kevin Boyle.

Iowa called another timeout to "ice" Palombizio before he could step to the free throw line for his 1-plus-1 free throw.

Palombizio eyed the basket and cooly made the free throw. He didn't get a chance for the meaningless bonus because the rush of players and fans rendered the floor unplayable.

Purdue trailed Iowa at halftime, 34-31, as Hawkeye Bob Hansen downed 12 points. Iowa shot a sizzling .652 for the half, and finished the game at .587.

The Boilers shot a solid .523 for the game, but it was their free throw shooting which saved the day. Purdue made a hefty 87 percent from the line on 20 of 23 shots.

Purdue and Iowa both made 13 turnovers in the clean ballgame.

Hansen led Iowa with 16 points, but Palombizio helped to hold him to only four second-half points. Freshman center Greg Stokes had a season-high 15 points, while fellow sophomore guard Steve Carfino fired in 14.

Purdue will find out tonight, after the NCAA has made its 20 at-large selections, if it is going to the NIT.

If Purdue is picked for the NIT, it will probably have to play its first-round game Wednesday or Thursday on the road.

The NIT's final four teams play March 22-24 at Madison Square Garden in New York City.

KEADY: WE HAD THIS ONE COMING

By Bob Scott

March 7, 1982 – Coach Gene Keady believes life and basketball have a way of "balancing out."

After Purdue won a thrilling, 66-65 game over Iowa Saturday, Keady strongly intimated that the Boilers were due a victory like that after so many close defeats.

Trailing by as many as nine points in the second half, Keady was proud his team "never gave up. We told our kids to keep pressure on them and they would crack, and we got a couple of breaks."

In his post-game press conference, Keady did not refer specifically to the controversial call, or the officiating, which gave Dan Palombizio a game-winning free throw.

"I was looking at the ball and didn't see the foul. I've always been a defensive back, anyway," joked the one-time pro football player.

Keady patted the crowd on the back for its enthusiasm, despite the students being on spring break.

"The crowd got behind us, and we happened to get momentum at the right time. This type of thing can happen to anyone on the road, especially at Mackey Arena. It's a tough place to play."

"I was glad to have Dan (Palombizio) at the line. He did well at Ohio State from the line," said Keady.

The second-year Purdue coach also put in a plug for his team's chances in the National Invitation Tournament.

"The NIT has to consider we finished strong and how tough our nonconference schedule was," said Keady. "We'll have a great crowd for an NIT game, but they'll pick whoever they want. I'm not real optimistic about a bid, but they must look at us real hard now.

Keady also noted Keith Edmonson's jump shot which tied the game was the same play Purdue tried to run at the end of the recent win at Michigan State.

In commenting of Michael Scearce, who picked up foul No. 4 with 11:54 left in the game, Keady said, "I told Michael I was going to leave him in because he was a senior and we needed him on the boards."

Edmonson scored 17 to win the Big Ten scoring championship with a 20.5-point average. His last game in the Big Ten, however, found him shooting 7 of 20 from the field for 35 percent.

"I was tired. Iowa didn't give me many uncontested shots, and most of the time I was double-teamed.

"I'm happy my family could come up from San Antonio for this last game. The fans really came out and supported us. They've been just beautiful to me during my four years at Purdue," said Edmonson, who wants a career in television after a few years in pro basketball.

Palombizio, the Boilers' latest hero, said he didn't really feel any pressure during his clinching free throw.

"I felt I had my rhythm. There was nothing to lose. If I missed, it's overtime. My teammates had a lot of confidence in me. It was the greatest feeling in my life when it went through, because we haven't beaten Iowa in two years," said the freshman.

Palombizio, who played 21 minutes, only scored one point, the winner, but he was proud of his defense on Iowa's Bob Hansen.

"I was all over Hansen. He was killing us (12 points in first half), so I just decided to stay on him during the entire second half," said the young forward.

Scearce, who is ready for another NIT drive, said the Boilers "will live if we don't get an NIT bid. We'll take it like everything else this season."

The senior forward also wanted to "thank God first of all for four good years at Purdue. I also want to thank my mother and father for raising me to be a first-class gentleman at all times."

Russell Cross said, "Wanting the NIT inspired us this week. The difference between the early part of the season and now has been the play of Mike (Scearce) and Dan (Palombizio). Rick (Hall) also has come along great. I'm proud of this team."

BRADLEY TRIPS BOILERS FOR NIT TITLE

By Bob Scott

March 25, 1982 – NEW YORK – It took a heckuva long time, but Purdue's basketball season has ended.

Bradley's Braves brought it to a screeching halt Wednesday night with a 67-58 win over the Boilers for the National Invitation Tournament championship.

The Braves finished 26-10, while Purdue would up with an 18-14 mark after the 45th annual NIT – the oldest college postseason tournament.

Purdue, winner of nine of its last 11 games, collided with a fierce Bradley defense which muzzled the Boilers' top gun, Keith Edmonson.

Bradley also received stalwart scoring from its two starting guards, Willie Scott and Barney Mines. The duo combined for a regular-season average of 16.1 points, but the tandem drilled Purdue for 34 points – 17 for each player.

The tourney's Most Valuable Player, Mitch Anderson, popped in 16, while David Thirdkill scored 15 to give Bradley four starters in double figures.

Edmonson, the Big Ten's leading scorer, got just 11 points, while teammates Mike Scearce and Russell Cross hit for 16 each. Purdue starters Ricky Hall and Greg Eifert failed to score.

As a Madison Square Garden crowd of 9,572 watched, the game quickly became a battle of styles. Who would control the tempo and dictate the play?

Purdue and Bradley knocked heads in the first half, but were tied, 31-31 at intermission. Scearce, sore back and all, hit for 10 in the half, as did Scott.

The Boilers trailed 27-19 with 6:14 left in the first half, and Bradley appeared ready for Purdue's jugular. But two quick jumpers by designated bomber Kevin Stallings put Purdue back in the game at 27-23.

Cross' aggressive center play spelled trouble for Bradley's centers.

Braves strongman Donald Reese sat out nine minutes of the first half with three fouls and eventually fouled out with 4:37 remaining in the contest. His backup, Carmel's Kerry Cook, also fouled out with about two minutes to go.

The Boilermakers had managed to get within one point in the second half at 43-42 on a jumper by Mike Scearce. After rebounding a missed shot, Purdue had a chance for its first lead since an early 8-6 advantage. Scearce, however, was called for an offensive foul and Thirdkill's three-point play started an 11-2 run that gave Bradley a 54-44 lead with 6:31 left.

The Boilers' second-half effort was erratic as they canned 8 of 20 field goals for a poor .400 mark. Bradley, however, blistered the cords with 10 of 16 and a .625 figure.

The Boilers' gritty determination surfaced once again, though, in staying close and averting a blowout. They came back to trail 59-56 at the 2:08

mark, and the small Boiler contingent had hope again.

Purdue called timeout with 1:27 left to figure out a strategy against Bradley's time-consuming spread attack. Fouling the Braves was Purdue's only option.

But the Missouri Valley Conference team sank six free throws and a basket from that point on, and Purdue's hopes were dashed.

Bradley was the NIT champion for the fourth time in 14 tourneys, and Purdue had to settle for its second runnerup trophy since 1979.

Purdue shot .467 for the game, while Bradley was a red-hot .583. Thirdkill was an amazing 7 of 7 from the field to spice Bradley's statistics.

Hall led all players with six assists, while Scearce was the high rebounder at 11. Purdue owned the boards, 29-23.

Bradley made 10 turnovers to Purdue's 15.

Edmonson and Cross were picked on the All-NIT team, along with Scott. Oklahoma's Chuck Barnett and Georgia's Eric Marbury rounded out the team.

Bradley Coach Dick Versace (as in "face") was named the top coach in the NIT. The Braves' 1,000-plus red-clad fans won the mythical "Sixth Man Award" for their noisy enthusiasm.

All the players in the NIT received wristwatches as souvenirs.

Purdue's "Night Owl Express" landed in West Lafayette around 2:30 a.m. today and was greeted by about 100 diehard supporters standing in a drizzling rain.

Keady already is pointing to next season. His team will start its off-season weight-lifting program Monday.

"BRADLEY PLAYED BETTER," PURDUE'S KEADY SAYS

By Bob Scott

March 25, 1982 – NEW YORK – Purdue Coach Gene Keady made no excuses. His Boilermaker basketball squad had been beaten by a better team Wednesday night in the NIT title game.

Bradley's Braves won the war of wills, which Coach Dick Versace mentioned in a press conference this week.

Versace's team was able to dictate the style of play, grab a lead and hold on for a 67-58 victory.

Keady, however, wasn't about to whine to a crammed press room after the game.

"Bradley played better. Their rebounding hurt us, along with our missed free throws in the first half," said Keady. "Bradley's quickness took us out of our offense. We couldn't run our plays like we wanted."

Keady also gave credit to Bradley's defensive ace, 6-foot-7 David Thirdkill. The jumping-jack put a blanket on Purdue's Keith Edmonson and limited the Boilermaker scoring leader to only 11 points.

"Keith wasn't in the flow of things. I don't know why. I wasn't inside his head," Keady commented.

The most logical reason was Thirdkill's hyperactive defense coverage. He blocked Edmonson's first shot, and then blocked another one minute later. That seemed to make the Boilermaker hesitant to put up his shots.

Edmonson admitted Thirdkill was a superior defensive player.

"He is something else," said the Texan. "Maybe I should've faked a few times, but I've never met a guy guarding me who could outjump me.

"I must give credit to the whole Bradley defense, though. It was a team defense with a good matchup zone."

While Edmonson struggled, teammate Mike Scearce sucked it up and scored 16 points with 11 rebounds. His back muscle was in spasms and it was even-money he would not start.

"Mike makes the decision when warming up if he will play or not," said Keady. "Mike showed a lot of courage to come back with the painful back. The kids battled back all year and I'm proud of them.

Scearce matter-of-factly stated, "We all have to play with pain once in awhile. Bradley was just a little better than us. It's been fun for four years.

Russell Cross also scored 16 points, but credited Bradley's second-half defense for winning the game.

"I couldn't move. They pinned me on all sides," he said. "It was rough out there, but I thought we gave it a good shot."

Bradley's Versace was all smiles after the game. In a way, he was vindicated for not being invited to the NCAA tourney.

But he wanted to bury that issue. At least he said he did.

The controversy over the NCAA snub was over, according to Versace.

"I put it to bed a long time ago," Versace said. "You people wouldn't let it die. The NIT is a great tournament. I hope it never dies."

Versace was asked if he was going to New Orleans now for the Final Four.

"The only way I would go to New Orleans is if I was one of the four. I played in the Superdome before, but playing in this arena with the greatest basketball tradition in the world is just as exciting to me," Versace said referring to Madison Square Garden, home of the NIT.

Versace told a reporter it was time to rest. He won two airline tickets to anywhere in the world supplied to the winning coach of the tournament by a major airline.

"I'm going to go to Athens, Greece, for a week, live in a cave and send all of you a bottle of wine," he said.

The Braves' boss saw the game as two coaching styles in conflict.

"We wanted the game to be uptempo and keep Purdue off-balance. We didn't want a power game, which did happen a few times.

"We didn't want Purdue to have an easy time looking for the open man in a 5-on-5 game.

"The key of the game was our ability to come up with the big basket. Cross' fourth foul was another key when (Mitch) Anderson made a three-point play. Our subs also didn't let Purdue take control," he said.

BOILERMAKER SCRUB PATROL SHINES IN WIN

By Tom Kubat

February 24, 1983 – CHAMPAIGN, ILL. – Call 'em the Comeback Kids, the Cardiac Kids or what have you – the Purdue Boilermakers outdid themselves Wednesday night.

Reserve Jim Rowinski banked in an 18-foot jumper from the top of the key as time ran out to cap one of the most incredible and unusual comebacks in Purdue basketball history as the Boilermakers edged Illinois, 56-54.

Rowinski got his chance to be the hero when Purdue Coach Gene Keady benched his starters, except for center Russell Cross, with 12:41 to go in the game and the Boilermakers apparently out of it at 47-29.

Rowinski, a 6-8 junior forward-center, came in along with Ted Benson, Herb Robinson and Mack Gadis as Dan Palombizio, Greg Eifert, Steve Reid and Curt Clawson sat down.

An Illinois basket stretched the lead to 20 at 49-29 before the Scrub Patrol began to stem the tide.

After the Boilermakers cut the lead to 53-38, Bruce Douglas hit a free throw for Illinois with 9:38 remaining, and that was it for the Illini.

Purdue outscored them 18-0 the rest of the way, with Rowinski taking an inbounds pass at midcourt with 3 seconds to play and, wide open, dribbling into the top of the key area and banking it home.

"It was a play we had set up," Keady said, with tongue probably at least partly in cheek. "We don't care who shoots it, as long as it goes in the hole.

"I emptied the bench because those guys have been playing better in practice and, at that point, I figured what do we have to lose. And, I'll be darn if we don't have one of those unbelievable finishes that just might have gotten us into the NCAA tournament."

The victory boosted Purdue's season record to 18-6 and enabled the Boilermakers to break out of a third-place tie in the Big Ten with the Illini. Purdue is now 9-5 in league play, behind 10-3 Indiana and 9-4 Ohio State. Illinois fell to 18-9 overall and to 8-6 in the conference.

"It wasn't designed to go to me," said a smiling Rowinski of the final play. "I don't think they thought I would shoot it. I wanted the ball because I knew I was wide open. I yelled at Herb to throw it to me."

It was starting guard Ricky Hall, the substitute for Benson with 8:07 to go, who made the play that enabled Rowinski to hit the winning shot.

After freshman forward Robinson had tied the score at 54-all with a three-point basket at the 4:53 mark, the Illini took the air out of the ball and ran the clock down until Rowinski ended up with a deflected pass and the Boilermakers called timeout with 2:35 to go.

Hall tried to drive along the right baseline for a layup but had the ball taken away in mid-air and the Illini had the ball back with two minutes left. This time Illinois ran the clock down to 14 seconds before calling a time out.

Illinois Coach Lou Henson sent four players underneath and had guard Derek Harper going one-on-one against Hall. But as Harper started to go up for a shot at the top of the key, Hall flicked the ball away, caught it and called timeout, with three seconds left.

"It's not many times you can have a 20-point lead with nine minutes to go and lose it," said Henson. "I think our inexperience showed. We just didn't play like a veteran team, like you have to, down the stretch. We didn't play with poise."

Until the Boilermaker Scrub Patrol took over, the game belonged to the Illini. Illinois spurted to a 12-4 lead and upped that to 18-8 as the Boilermakers managed just seven points in the opening 10 minutes of the game.

Purdue fought back to within two, 24-22, but the Illini scored eight straight points to regain control before the half. The Boilers got the last basket before intermission, but Illinois still had an eight-point lead, 32-24, at halftime.

The Boilers also got the first basket of the second half, but a little later the Illini ran off 13 straight points for their 20-point lead.

Then the Scrub Patrol went to work, outscoring Illinois 27-5 down the stretch, with Rowinski's final basket giving Purdue its only lead of the game.

The only one that mattered.

PURDUE SAVED BY UNLIKELY HEROES

By Tom Kubat

February 24, 1983 – CHAMPAIGN, ILL. – Just when you think you've seen everything in sports, along comes a game like Wednesday night's 56-54 Purdue victory at Illinois.

The Boilermakers' comeback, from 20 points down with less than 10 minutes remaining, was one of those things that you still can't quite believe even after you've seen it.

Especially since Purdue Coach Gene Keady had all but thrown in the towel, going to his bench in a desperation move.

The starters ended up scoring just 26 points, less than half of Purdue's 56 total.

Center Russell Cross, coming off games of 31 and 27 points, picked up two quick fouls and had three by halftime, and scored just 13 points, five below his average.

For the other starters it was Dan Palombizio with 8, Jim Bullock with 3, Steve Reid with 2 and Ricky Hall was shut out.

But the guys off the bench chipped in with 30 points — Mack Gadis had 8, Curt Clawson 7, Jim Rowinski 6, Herb Robinson 6 and Greg Eifert 3.

UNLIKELY HERO

When Rowinski was introduced to the press after winning the game with his 18-foot bank shot, one writer joked, "Jim who?"

That's a question most Big Ten fans will probably be asking when they read accounts of the game in their newspapers today.

Before Illinois, the muscular Rowinski had appeared in only 10 of Purdue's 13 league games for a total of just 74 minutes of playing time – less than two full games.

The junior from New York had scored just four points in Big Ten play for an 0.4 average on 2-for-9 shooting from the field and 0-for-7 shooting from the free-throw line.

But Rowinski, who was 6-foot-3, 185 pounds when he came to Purdue as a walk-on and is now 6-8 and 235, still wanted the ball at the end.

"I'm not a bad shooter from outside, in my opinion," he said.

Rowinski said he thought he was fouled during his winning shot. But no matter.

"If I hadn't been fouled, I would've probably swished it," he said.

GUILTY PARTY?

Illinois Coach Lou Henson wouldn't say who was supposed to pick up Rowinski.

"Oh, I don't want to get into that," he said. "Why embarrass the kid?

"Let's just say that we didn't do it the way we wanted to. However, their better shooter wasn't shooting the ball."

HOT SHOTS COOLED OFF

Cross and Illinois guard Derek Harper both came into the game off of two big games last week, but both had off nights.

Cross scored 58 points in victories over Michigan and Michigan State, while Harper had 52 points in wins over the same two teams.

Cross and Harper shared the Big Ten Player of the Week honor and Harper was also named the College Basketball Player of the Week by *Sports Illustrated*.

The officials helped hold Cross in check but Ricky Hall's defense did the job on Harper.

Cross had two fouls before the game was barely three minutes old, sat down for over five minutes, and then picked up his third personal with still almost seven minutes to play in the first half.

Although Cross wasn't whistled for any more fouls, he managed to score just 13 points, and Keady said it was a factor in his team's play.

"On behalf of the players who started, I think the two quick fouls on Russell made them play tentative," Keady said.

The only substitution Keady made down the stretch was to insert Hall for Ted Benson. The move paid off since Hall stole the ball from Harper to set up Rowinski's winning shot.

Harper came into the game with a streak of 18 straight field goals and had it snapped after he hit his first shot of the game. Harper hit his last seven shots last Thursday against Michigan and then went 11 for 11 Saturday against Michigan State.

The collegiate record is held by Ray Voelkel of American University who hit 25 field goals in a row over nine games in 1978.

With Hall guarding him most of the time Harper finished 4 for 12 from the field against the Boilermakers.

Russell Cross slam dunks against Illinois as Jim Rowinski (#41) watches.

ROWINSKI HAD NOTHING TO LOSE ON FINAL SHOT

By Bob Scott

February 24, 1983 – CHAMPAIGN, ILL. – Jim Rowinski wanted the basketball. Too bad for Illinois.

The muscular 6-foot-8 Purdue junior beat host Illinois Wednesday night at the buzzer, 56-54, with an 18-foot bank shot off the backboard's "window."

"Russell (Cross) was buried underneath and I wanted the ball," he said in the Boilermakers' jubilant locker room.

"I wanted the ball. I was wide open and figured there was nothing to lose. If I miss we have an overtime anyway. We played like that when we got way behind."

Purdue rallied from a 20-point deficit (49-29) early in the second half and outscored the Illini 27-5 in the final 12:27. Illinois was scoreless over the last 9:38.

Rowinski isn't renowned for his velvet shooting touch. "But, I always beat these guys in 'Horse,'" he said of his teammates. "I grew up playing guard or small forward. Therefore, I learned how to play facing the basket. I never played as a true center with guys on my hip."

Rowinski, who totaled 6 points, said he "didn't know we were down 20 points. But I remember looking up and we were only down 3 points (54-51)."

Freshman Herb Robinson then calmly sank a 3-point basket at 4:53 to tie the game at 54-54. Robinson, who scored a season-high 6 points in 14 minutes of action, was averaging only 4.3 minutes of playing time.

"This win is my biggest thrill ever in basketball," he said. "I make a lot of long shots during practice as a member of the 'gold squad' because I always play the role of a shooting forward.

"I really didn't know what the score was when I made the 3-pointer. The shot seemed to give us more incentive to go on.

"Coach Keady knew we (reserves) would play hard when we went in. Give credit to our teammates for always cheering us from the bench."

Robinson and fellow freshman Mack Gadis scored 14 of Purdue's 32 second-half points. Gadis also is on the "gold squad."

"A win like this can do nothing but help the younger players' confidence," Gadis said. "Our team plays hard against each other in practice, so we are always ready.

"When Coach Keady started substituting, we were so far behind, we played for pride. We wanted to keep the score respectable."

Center Cross, who led Purdue with 13 points, was jubilant in the Boilers' chaotic locker room. "Unbelievable. What a game! What a game!" the 6-10 junior shouted.

"I looked at the clock and we're down 49-29," Cross recalled. "I have 3 fouls and I think, 'We got to come out and play some basketball.'

"I'm proud of those guys coming off the bench. My role was to go and get them going, but they got me going, instead."

And junior guard Ricky Hall, who led all Boilers with 28 minutes, battled Illini guard Derek Harper and won, despite going scoreless himself.

Harper, *Sports Illustrated*'s "Player of the Week," had 18 straight baskets entering the game. Hall stopped the streak at 19.

Harper had 10 points, but no assists.

PURDUE—ILLINOIS BOX SCORE

Purdue 56—Illinois 54

Purdue	FG	FT	R	F	P
Palombizio	3-9	2-2	4	2	8
Bullock	1-3	1-2	2	4	3
Cross	5-7	3-5	6	3	13
Hall	0-2	0-0	4	3	0
Reid	1-5	0-0	0	1	2
Gampfer	0-0	0-0	1	1	0
Rowinski	3-4	0-2	3	2	6
Clawson	2-4	2-2	3	1	7
Eifert	1-3	1-2	3	0	3
Robinson	2-4	1-2	2	2	6
Gadis	3-6	1-1	2	0	8
Benson	0-1	0-0	1	0	0
Team			1		
Totals	21-48	11-18	32	19	56

Illinois	FG	FT	R	F	P
Welch	4-8	2-4	5	2	10
Winters	2-5	3-4	3	4	7
Leonard	3-4	2-2	4	5	8
Douglas	5-9	3-4	4	2	13
Harper	4-12	2-5	4	3	10
Montgomery	3-7	0-0	4	4	6
Meents	0-4	0-0	2	3	0
Bontemps	0-0	0-0	0	0	0
Team			2		
Totals	21-49	12-19	28	23	54

Halftime Score: Illinois 32, Purdue 24
FG Percentage: Purdue .438, Illinois .429
FT Percentage: Purdue .611, Illinois .632
Three-Point Shots: Purdue 3-7 (Clawson 1-2, Robinson 1-2, Gadis 1-2, Reid 0-1), Illinois 0-0
Assists: Purdue 15 (Ricky Hall 5), Illinois 14 (Douglas 10)
Turnovers: Purdue 14 (Ricky Hall 5), Illinois 9 (Harper 4)
Steals: Purdue 7 (Hall 3), Illinois 10 (Harper 4)
Blocked Shots: Purdue 1, Illinois 4

Brian Cardinal

Trying to steal the ball at every opportunity, regardless of the impact it has on his body, Brian Cardinal was dubbed "Citizen Pain" in a nickname contest.

Chad Austin

Chad Austin, who broke Cuonzo Martin's Purdue record for 3-point shots made, also displayed great skills around the basket, hanging in the air to free himself from would-be defenders.

Porter Roberts

Porter Roberts dribbles between a pair of Northwestern defenders en route to a third straight Big Ten championship.

Michael Robinson
Forward Michael Robinson dunks verses the Delaware Blue Hens in the 1998 NCAA Tournament.

Gene Keady
Gene Keady has a great sense of humor, especially away from the basketball court.

Gene Keady - Game Time

Carolyn Peck

In her first year as a collegiate head coach, Carolyn Peck led Purdue to the Big Ten Post-Season Tournament Championship in 1997-1998.

Stephanie White

Stephanie White's offense features an array of dazzling moves to the basket, along with a potent long-range jump shot.

Nell Fortner

Nell Fortner helped produce an unlikely Big Ten tri-championship in 1996-1997 as Purdue successfully rebuilt a team that had been decimated by player departures.

PURDUE
BOILERMAKERS

Glenn Robinson

Glenn Robinson scored 44 points against Kansas in 1994, a school record for an NCAA tournament game.

Glenn Robinson

Glenn Robinson was unstoppable with the ball in 1993-1994. He won the John Wooden Award as the top player in the nation.

Cuonzo Martin

Not all of Cuonzo Martin's field goal attempts came from long distance.

WHEW! ANOTHER BOILER MIRACLE

By Tom Kubat

March 18, 1983 – TAMPA, FLA. – Purdue "super sub" Steve Reid became a "super starter" Thursday night to lead the Boilermakers past little Robert Morris College in a first-round game of the Mideast Regional.

Reid, an unexpected starter when Ricky Hall was sidelined with a sore throat and headaches, canned a 23-footer from the top of the key with five seconds left to give Purdue a 55-53 victory in its opening NCAA Tournament game.

The win sends the Boilermakers into second-round action Saturday at the University of South Florida's Sun Dome against 25-3 Arkansas, which drew a first-round bye.

Reid, who sputtered during four starts near the end of the regular season, was in high gear this time. The 5-10 sophomore hit 9 of 11 long-range bombs and finished with a game-high 20 points and 7 assists while playing all but the last minute of the first half.

"I kind of prepared myself that I might be a starter," said Reid. "I knew that Ricky had been sick since getting up this morning."

The Boilermakers needed Reid's sniping to run their record to 21-8 and to stay alive in the tourney as Robert Morris used a full-court press to come back from a 13-point deficit and tie the score at 53-all on a basket by Tom Parks with 3:28 remaining in the game.

But Purdue then took the air out of the ball, working the clock down to 22 seconds before calling a timeout.

"Our last play was set up for Reid to penetrate, and then shoot or pass off if they picked him up," said Coach Gene Keady. "Actually, he shot it a little quickly."

Reid said he didn't penetrate because he was afraid of getting the shot blocked "and when I saw the time down to single digits I didn't panic but I just wanted to get a good shot off."

A good one it was, and Reid said he thought he had it all the way. "Yea, it looked pretty good," he smiled.

After Reid's go-ahead basket, Robert Morris didn't get a timeout called until just 2 seconds showed. A desperation half-court shot missed.

For most of the game, it didn't look like the Boilermakers would need any last-second heroics as they used Reid's 6-for-6 shooting to take a 33-24 halftime lead.

Purdue hit 15 of 21 field goals in the first 20 minutes for 71.4 percent, and had its biggest lead of the game at 33-20 with 1:13 left in the first half.

The Boilermakers still had a 10-point (42-32) lead with 13:42 to go in the game and a 9-point (50-41) advantage with 7:18 on the clock.

But then the Robert Morris press, spearheaded by super quick guards Chipper Harris and Forest Grant, began giving Purdue fits – the Boilermakers had 20 turnovers for the night – and the Colonials began to chip away at the lead.

Until Reid finally sent the Colonials home, with only their second loss in their last 21 games, and with a 23-8 season record.

"It's hard to find the right words right now," said Robert Morris Coach Matt Furjanic, whose team was routed last year 94-62 by Indiana in its first NCAA tourney appearance and had to beat Georgia Southern (64-54) in a preliminary round game Tuesday night to get into this year's 48-team field.

"It's sure tough as hell speaking right now," said Furjanic. "But I'm very proud of my players. A lot of people thought we'd get blown out tonight, but we fooled a lot of people."

But not Keady.

"I told our kids to expect the same kind of game like we had against Rollins and Stetson in the Tangerine Bowl tournament," he said. "We felt like they would give us exactly this type of game.

"I felt like the fact that Ricky Hall didn't play hurt our ability to bring the ball up the floor. We played tentative. And then Russell Cross hurt his back right before the half. The back spasms that have bothered him all year acted up again."

Cross had 9 points in the first half and finished with 14 as the only other Boiler in double figures. Harris paced Robert Morris with 17.

Purdue outrebounded the smaller Colonials, 28-20, getting good balance from its front line, with Jim Rowinski pulling down 8 rebounds, Cross 7 and Jim Bullock 6.

The Boilermakers didn't shoot well from the free throw line, but they needed every one they made since Robert Morris outscored them from the field, 24 field goals to 22. Purdue was 11 for 20 from the line, while the Colonials were 5 for 6.

"Our kids are gutty," said Furjanic. "What we lack in size they make up in heart.

Reid agreed saying. "They're a good team, they refuse to quit. They're a lot like us."

Head Coach Gene Keady and his Boilermaker players know how to celebrate a victory.

REID: LITTLE TOO CAUTIOUS BUT CLOSE GAMES HELPED

By Tom Kubat

March 18, 1983 – TAMPA, FLA. – David almost felled Goliath, but in the end it was Purdue's own version of David – little Steve Reid – who had the final say.

Robert Morris College, "fondly" known as Bobby Morris, tried to pull an upset in first-round NCAA tournament play Thursday night, but for the seventh time this season, Purdue avoided disaster with a last-second winning shot.

Reid, who beat Iowa 60-57 with a three-point field goal at the buzzer back on Feb. 5, kept the Boilermakers alive Thursday night in Mideast Regional play with a 23-footer, with five seconds on the clock, for a 55-53 win over "Mr. Morris."

"We have 14 guys who want the ball for the last shot," said Purdue Coach Gene Keady. "They're not afraid to fail, and I like that. They're a unique bunch of guys."

There's no 3-point shot in NCAA tourney play, but Reid was bombing away from long range all night, hitting 9 of 11 shots.

"I didn't even think about the 3-point line," he said, but the official play-by-play sheet listed Reid's baskets from 21, 22, 20, 21, 25, 22, 15, 21 and 25 feet away.

"The way they had their zone packed in the middle, they were all but saying they were not going to give us anything inside," said Reid.

Because of that tight zone, Purdue worked over three minutes off the clock after Robert Morris tied it at 53. The Boilermakers called a timeout

with 22 seconds to go to set up Reid's winner.

"I think we probably tried to protect our lead a little too much," said Reid, "but I think the fact that we have been in so many close games probably helped us out.

"It really wasn't planned to run so much time off the clock, but we couldn't get the ball inside so I think we all just figured we'd work the ball around. But no one really said to go for just one shot or anything like that."

Robert Morris Coach Matt Furjanic said he thought about pulling his team out of its zone near the end. "But when we played man earlier they were able to get the ball inside rather easily.

"But after we went to a zone, they had to beat us with 20- and 25-footers the rest of the night."

Keady wasn't surprised the Colonials didn't come out of their zone to contest the ball more.

"They couldn't cover us man to man," he said. "They didn't have a choice."

SMALL GUYS TOUGH

Purdue center Russell Cross said he wasn't frustrated by not being able to get the ball inside as much as he was just playing against Robert Morris' smaller front line.

"Those smaller players can put their butt on your knee and move you right out of there," he said.

"Yes, that's what I was saying in the locker room," said forward Jim Rowinski. "Those smaller guys can get under you and it's really hard to hold them off. And the officials tend to call the fouls on the bigger guys when they try to fight back."

Cross' back spasms, which have bothered him most of the season, acted up just before the end of the first half, but he still played the entire game.

"Rowinski passed the ball to me and I turned and I felt something, although I really didn't notice it until the next timeout," said Cross. "I don't know how long it will take to get better, but I'll be ready for Saturday. Right now it's more stiff than it hurts."

SATURDAY'S CARD

Second-round play Saturday afternoon will match 22-8 Ohio University against 21-7 Kentucky in the first game, followed by Purdue, now 21-8, and 25-3 Arkansas in the second game.

Ohio advanced by defeating Illinois State 51-49 Thursday night on a last-second shot.

There has been some confusion about Saturday's game times. First Purdue was playing in the first game, then the Boilers were in the second contest.

And CBS-TV has been promoting the starting time for the first game as 2 p.m., but tourney officials have been saying 2:30.

Word Thursday night was that it would be Ohio-Kentucky at 2:30 and Purdue-Arkansas around 4:45 p.m., with CBS televising the Boilermaker-Razorback game back to the Big Ten and Southwest Conference states.

Saturday's session is listed as a sellout in the Sun Dome, which seats just over 10,000.

But the crowd was slow in arriving Thursday night. Officials said over 8,000 tickets had been sold in advance, but at the start of the first game between Purdue and Robert Morris there were probably no more than 2,000 fans in the stands. At game's end, there were around 6,000.

TEACHER VS. PUPIL

Saturday's Purdue-Arkansas game sets up a meeting between Keady and his former boss Eddie Sutton.

It's a head-to-head confrontation Keady has said he'd rather not have, and Thursday night Sutton agreed.

"I have mixed emotions about playing Purdue," said Sutton. "But when you're going for a national championship you have to forget about that."

PURDUE MAKES IT TO THE TOP

"Keady's Kids" Beat Illinois Behind Rowinski's 24 Points

By Tom Kubat

February 26, 1984 – Unlike most past Super Bowls, the Big Ten basketball showdown Saturday in Mackey Arena lived up to its advance billing.

With a sellout crowd of 14,123 fans rockin' the place like it's seldom been rocked before, Purdue held off Illinois 59-55 to take sole possession of first place with four games remaining.

"There's no doubt about that," Purdue coach Gene Keady said when asked if it was the biggest game he's ever coached.

But at the same time he warned, "But this won't mean anything if we don't win our next four."

The victory gives the 13th ranked Boilermakers, 19-5, a 12-2 mark in conference play, while the sixth-ranked Illini, 20-4, fell into a second-place tie with Indiana at 11-3.

In the electrically-charged atmosphere it was perhaps fitting that Purdue center Jim Rowinski, still wearing a battery-powered electrical stimulator on his bad back, led the Boilermakers.

The muscular 6-foot-8, 245 pound senior scored 24 points and pulled down 13 rebounds, both game highs – with 20 points and nine rebounds coming in the second half.

"Rowinski probably played the best game of his career," Keady said, admitting that he didn't expect him to dominate the way he did. "Not that much, no. But he just took it to them."

Illinois coach Lou Henson, who said the Illini "were just decimated inside," agreed that Rowinski was the difference.

"The key in the ball game was Rowinski," Henson said. "He did a real good job and we didn't do a very good job defending him."

Rowinski has been bothered by back spasms for two weeks, but said his back seemed to loosen up in the second half.

"Offensively and defensively, put them together, and it probably was my best all-around performance," he said.

Because forwards Greg Eifert and Mark Atkinson were in foul trouble, Keady put Rowinski on Illinois forward Efrem Winters in the second half. Winters had 13 points in the first half, but got only four more against Rowinski.

With Illinois guard Bruce Douglas stealing the ball four straight times, the Illini came back from an 11-point deficit to cut it to 48-45 with 2:33 left.

It was 55-53 Purdue when Rowinski did his guard imitation and brought the ball upcourt against the Illinois press. He was fouled with 10

Ricky Hall had 5 points in the 59-55 victory over Illinois.

PURDUE—ILLINOIS BOX SCORE

Illinois	FG	FT	R	F	P
Altenberger	2-7	2-2	3	2	6
Winters	6-12	5-6	4	1	17
Montgomery	2-4	1-2	7	4	5
Douglas	4-7	3-4	4	4	11
Richardson	4-10	4-4	2	4	12
Meents	0-3	2-2	0	0	2
Wysinger	1-1	0-0	0	2	2
Team			0		
Totals	19-44	17-20	21	21	55

Purdue	FG	FT	R	F	P
Atkinson	1-1	2-3	3	4	4
Eifert	0-1	1-2	1	3	1
Rowinski	10-13	4-4	13	2	24
Hall	2-7	1-2	2	2	5
Reid	6-15	2-2	2	2	14
Bullock	4-6	0-0	3	4	8
Clawson	1-2	1-2	1	0	3
Team			2		
Totals	24-45	11-15	27	17	59

Illinois			25	30	55
Purdue			26	33	59

Assists – Purdue 12 (Reid 9), Illinois 9 (Douglas 3)
Steals – Purdue 5 (Reid 3), Illinois 9 (Douglas 8)
Turnovers – Purdue 15 (Reid 7), Illinois 11 (Montgomery 4)
Officials – Weller, Hightower, Kavulich
Attendance – 14,123 (sellout)

seconds to go and sank both ends of a one-and-one situation.

After the Illini's Quinn Richardson answered with two free throws with seven seconds left, Illinois' Tony Wysinger was called for a deadball foul on the inbounds play and Boiler guard Steve Reid, who scored 14 points and had nine assists, finally clinched it with two free throws.

Although it led 26-25 at halftime, Purdue trailed most of the first half, until Reid hit a 15-foot jumper from the foul line to put the Boilers on top 18-17 with five minutes to play.

Purdue took the lead for good at 34-33 on a Rowinski layup. The Boilermakers were leading 36-35 when Illinois went more than nine minutes without a field goal and Purdue outscored the Illini, 12-2, to lead 48-37. Rowinski, who started the run

with a three-point play, scored seven points during the spurt.

Illinois was 19-of-44 from the field for .432, while Purdue was 24-of-45 for .533. The Boilermakers also outrebounded the Big Ten's top rebounding club, 27-21 —only the fourth time all season and second time in league play that the Illini have lost the battle of the boards.

"This definitely gives Purdue the inside track," Henson said. "Indiana has an outstanding ballclub and the game here could go a long way towards deciding it. It's still up for grabs."

The Boilermakers will have to settle down in a hurry since arch-rival Indiana, the other remaining contender, visits Wednesday night for another showdown.

Purdue beat Illinois with plays like these; Steve Reid (above) battling for a loose ball, and Jim Rowinski, who had 24 points and 13 rebounds, playing strong underneath the basket.

DOUBLE FEATURE: STORYBOOK BIG TEN SEASON HAS HAPPY ENDING FOR BOILERS

By Tom Kubat

March 12, 1984 – MINNEAPOLIS – Purdue's Cinderella basketball team tried on the Big Ten's glass slipper for the last time Sunday – and it fit.

The Boilermakers held off a furious Minnesota rally to edge the Gophers 63-62 on national television to gain a share of the Big Ten championship with Illinois. Both finished 15-3 in conference play.

Afterward, Purdue received a bid to the National Collegiate Athletic Association tournament and was seeded third in the Midwest Regional at Memphis, Tenn. The 22-6 and 11th ranked Boilermakers were awarded a bye and will open NCAA play Saturday against the winner of Thursday's game between Memphis State and Oral Roberts.

"I suppose it will take a couple days for all this to sink in," Purdue coach Gene Keady said. "This has been a miracle season by a miracle bunch of guys."

The Boilermakers were tabbed as second-division finishers in most pre-season polls and, despite their surprising success, people kept waiting for them to turn into pumpkins.

Instead, they wrote one of the most unusual chapters in Big Ten history.

"The great part about it was this team played loose because we weren't supposed to win," Keady said. "This team's got talent. People misjudged it.

These kids play smart and they play hard. They're a deceptive team."

And good enough to bring home Purdue's 16th conference crown, breaking a tie with Indiana for most Big Ten titles, and only third Boilermaker championship since 1940.

But the Gophers, 15-13 and 6-12, made the Boilermakers earn it, rallying from 14 points down in the second half.

Three three-point plays – by center Jim Rowinski and forwards Mark Atkinson and Greg Eifert – in the first four minutes of the second half helped the Boilers stretch a 32-27 halftime lead to 51-37 with just over 12 minutes remaining.

But then Minnesota guard Tommy Davis, who topped all scorers with 20 points, started bringing the Gophers back with some long-range firing. Shooting from 25-30 feet out, Davis connected on 6-of-7 shots in the second half.

"Those were the longest shots I've seen made against us all year," Purdue guard Curt Clawson said.

It came down to two Clawson free throws – the first one bounced in with 12 seconds left, making the score 63-60 – before Keady and the Boilermakers could relax.

"I really wanted to shoot those free throws," Clawson said. "Two years ago when Minnesota won the Big Ten title, we had a game just like this and I missed two free throws with 10 seconds left."

This time he didn't miss, and Purdue had its first victory in Williams Arena since 1979. It was also Keady's first victory in four tries at Minnesota, the only place in the Big Ten he hadn't won.

"The second free throw had good arch and I knew it had a chance, but the first one was flat," Clawson said.

Marc Wilson followed with a jumper from the free throw line with six seconds to go, but time ran out on the Gopher upset bid.

A three-point play by Wilson with 56 seconds left pulled Minnesota to within 59-58, and for a while it looked as if that slipper might fall off.

After Ricky Hall sank two free throws and Davis bombed another one in, Steve Reid missed the front end of a one-and-one with 25 seconds left. But the 6-foot-1 Hall got the rebound for the Boilers, his second on a missed Purdue free throw in the final two minutes, to set up Clawson's clinching free throws.

Purdue led by 3-4 points most of the first half before Minnesota grabbed its first lead, 22-21, after 15 minutes. But, with the score tied at 23, Jim Bullock scored five straight points for the Boilers, on a three-point play and a fast-break layup on a pass from Reid.

Rowinski topped Purdue with 19 points and forward Mark Atkinson, playing with two badly sprained fingers from a Friday workout, had eight rebounds.

Minnesota, which made six more baskets than Purdue, shot 61 percent in the second half and .509 overall. The Boilers finished at an even .500 after hitting 56 percent in the first half.

Purdue won it at the free throw line with .826 shooting (19-of-23). The Gophers were 6-of-10 from the stripe.

"That's that," Rowinski said. "We've been in a lot of close games and we've won most of them, so I was confident we'd pull it out."

In other words, if the shoe fits, wear it.

MORE THAN 1,000 GREET TRIUMPHANT BOILERS

By Tom Kubat

March 12, 1984 – It was bitter cold outside, but Purdue's basketball team received a heartwarming welcome home Sunday night.

When their chartered airplane touched down at Purdue Airport shortly after 7 p.m., a crowd estimated at more than 1,000 fans greeted the Big Ten co-champions.

About four hours earlier, the Boilermakers had clinched a tie for first place with Illinois by winning at Minnesota, 63-62, to finish the season 22-6 and 15-3 in league play.

Purdue coach Gene Keady and the players all boarded the Boilermaker Special to say a few words.

"It was a tough victory and I just wish all you people could have been there to enjoy it like we did," Ricky Hall said.

From the roar of the crowd, it sounded like they definitely were there in spirit.

And, it was a spirited flight back from Minneapolis, with a champagne toast and Keady walking up the aisle congratulating each player.

But it was frustrating, too, since there was no way of knowing how the NCAA draw had come out, since the pairings were being announced while the Boilermakers were in flight.

Keady repeatedly said, in the post-game press conference and on the plane, "I don't care who we play or where we go, I'm just happy we're in. I just want to play."

At one point, Keady went into the cockpit, where the pilot was trying to obtain information from the control tower about the draw.

After a few minutes, he came out, went to the back of the plane and took the stewardesses' microphone to announce that Purdue received a bye, was in the Midwest Regional and would play the winner of the Memphis State-Oral Roberts game, probably in Memphis.

Shortly thereafter, word came that Purdue was the No. 3 seed, with DePaul No. 1, Houston No. 2 and Wake Forest No. 4.

"It could have been worse," Keady said. "Playing Memphis State at Memphis will be tough, but what can you do? You just gotta play. We didn't get too bad a draw."

But then word came that Illinois, the other Big Ten co-champ that figured to stay close to home in the Mideast Regional, also had been shipped to the Midwest.

That seemed unlikely, and cast a cloud of doubt over all of the previous information.

"I'm not going to worry about it," Keady said. "We just won the Big Ten championship and I'm gonna sit back and relax."

Shortly before landing, the pilot informed everyone that "the control tower just extended its congratulations."

Finally, the triumphant Boilermakers deplaned to the roar of the crowd, which had started to gather well before the announced 6:30 arrival time. Some had left after being told the plane had been delayed and wouldn't arrive until 7:40 p.m.

Some estimates of the original crowd ran as high as 2,000, many of whom will likely be disappointed with today's announcement that there will be no public sale of the Boilermakers' small allotment of NCAA tourney tickets.

"This is really something," Curt Clawson said. "I want to publicly acknowledge coach Keady and the job he's done. CBS named him the coach of the year, but as far as the players are concerned he's the coach of the decade."

CBS-TV, which televised Sunday's game live, announced Saturday it had picked Keady national coach of the year by a vote of the network's basketball announcers, producers and directors.

After confirming the information about the draw that he had received on the plane, Keady repeated, "We just want to play. I know Memphis State has a great player in Keith Lee and Oral Roberts is a good team. Everyone's good at this stage, so it doesn't make much difference."

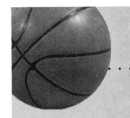

TIGER DEFENSE, POOR SHOOTING BURN BOILERS

By Tom Kubat

March 18, 1984 – MEMPHIS, TENN. – Which came first, the chicken or the egg? That's what Purdue players were trying to figure out after Memphis State waltzed past the Boilermakers, 66-48, Saturday night to advance in NCAA Midwest tourney play.

Was it poor shooting or a tough Memphis State zone defense that caused the Boilers to shoot a dismal 28 percent?

"We made their zone effective," Purdue guard Steve Reid said. "I can remember me, or Ricky (Hall), or one of the guys having a bad shooting night, but never all of us at once.

"We've never collectively shot this bad."

Reid was 2-for-8 in the first half and finished with 12 points, hitting only 4-of-14 shots.

"This is the first time I can remember a team putting three and four players in the lane and daring us to shoot from outside," said Curt Clawson, who went 3-for-13.

"Their zone took 'Row' (Purdue center Jim Rowinski) out of the game. We couldn't pull them out."

Because of their poor outside shooting, guard Ricky Hall said it was next to impossible to get the ball inside to Rowinski.

"We changed offenses several times to try to get Rowinski open, but nothing worked," he said. "It was like they had five guys on him."

"They collapsed on me and did a great job," Rowinski said. "They have a lot of tall people in

there. If we could have hit some outside shots, we might have been able to bring them out a little."

One of MSU's "tall people" was 6-10 forward Keith Lee, who finished with 29 points and 16 rebounds.

Rowinski spent most of the second half guarding him, after Greg Eifert and Jim Bullock tried in the first half.

"He has such long arms he just holds the ball above you and takes that little turnaround jumper," Rowinski said. "That's his main shot and he hit it well tonight."

Eifert, who has taken on the opposition's best forward all season, started out on Lee, but two fouls in the opening three minutes put him on the bench quick.

He played only nine minutes, but he saw enough.

"I tried to force him outside the lane and I could do that pretty easy," he said. "But even from outside, he was still effective.

"We put Rowinski on him later figuring that he could be more physical and maybe wear him down."

Before the game, the Boilers compared Memphis State to Kentucky, which beat Purdue 86-67 earlier in the season.

"Kentucky's very deep," Keady said. "Nobody has the depth Kentucky has. But Keith Lee is a great basketball player and we wish Memphis State all the best the rest of the way."

ROAD ENDS IN MEMPHIS

By Tom Kubat

March 18, 1984 – MEMPHIS, TENN. – Purdue basketball coach Gene Keady said he didn't know if it was possible to stop Memphis State's 6-foot-10 All-American forward, Keith Lee.

He found out the hard way that he was right.

Lee put on a one-man show Saturday night, scoring 29 points and grabbing 16 rebounds in leading Memphis State to a convincing 66-48 victory over Purdue in the NCAA Midwest Regional.

"I was very impressed with Memphis State," Keady said. "It was too much Keith Lee and too much Memphis State rebounding."

For the 16th-ranked Tigers, at 26-6 the winningest team in Memphis State history, it's on to St. Louis to face fifth-ranked Houston next Friday night.

For the No. 10 Boilermakers, 22-7, it was a rude ending to their Cinderella season.

Lee has been on a tear the last three games, including the Metro Conference championship game and Thursday night's first-round NCAA game.

In those victories – over Virginia Tech, Oral Roberts and Purdue – the long-armed junior has scored 90 points and pulled down 40 rebounds.

Lee, who is third on Memphis State's scoring list with 1,706 career points, also has 1,003 rebounds.

He's only the second MSU player to go over the 1,000 plateau in both categories.

"We tried everything," Keady said. "We pressed, we played zone and we collapsed, but nothing worked."

But Memphis State's collapsing 2-3 zone shut the door on Purdue.

Boilermaker center Jim Rowinski was being clawed by two and three Tigers inside, and his teammates couldn't come to his rescue by hitting over the zone.

The Boilers nearly set an NCAA tourney record for lowest shooting percentage.

Purdue was 8-of-30 from the field in the first half and 11-of-38 in the second half for a 19-of-68 total, 27.9 percent.

Memphis State, hitting from in close, was 26-of-48 from the field for 54.2 percent.

"Our poor shooting against their great defense is what beat us," Keady said.

That, and Memphis State's domination of the boards. Seven-foot center William Bedford and 6-7 forward Baskerville Holmes combined with Lee for 30 rebounds as the Tigers owned the boards, 49-32.

Bedford had eight rebounds and Holmes six.

Lee and Memphis State wasted no time. With Lee scoring their first six points, the Tigers never trailed.

Rowinski, working against a man-to-man defense early, answered Lee, scoring Purdue's first seven points.

When Steve Reid hit two free throws after Kirk was slapped with a technical with the game not even three minutes old, the Boilermakers trailed only 10-9.

But six minutes later, Memphis State was up by 10. Purdue guard Ricky Hall hit an 18-foot jumper to cut it to eight, but that was close as the Boilers came.

With Lee getting 19 points, the Tigers stretched their lead to 35-22 by the intermission.

"We got their attention early," Kirk said.

And they never let up, taking their biggest lead early in the second half at 41-22. The closest Purdue came in the second half was 11 points, 53-42 with seven minutes remaining.

"We played extremely well," Kirk said. "All in all, we played an excellent game against an excellent club.

"They were trying to deny our forwards the ball, and that opened up the middle. Instead of passing forward to center, we went guard-center, and that left Lee open one-on-one. It's hard to guard him that way."

Rowinski finished with a team-high 14 points for the Boilermakers. But Purdue's outside threats, forward Mark Atkinson and guards Reid, Hall and Curt Clawson, shot a combined 11-of-47 from the field.

"We came into a difficult situation here," Keady said. "Memphis State's fans were unbelievably hyper and I don't think anyone could have stopped Lee tonight.

"But I'm extremely proud of this team and these seniors.

"I think we have to be the top story in college basketball in the nation."

Steve Reid shows the form that made him so effective from long distance, although his touch disappeared against Michigan State.

137

ICE-COLD BOILERS OUT OF TOURNEY

March 18, 1984 – MEMPHIS, TENN. – Purdue's hopes of advancing in the National Collegiate Athletic Association Division I basketball tournament were dashed in convincing style Saturday by the Memphis State Tigers.

All American Keith Lee scored 29 points and grabbed 16 rebounds as Memphis State eliminated the cold-shooting Boilermakers, 66-48, at the Mid-South Coliseum, the Tigers' home floor.

"We worked to stop Lee, but it just didn't work," Purdue coach Gene Keady said. "He was just too big for us. I'm not sure anybody could have stopped him today."

Purdue hit only 27.9 percent from the floor, on 19-of-68 firing, including 8-of-30 (26.7 percent) in the first half. The team had hit 49.6 percent of its shots while building a 22-6 regular-season record.

In contrast, Memphis State, which takes a 26-6 record against No. 5 Houston in St. Louis Thursday, hit 26-of-48 attempts, 54.2 percent.

With Lee leading the way, Memphis State outrebounded Purdue 49-32.

For Lee, it was the third consecutive solid performance, following a pair of games in which he had totaled 63 points and grabbed 24 rebounds.

Purdue's defensive ace, Greg Eifert, shadowed Lee early, but Lee scored the Tigers' first six points and had 19 at intermission, when Memphis State took a 37-22 lead.

Purdue played even with the Tigers in the second half, but could never get closer than a 53-42 deficit with 7:02 remaining. But Keady drew a technical foul while disputing a referee's call, and Lee sank both free throws, then followed with two quick baskets to end the comeback bid.

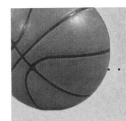

BOILERS BEAT IU AS BOBBY BOILS

By Tom Kubat

February 24, 1985 — BLOOMINGTON, IND. — Purdue's Boilermakers spent much of the time Saturday trying to dodge flying chairs and coins in Indiana's Assembly Hall, but they still managed to come away with a 72-63 Big Ten Conference basketball victory over the rival Hoosiers.

The game was only five minutes old when Indiana coach Bob Knight was ejected after throwing a chair across the playing floor and picking up three technical fouls while protesting a foul.

Later, early in the second half, Purdue guard Steve Reid was struck on the arm by a penny thrown from the stands, and Pat Keady, wife of Purdue coach Gene Keady, sitting behind the Boilermaker bench, was hit in the eye by a dime. She was treated at the first aid station and left the arena wearing an eye patch.

With the crowd yelling "Bob-BEE, Bob-BEE, Bob-BEE" as Knight walked off the floor, assistant coach Jim Crews took over.

Knight wasn't around after the game, and IU officials weren't talking either.

Ralph Floyd, Indiana's athletic director, issued a one-sentence written statement: "Dr. Ryan has requested that I prepare an immediate report to the conference commissioner, with a copy forwarded to Dr. Ryan, and there will be no further comment from Indiana University officials regarding today's incident."

Dr. John Ryan is president of IU. Ryan and Floyd both followed Knight to the locker room after the coach was ejected.

Keady's opening comments to the throng of sportswriters and broadcasters after the game was a plea of sorts.

"I think the main thing that I want to tell you is that our victory is the main headline," he said. "I hope you get my drift. My kids have done a good job, and they deserve it. I'd appreciate it, and I've been good to you guys."

Keady refused to comment on the Knight incident.

Crews praised Purdue's efforts, but sidestepped questions about Knight. He did say that Knight talked to his team at halftime, but he wouldn't reveal what was said.

Crews, a former player at IU under Knight, admitted it was a tough job filling in on such short notice. "I don't think anybody can step into that situation," he said. "He's the best coach in the country."

Steve Reid was the man at the foul line when Coach Bob Knight heaved a chair onto the court.

IT'S TIME FOR KNIGHT TO RESIGN

by Lee Creek

February 24, 1985 - It's time for Bobby Knight, the Indiana University basketball coach, to call it quits.

Knight's latest escapade included throwing a chair across the floor, getting three technical fouls, and being ejected from Saturday's Purdue-Indiana basketball game.

It was fortunate that no players were hurt when Knight threw his tantrum. But what may suffer is the image of Indiana University, one of the nation's finest.

The referees did the right thing. They sent Knight to his room, just as many parents do when their children become unruly. But Knight isn't a child, just childish. He should be treated as an adult.

Most adults who behave on the job as he did Saturday would have hell to pay with their superiors. They might even lose their jobs. It will be interesting to see if Indiana officials once again pass it off by saying that's just Bobby's way and that they don't interfere with his basketball program.

Accountability is a difficult thing to escape, and Knight has dodged the bullet all too many times. Woody Hayes ducked a few shots in his coaching career, too, but one day he took one right between the eyes. Perhaps it's Knight's turn.

There has been talk in recent years that Knight was getting tired of coaching. He's done it all, they say. He's coached champions and raised the level of basketball nationwide to its zenith.

The problem with people who have that power is that they also have the power to create an opposite reaction. For a few seconds Saturday, Knight lowered college basketball to the depths.

A few years ago Knight had a mule named Jack on his weekly television program and made some not-so-kind references to Purdue. In retrospect, it isn't all too difficult to think that the reason Jack was on the show was because he and Knight have so much in common.

To call for Knight to hang it up and not recommend a replacement doesn't seem fair, so here is one possibility: Mike Krzyzewski of Duke. Although I'd hate to see him leave my beloved Blue Devils, he is an excellent coach, recruiter and a gentleman. And, yes, for those die-hard Hoosier fans, he was Knight's assistant for a time.

At least with Krzyzewski, they could put the "cl" back in class when describing the IU coach.

Gene Keady and Bob Knight share a laugh during happier times.

PURDUE TOPS INDIANA

Keady gets 100th Boiler Win

By Tom Kubat

February 24, 1985 — BLOOMINGTON, IND. — Purdue's 72-63 victory Saturday over rival Indiana was coach Gene Keady's 100th with the Boilermakers, and it's doubtful he's ever had another under more difficult circumstances.

With an overflow Assembly Hall crowd of 17, 279 whipped to a frenzy by Indiana coach Bob Knight's sideline antics, the Boilermakers managed to fight off an IU rally and win the physical Big Ten Conference game.

With forward Mark Atkinson holding Steve Alford to eight points, and forward Todd Mitchell, a freshman starting for the first time, leading everyone with a career-high 21 points and 12 rebounds, the Boilermakers managed to steal at least some of the spotlight away from Knight.

Purdue, 18-7 and 9-6, kept alive its hopes for an NCAA tournament bid, while the loss was a serious setback to Indiana's tourney hopes. The Hoosiers fell to 14-10 and 6-8.

Purdue was leading 11-6 when Knight became enraged at a foul called on Marty Simmons with the game five minutes old. And it didn't help when Daryl Thomas was called for a foul just a second later.

After Knight threw a chair and picked up three technical fouls, which got him ejected, Purdue had a chance to add eight points to its lead on six free throws, two for each technical, and possession of the basketball.

But Steve Reid made only three free throws and the Boilermakers failed to convert. The Hoosiers, urged on by the delirious crowd, began trying to rally from a 14-6 deficit.

Purdue actually increased its lead to 22-12 before IU outscored the Boilermakers 16-4 to take its only lead, 28-26, with 5:15 left in the first half.

But Purdue had a surge of its own and led 35-32 at halftime. Another Boilermaker surge to start the second half eliminated any doubt.

The Boilermakers stretched their lead to 58-45 at 7:12, and the closest Indiana got thereafter was a 60-55 with 4:18 to play.

Purdue played a box-and-one defense, with Atkinson, who played 38 minutes, assigned to Alford.

"He scored 18 points in that first game, so I was just trying to hold him to that today," Atkinson, who at 6-feet-8 is six inches taller than Alford, said. "The only thing I did differently today was to try to block some of his shots."

Indiana's 7-2 center Uwe Blab, averaging 16 points a game, had 10 points and five rebounds.

The victory gave Purdue its first two-game sweep of IU since 1977, and the loss was the first time the Hoosiers have lost three in a row in Assembly Hall since it opened in 1972.

The Boilermakers joined Illinois as only the second Big Ten team to beat Indiana in Assembly Hall two straight years.

Keady, now 100-48 in his fifth season at Purdue, said Knight's tirade motivated the Boilermakers.

"We wanted to beat them by 30 then," he said. "Well, not by 30, but you know what I mean. It fired us up. We wanted to play hard and be aggressive.

"I'm very proud of my players. They came back after a difficult loss Thursday and won under difficult circumstances here."

ESPN will repeat the game at 10 a.m. Monday. It is the network's only showing.

Steve Reid knows how to celebrate a victory.

BOILERS FALL TO TIGERS IN TWO OVERTIMES

By Tom Kubat

March 14, 1986 — BATON ROUGE, LA — Anthony Wilson hit five free throws in the final four seconds of the second overtime Thursday night as Louisiana State defeated Purdue 94-87 in first-round play of the NCAA tournament's Southeast Regional.

Troy Lewis, who had 20 points, pulled Purdue to within 89-87 and then fouled Wilson with four seconds left.

Purdue coach Gene Keady picked up a technical on the play, his second, and Wilson, who scored a career-high 25 points, made 3 of 4 free throws for a 92-87 lead.

Wilson was fouled on the inbounds play and finished off the scoring with two more free throws.

The loss was the fourth straight first-round defeat for the Boilermakers, who finished 22-10.

Louisiana State, 23-11, which will advance to second-round play Saturday against 12th-ranked Memphis State, jumped out to an 11-point lead in the second overtime.

Purdue then outscored the Tigers 11-2 until Wilson won it at the line.

The Boilermakers sent it into overtime when Todd Mitchell, who scored a career-high 31 points, saved a missed shot by Everette Stephens and Jeff Arnold scored with 1:05 left.

Purdue then scored first in overtime, taking a 71-69 lead on Lewis' long jumper. Purdue got the ball back but lost possession on a shot-clock violation, and LSU tied it on Don Redden's rebound basket with about two minutes left.

Stephens had hit a long jumper with 1:40 left in overtime to give Purdue a 73-71 lead before Williams hit a short, turnaround jumper with about 1:20 left to tie it at 73 to set up the second overtime.

Purdue lost the services of freshman center Melvin McCants with 3:52 remaining in the first half when he reinjured his left ankle. Sophomore Jeff Arnold replaced him and had a career-high eight points.

Lee also had 20 points for Purdue, while Redden had 21, Derrick Taylor 20 and John Williams 16 for Louisiana State.

LOSS TO LSU WILL STAY IN BOILERMAKERS' THOUGHTS

By Tom Kubat

March 15, 1986— BATON ROUGE, LA — That knot in Purdue coach Gene Keady's stomach tightened several notches more with the Boilermakers' 94-87 double overtime loss Thursday at Louisiana State.

It marked the fourth straight year that the Boilermakers failed to get past first-round play in the NCAA basketball tournament.

The LSU defeat and last year's one-point loss to Auburn were especially hard to take.

Playing on their opponents' home court for the second time in three years also made Thursdays setback a bitter pill to swallow.

"It'll be a long summer, because Auburn left a bad taste in our mouths last year," Keady said. "It was a long summer and a long fall. We wanted to come back to the NCAA and do well.

"We felt like we paid our dues about playing on the home court at Memphis State. So why again? That's what bugged me. I didn't care about playing LSU. That's fine because they've got a great program.

"It's just something that kind of hangs in your craw. So we'll just have to come back and do it again. We've got young kids."

But Keady paid tribute to the winners.

"Let me say this, we had our chances to win it and didn't do it," he said. "That's basketball, and LSU just did a better job executing than we did. So you've got to hand it to them."

Louisiana State switched to a 2-3 zone late, and that gave Purdue fits and neutralized Todd Mitchell, who topped Purdue with a career-high 31 points.

Mitchell had only one basket in the two overtimes.

Keady said: "They have long arms, and they've got good athletes. It's hard to get the ball around them. There's not any better athletes than that in the Big Ten. They played a very active zone, did a good job, and we couldn't get the ball to Todd."

Purdue lost freshman center Melvin McCants in the first half when he reinjured his ankle, but Keady said that sophomore Jeff Arnold, who had eight points and three rebounds in 32 minutes, played well.

CHAPTER 46

LEWIS POURS IN 39 AS PURDUE ROLLS

By Michael Perry

January 6, 1987 - Purdue's Troy Lewis put Michigan in a hole Monday night, scoring a career-high 39 points and leading the sixth-ranked Boilermakers to an 89-77 victory in front of a sellout crowd of 14,123 at Mackey Arena.

The Wolverines made a late charge coming back from a 21-point deficit, but the Boilermakers hit 5 of 6 free throws in the final 1:06.

Lewis was 12 of 15 from the floor, including two three-pointers, and 13 of 15 from the foul line to score more points than any Boilermaker in one game since Joe Barry Carroll scored 41 in 1979.

"It was definitely a team effort even though I got 39," said Lewis, who had been in an early-season slump. "I give credit to my teammates. I also give credit to my brother Kendrick because he stayed with me last weekend and psyched me up."

Purdue, 10-1, 2-0 in the Big Ten Conference, used a 17-4 run midway through the second half to pull away from an eight-point lead.

The Boilermakers were ahead 61-53 when Melvin McCants got a layup, Everette Stephens took an alley-oop pass from Lewis for another layup, and McCants and Tony Jones followed with two more layups.

Michigan scored twice before Purdue ran off nine more points in a row — five by Todd Mitchell.

The Boilermakers played more than 13 minutes of the second half without Doug Lee, who picked up his fourth foul 16 seconds after halftime.

"It was about like we expected," Purdue coach Gene Keady said. "We battled hard. It seemed like we went in valleys and peaks a lot. We didn't play as smart in the late going as I wanted."

From the 16:24 mark of the second half to the 12:37 mark, Lewis scored all 10 of the Boilermakers' points.

"I'm never going to mess with the guy's shot too much," Keady said. "With Troy, you have to keep encouraging him because he's not going to force his shots."

Purdue led 45-35 at halftime after Lewis rebounded a missed long-range jumper by Stephens and hit a jump shot in the lane with two seconds left.

Lewis scored 22 points in the first half, hitting 7 of 9 field goals and 7 of 8 free throws.

Michigan, 8-5, 0-2, trailed early by seven points but came back to tie it 27-27 on a layup by Mike Griffin with 6:53 remaining before intermission. The Boilermakers came right back with jump shots by Lewis and Mitchell, and two free throws by Lewis during an 8-1 run.

CHAPTER 47

BOILERS WIN IN A NAILBITER

by Michael Perry

January 23, 1987 — Have you got an hour or two or three to recap fifth-ranked Purdue's 87-86 overtime victory Thursday night against No. 9. Illinois?

It's needed.

Kip Jones sank the second of two free throws with no time remaining, apparently giving the No. 5 Boilermakers a crucial Big Ten Conference victory.

This game not only wasn't over until it was over. It wasn't even over despite the zeros on the scoreboard.

The referees called a technical foul on Purdue when all of its players rushed on to the floor, thinking they had won.

Not so, said the refs, who sent Illinois' Doug Altenberger to the foul line for one shot. Altenberger, a fifth-year senior and 78 percent free throw shooter, missed. But the Illini had one last shot, a 30- to 40-footer by freshman Steve Bardo, that fell way short at the buzzer.

"It was just one of those games that you have about once every five years," Purdue coach Gene Keady said. "People, if they want their money back on this one, they're sick.

"I'm kind of speechless. We were out of the game, and we came back. We got a lot of people in foul trouble, and we played our hearts out."

The Boilermakers tied it at 86 with 54 sec-

onds left in the extra period when Illinois' Phil Kunz was called for goaltending on a shot by Doug Lee. Lee was fouled but missed the free throw, and Illinois called a timeout.

Then, with 20 seconds remaining, a pass from Bardo went through the hands of Glynn Blackwell and out of bounds.

Gene Keady hollers out instructions during the win over Illinois.

Boilermakers' ball.

Purdue's Jeff Arnold missed a short jumper, and the rebound came out past the three-point arc, to Boilermaker freshman Tony Jones, whose shot was blocked by Ken Norman.

Altenberger got the ball, but he was called for traveling in the far right corner by the Purdue basket with three seconds left. Tony Jones inbounded to Arnold at the foul line, who passed to Kip Jones driving to the basket.

Norman fouled Jones, whose first foul shot hung on the rim before falling out. The second shot gave Purdue the winning point.

"I relaxed a lot more on the second one," said Jones, a 48 percent free throw shooter.

"They all kept telling me to relax. They know I'm a pretty hyper and nervous person. It was the weirdest thing. I wanted to win so bad; the nervousness just went away.

"There's nothing better than winning it at the very end. There can't be."

Purdue sent it into overtime when Lee hit a three-point shot from the left of the arc as time expired. It was the Boilermakers' only field goal in the final 5:47.

Illinois had gone ahead 80-77 when Bardo hit two free throws with six seconds left.

"I think the shot that Doug hit was unbelievable," Keady said.

The Boilermakers, 15-2, improve to 6-1 in the conference, while Illinois drops to 13-4, 5-2.

Purdue staked the Illini to a 10-0 lead after turning the ball over on its first five possessions. Illinois shot 73 percent in the first half and had the Boilermakers playing catchup until they took their first lead at 70-69 with 5:07 left in regulation.

Troy Lewis scored 22 of his game-high 31 points in the first half and played the second half with a badly bruised thigh.

Illinois played the final 9:57 without starting guard Tony Wysinger, who dislocated his shoulder.

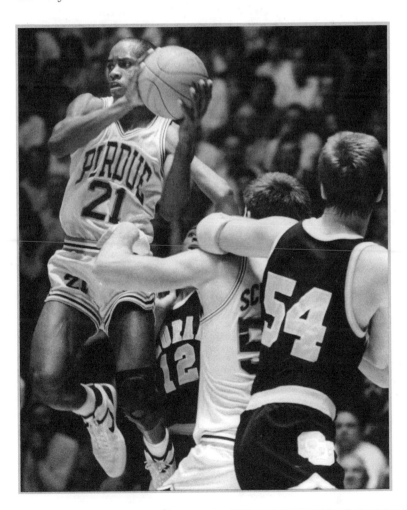

Everette Stephens averaged 12 points a game his junior year, when Purdue nipped Illinois twice in overtime.

CHAPTER 48

PURDUE DEFEATS ILLINOIS IN OT

By Michael Perry

February 24, 1987 — CHAMPAIGN, ILL. — Sixth-ranked Purdue ended three years of frustration at Illinois' Assembly Hall by beating the No. 14 Illini 76-75 in overtime Monday night.

The Boilermakers, 21-3, pulled within 1 1/2 games of a first-place Indiana in the Big Ten Conference at 12-2. The Hoosiers visit Mackey Arena on Thursday night.

Purdue broke a 67-67 tie in overtime on a Troy Lewis jumper with 1:53 left and a 3-pointer by Everette Stephens with 55 seconds remaining.

A 3-pointer by Tony Wysinger with 15 seconds left pulled Illinois within 74-72, but Todd Mitchell hit two free throws.

Doug Altenberger's sixth 3-pointer at the buzzer cut the final margin to one point.

"I'm grateful to my kids for the courage they showed," Purdue coach Gene Keady said. "A lot of people on our team had a lot to do with who won the game.

"It was a great win for us, and thank goodness we're going home."

Mitchell, who scored 15 of his team-high 19 in the final 25 minutes, said: "Championship teams want to win, and I think that's what this team wants to do.

"I think we were hungry after being off nine days. We just really wanted to come out and play hard."

Everette Stephens hit a key three-pointer in overtime to help Purdue win in Champaign.

Fourth-place Illinois, 19-7, 9-5, had won the past three meetings with Purdue in Assembly Hall by an average of 26.3 points.

Illinois led 46-30 with 11:57 left in regulation, but Purdue scored 11 straight during a 23-6 run.

The Boilermakers went ahead with 3:28 left when Mitchell blocked a Lowell Hamilton shot, and Stephens took the rebound all the way for a layup.

Purdue had built a 61-55 lead with 1:05 left, but Illinois came back.

Glynn Blackwell grabbed a loose ball near the Illini basket and hit a jumper, and Altenberger hit a 3-pointer with 26 seconds left to trail 61-60.

Lewis hit two free throws, but Altenberger hit another 3-pointer with eight seconds remaining to send it into overtime.

Lewis missed a 3-point attempt at the buzzer of regulation.

"If anybody had told me we'd win all three road games, you'd have made a lot of money off me," Keady said, referring to his team's recent victories at Iowa and Minnesota.

"The 3-point play kept them in the game. It doesn't help us as coaches; it just makes our job harder. It is fun for everybody sitting around and watching, but it's ridiculous."

Illinois was 0 of 6 from 3-point range in the first half but finished 7 of 18.

Altenberger, who was 6 of 13 on 3-pointers, led the Illini with 23 points. Ken Norman, who averages 20.6 points, was held to 10.

Lewis scored 18 for Purdue, while Doug Lee added 14, nine rebounds and seven assists. Melvin McCants had 12 points and Stephens 11.

Illini coach Lou Henson said: "I'm kind of getting used to playing top teams and losing. I think the players are getting used to it, too.

"I thought we put great effort into the game with the exception of those two or three minutes. We had all kinds of opportunities to win it, but what else is new? This ballclub - we don't play with confidence down the stretch."

Garrett Confident IU will win title

by Michael Perry

February 24, 1987 - After Indiana's victory Saturday against Iowa, Hoosier center Dean Garrett expressed his confidence in his team's chances to win the Big Ten Conference title.

"We want this Big Ten championship," Garrett said in a *Chicago Sun-Times* story Monday. "We've come a long way to get where we are, and nothing is going to stop us — not Purdue, not anyone.

"I don't think Purdue wants this as much as we do. No one wants this as much as we do."

GATORS CHEW BOILERS DEFENSE

by Michael Perry

March 16, 1987 — SYRACUSE, NY — Seven months ago, the Purdue basketball coaches were worried about their team's defense.

And their concerns became a reality as the season closed.

Florida pounded the seventh-ranked Boilermakers 85-66 Sunday at the Carrier Dome, eliminating them from the NCAA Tournament's East Regional.

In its final three games, Purdue's defense — which was ranked No. 2 in the Big Ten Conference — gave up an average of 94.7 points a game. Its opponents scored an average of 69.2 during the regular season.

"Our biggest fear last August was, 'Yeah, we've got some pretty good offensive players, but can we stop anybody?'" Purdue coach Gene Keady said.

"Our biggest fears came to be realistic. I guess when we get against great talent, we can't stop them."

Instead, the Gators, 23-10, stopped Purdue by shooting 67 percent from the floor in the second half.

Florida led 54-46 with 12:48 to play and then pulled away with a 14-1 run while the Boilermakers went 6 1/2 minutes without a field goal.

Purdue was just 16 of 35 from the floor in the second half and finished 5 of 21 from 3-point range.

Doug Lee, who scored a career-high 29 points Friday against Northeastern, was 2 of 9 from the field for four points.

The Gators outrebounded Purdue 37-31, and 7-foot-2 freshman Dwayne Schintzius scored 15 of his 21 points after intermission.

"We just didn't do the job on the defensive end," said Troy Lewis, who scored 15 points for Purdue. "We were too casual. We let things happen instead of making things happen.

"We dug ourselves in a hole we really couldn't get out of."

The Boilermakers were sluggish from the start, falling behind 13-6 after turning the ball over seven times in the first six minutes.

Purdue used a 10-0 run to take its biggest lead at 18-13, but Florida came back and went ahead 31-29 at the half.

"I thought we were ready," Keady said.

Everette Stephens, who had 15 points and 10 assists, said: "These guys came out here, and they were just totally hot. They just hit all their shots, and it killed us.

"I thought our defense was going to be the key to the game, but we didn't shut them down. We weren't playing aggressive at all. They were getting all the loose balls."

SEVEN-FOOTER TOOK SPOTLIGHT FROM GUARDS

by Michael Perry

March 16, 1987 — SYRACUSE, NY — Watch out for the M 'n' M combination, everyone said. They may be the best backcourt in the country.

And the Purdue Boilermakers were watching Florida's Vernon Maxwell and Andrew Moten on Sunday.

But while they were, a 7-foot-2 freshman, whose name is harder to spell than it is to pronounce, tried to steal everyone's attention.

Dwayne Schintzius tied career highs of 21 points and six assists during the Gators' 85-66 victory against Purdue. He was 7 of 10 from the field, 7 of 8 from the foul line, and he had four rebounds and one blocked shot.

He came into the game with a 10.7 scoring average and was yanked by coach Norm Sloan in the opening minutes for reserve Kenny McClary.

"I think he just wanted to settle me down," Schintzius said of Sloan. "I was just making some mental errors.

"I just settled down, and I started to play my style of game. I got the team involved instead of trying to do it myself."

He hurt Purdue most after intermission, scoring 15 points and controlling the paint.

The Boilermakers, who got two of their first three baskets from center Melvin McCants, stopped going inside late in the game. McCants and reserve center Jeff Arnold combined for only five field goals and 14 points.

"The shots he would normally miss he was hitting because I didn't have him pushed out far enough," McCants said. "He surprised me a lot. For a freshman, he's pretty good. He's got a lot to learn, but overall he's going to be a great player."

Purdue coach Gene Keady said: "A couple coaches thought he might be our starting center in the Olympics, so he's got potential."

Todd Mitchell averaged 15.6 points a game in 1986-87, his junior year.

Maxwell also hurt Purdue, collecting 24 points, five assists and four rebounds. Moten, who has a bruised thigh and played just 24 minutes, had five points and five assists.

Florida was 18 of 27 in the second half for 67 percent and finished shooting 53 percent from the field. Purdue shot 47 percent from the floor, including 24 percent from 3-point range. In the end, Purdue seemed to be outnumbered.

The Gators' bench outscored the Boilermakers' 24-10, and some suggested Purdue was tiring late in the game.

Forward Joe Lawrence said: "I would say our bench strength has been a positive factor all year, especially today. They seemed a little tired about the 10-, 15-minute mark of the second half."

Keady said his team is the best conditioned in the Big Ten Conference, but that it would have to improve its bench play next season.

"Especially in the tournament, you've got to have depth," he said. "You can't win a national championship without depth.

"We thought they had great depth."

Tony Jones was a first-year player on the 1986-87 team that won 25 games before losing to Florida in the NCAA tournament.

PURDUE EARNS BIG ROAD VICTORY

by Michael Perry

February 8, 1988 — ANN ARBOR, MICH. — The Purdue basketball team benefited from its experience Sunday afternoon.

The No. 6 Boilermakers upended 11th-ranked Michigan 91-87 to take sole possession of first place in the Big Ten Conference.

A national television audience and a sellout crowd of 13,609 in Crisler Arena — Purdue's Temple of Doom last season — watched the Boilermakers improve to 19-2, 8-1 in the league at the halfway mark. The talent-rich Wolverines, who beat Purdue by 36 points in Crisler last year, dropped to 18-4, 7-2.

"I told Gary Bender and Dick Vitale (of ABC) that I thought this was going to be a classic," Purdue coach Gene Keady said.

"And I thought it was a very good game to watch."

Indeed it was.

But it came down to experience, and the Boilermakers outnumbered the Wolverines in seniors 3-1.

A composed Purdue team, which lost to Indiana on January 30 in the final 63 seconds, won Sunday by executing at both ends of the floor down the stretch.

After a three-point shot by Michigan's Gary Grant tied it at 82 with 3:38 left, Melvin McCants put Purdue ahead with a bank shot after an offensive rebound.

Terry Mills missed for the Wolverines, and the Boilermakers went into their control game and started running time off the clock.

With 2:15 to play and about four seconds left on the shot clock, Troy Lewis hit a right-side baseline jumper to give Purdue an 86-82 lead.

Glen Rice tipped in a Grant miss to pull Michigan within two, and Purdue again went into a delay.

With the shot clock almost expired, Everette Stephens hit a baseline jumper from the left corner with Rumeal Robinson's hand in his face to make it 88-84 with 1:05 remaining.

"Yeah, it was a tough shot," Stephens said. "I was almost out of bounds.

"I didn't think I could work the ball around before time expired. I think I can hit those shots, and you're supposed to think that way out there."

Keady said, "I stood there and said I hope it goes in."

Robinson missed a shot at the other end, and Lewis rebounded for Purdue. McCants was fouled with 41 seconds left. After Michigan's last timeout, McCants missed the front end of a one-and-one, but the rebound went out of bounds off Wolverine Mark Hughes.

Lewis inbounded to McCants, who then had the ball stolen from him by Mills. It was only Purdue's second turnover in the half.

Rice connected on a three-pointer to pull Michigan within 88-87 with 27 seconds to play.

Following a Purdue timeout, Boilermaker guard Tony Jones was fouled immediately by Mike Griffin. Jones hit his first foul shot but then missed.

The Wolverines had a chance to tie or win with a three-pointer. The ball got down low on the right side to Loy Vaught, who missed a short hook shot from the baseline.

Purdue beats Michigan in 1988 and the fans rejoice.

"We wanted Glen (Rice) or Gary (Grant), they knew that," Michigan coach Bill Frieder said. "But the ball goes in to Loy, and he's wide open. He's got to take it."

The rebound from Vaught's miss fell into a crowd, and Jones came up with it for Purdue with three seconds left.

He then hit two free throws, shooting into a background of screaming fans waving gold towels, to clinch it.

"I wasn't really thinking about the pressure," Jones said. "I didn't let the crowd bother me. I just put my head down and tried to ignore it."

Keady said: "I was really proud of our players, the way they executed down the stretch. I think the Indiana loss helped us a little because we didn't make the mental errors that we made in the Indiana game.

"We made our free throws when we needed to, and it certainly was a tremendous game for us."

Michigan started the second half 11 of 14 from the floor, and with 7:54 left Purdue went into its matchup zone defense. The Wolverines were 5 of 14 the rest of the way.

"In my mind, it's (the zone) always questionable because you're not going to block out as well as you do in a man-to-man, and that was kind of a risk," Keady said. "But we tried to make them beat us from the outside if they were going to.

"Even though they hit a couple of big ones, they still missed some big ones and we got the rebound."

Todd Mitchell led Purdue with 22 points. Lewis, held to five points by Grant last year, scored 20 and had six rebounds, six assists and two steals.

Stephens added 16 points and McCants 15 for the Boilermakers.

Grant was 13 of 21 from the field and had a game-high 32 points. Michigan also got 23 from Rice, 11 from Robinson and 10 points and 14 rebounds from Mills.

Purdue tried the whole game to keep the tempo at a slower pace.

"We were trying to shorten the game," Keady said. "If we could keep their transition baskets to a minimum, we knew we had a chance."

The Wolverines rebounded from an early 15-10 deficit and took their first lead at 20-19 on a dunk by Vaught.

While McCants scored 11 straight Purdue points, Michigan was on its way to a 39-29 lead with 4:02 left in the first half.

Its 10-point advantage came after a dunk by Rice on a long lob pass from Robinson. Then, on a fastbreak, Robinson bounced a pass backwards, between his legs, to a trailing Vaught, who slammed it in.

But Purdue went on a 10-0 run to tie it, with Mitchell scoring seven of those points.

After an exchange of free throws, Michigan took a 43-41 halftime lead on a jumper by Robinson at the buzzer.

"We were trying to get back within four points, and we felt like if we hadn't have gone up on a fake that Robinson wouldn't have scored, and it would've been even," Keady said. "So it was even more than what we expected.

"We said at halftime we had to take our turnovers down and make our free throws to win."

Purdue finished with 14 turnovers and was 20 of 29 from the foul line.

PLAYERS HAVE SOMETHING TO PROVE

by Michael Perry

February 8, 1988 — ANN ARBOR, MICH. — This was the one Big Ten court on which they had yet to win.

It was the same arena where they lost by 36 points 11 months ago.

The game was for first place in the conference — at least temporarily.

Experience

Confidence.

Poise.

"Any time you play on national TV, you don't want to get embarrassed, and you want to win," said Purdue guard Troy Lewis after the Boilermakers defeated Michigan 91-87 Sunday in Crisler Arena in a nationally televised game.

"We wanted the nation to see we can play with anybody on any floor."

Lewis, too, wanted to show something.

In last year's fiasco, he was held by Michigan's Gary Grant to five points. It was the only time in the past 55 games Lewis has not scored in double figures.

On Sunday, he finished with 20 points on 9 of 14 shooting, six rebounds, six assists and two steals.

The Boilermaker senior spent all afternoon weaving around his teammates, trying to get open.

"That's my main game," Lewis said. "I know it's hard to guard somebody who's moving constantly."

Purdue coach Gene Keady said Kip Jones and Steve Scheffler set some screens that freed Lewis.

"We didn't run that type of offense last year," Keady said. "We didn't give him much help."

Grant, who scored 32 points, won the statistical battle but lost the game.

He said he had a tough time staying with Lewis.

"I haven't been screened like that before," Grant said. "Both insides of my jaw are cut. It's just incredible how those guys were screening me. I felt really bad sometimes when I hit those screens.

"They've got big guys setting screens, and they set those screens well. It was tough for me to fight through them, and it allowed Troy to have a lot of easy shots.

"A great player like Troy doesn't need time to shoot to make them. I give him a lot of credit."

Most of the accolades, though, belonged to Lewis and his fellow seniors, Todd Mitchell and Everette Stephens.

The Boilermakers, trailing 43-41 at intermission, shot 63.3 percent from the field and had just two turnovers in the second half.

"In the first half, the last five possessions we scored, and that was a big confidence builder," said Mitchell, who scored a team-high 22 points.

"The second half we went out and really tried to get the ball inside, hopefully getting some of their people in foul trouble."

Mitchell scored the first bucket after the break when he picked off a stray Grant pass and went all the way for a dunk.

Stephens scored twice in the next three possessions on dunks after an alley-oop pass from Lewis. Those sandwiched a reverse layup off the baseline by Mitchell.

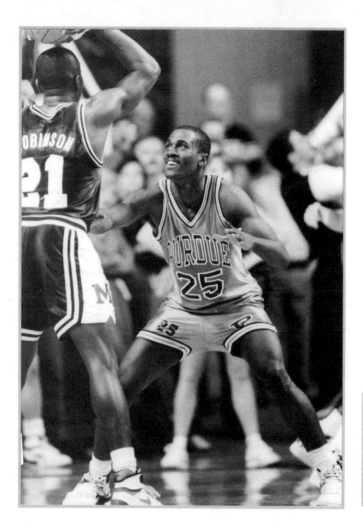

Tony Jones plays tough defense against Michigan's Rumeal Robinson. Jones made three free throws in the final 30 seconds to help clinch the victory.

"We were just going to go out and use the plays that we have all year, and we knew we'd get back in it," Mitchell said.

There were four ties and 11 lead changes after halftime. The final deadlock came at 82 after a three-pointer by Grant with 3:38 left.

The Boilermakers had gone ahead with a spinning layup in the paint by Mitchell and two free throws by Melvin McCants.

It was a McCants bank shot that gave Purdue the lead for good at 84-82, but Lewis and Stephens each hit pressure jumper shots in the final 2:15 to keep the Boilermakers in front.

Just eight days earlier, Purdue had blown a one-point lead against Indiana in the last 1:03.

"We all were a little nervous out there," Stephens said. "It went through my mind, about the Indiana game, but I've got a lot of confidence in my teammates.

"It was a new situation, so we just had to learn from our mistakes."

Lewis said the Boilermakers had great confidence in each other down the stretch, and that helps in situations like Sunday's.

"When Todd has the ball, I have the same confidence as if I had the ball," Lewis said. "Or Everette's the same way.

"And when you have that kind of confidence in each other, you tend to get each other open, and when somebody makes that basket you feel just as much joy as they do and it carries over on the defensive end because you get that high."

KANSAS STATE SHOCKS PURDUE

Boilers' Poise Missing in Action

by John Millman

March 26, 1988 — PONTIAC, MICH. — Purdue coach Gene Keady and his Boilermakers looked into a mirror Friday night.

It was the NCAA Midwest Regional semifinal game with Kansas State, a team Purdue had beaten 101-72 last December.

Such a long time ago.

That game became a turning point for the Wildcats and their coach, Lon Kruger.

Kruger, like Keady a K-State grad, rebuilt his offense after that loss to Purdue. The fast break was out. The passing game was in.

The Wildcats began mixing defenses.

The 29-point loss to Purdue became a turning point. The Wildcats finished strong. They entered Friday's game with Purdue on a 10-game winning streak.

The change of philosophy worked wonders.

"They're a lot like we are," Keady had said. "Kansas State is very mature with its four seniors and they do a great job of getting the ball to Mitch Richmond."

Purdue, with its three seniors — Troy Lewis, Todd Mitchell and Everette Stephens — also had been labeled a mature team.

So the Boilermakers, who brought a haughty 29-3 record into Friday's game with K-State, would have a battle on their hands.

But when the game started, it looked like the teacher, Purdue, would give the student, Kansas State, a lesson.

The Boilermakers jumped out to a 10-0 lead. They were ready.

But Kansas State maintained its poise and battled back.

Poise. That's the word Keady often uses to describe his players.

The Wildcats battled back with a deliberate offense and crisp passing game - Purdue's trademarks.

It was eerie.

Keady has said all year he wants his team to start out strong the first five minutes of the first and second halves.

This time, Purdue started the first half well, but it was Kansas State that opened the second half with a flurry.

Purdue prides itself on its play in the final five minutes of close games. The Boilers have a

Todd Mitchell scored 13 points in his final game at Purdue, the NCAA tournament loss to Kansas State.

tendency to win the close ones. They don't often make the little mistakes down the stretch.

Friday night, trailing by two with 19 seconds left, Stephens dribbled the ball off his knee working his way around a screen.

And Boiler guard Tony Jones couldn't find anyone open on an in-bounds pass with 44 seconds remaining and Purdue trailing 69-67.

He was forced to call Purdue's final timeout.

The poise, the mistake-free basketball which had made Purdue the favorite to win the regional, suddenly wasn't there.

Kansas State began making the key plays, the free throws down the stretch. It was eerie all right,

Kansas State ending Purdue's season with Friday night's 73-70 shocker.

That's a 32-point turnaround from December. Kansas State learned its lesson well.

"My hat's off to them," Keady said after the game.

Stephens said: "The Kansas State coaching staff did a great job improving that team. We just got beat by a better ballclub. They remind us of ourselves."

The Boilers looked into a mirror and what they saw was defeat. They were beaten at their own game.

SECOND-HALF COMEBACK LIFTS WILDCATS

by Michael Perry

March 26, 1988— PONTIAC, MICH. — The Purdue basketball team's storybook season concluded Friday night without a happy ending.

Unranked Kansas State abruptly eliminated the No. 3-ranked Boilermakers from the NCAA Tournament with a 73-70 upset victory before 31,309 fans in the Pontiac Silverdome.

The fourth-seeded Wildcats came back from a 10-point first half deficit to avenge a 101-72 loss that came three months ago in Mackey Arena.

Kansas State (25-8) set up its fourth meeting this season with unranked and sixth-seeded Kansas at 1:58 p.m. Sunday in the Midwest Regional final. The Jayhawks (24-11) defeated seventh-seeded Vanderbilt 77-64 in Friday night's other semifinal. Kansas State has won two of the previous three games.

"We couldn't execute or get the ball in the basket," said Boilermaker coach Gene Keady, who was done in by his alma mater.

"I looked in my players' eyes, and I could see they started to doubt themselves."

Purdue, which committed 10 second-half turnovers, had its chances in the final minute Friday night.

Trailing 69-64 with 1:42 to play, Everette Stephens hit a three-pointer to pull the Boilermakers within two.

Kip Jones fouled Kansas State's Charles Bledsoe with 58 seconds left, and he missed the front end of a one-and-one.

Purdue's Troy Lewis bounced a pass, intended for Todd Mitchell, off a Wildcat, and the shot clock was turned off with 44 seconds remaining.

The Boilermakers used one timeout to set up an inbounds play but had to call their final timeout when Tony Jones could not get the ball into play.

When they finally did inbound the ball, Stephens had a pass for Mitchell intercepted by Bledsoe. Mitchell fouled him immediately with 27 seconds left.

"Our bad passes hurt us," Keady said.

The Kansas State senior hit 1 of 2 foul shots for a 70-67 lead, still giving the Boilermakers a chance to tie. But Stephens lost the ball into the Purdue bench trying to set up for a three-point attempt.

Steve Henson, a sophomore guard, sank two free throws for Kansas State with 17 seconds remaining.

Stephens hit a three-point shot to make it 72-70 with eight seconds left, but the Boilermakers only could stop the clock by fouling Mitch Richmond.

The Wildcats' leading scorer, who averages 22.8 points a game, hit 1 of 2 free throws and finished with a game-high 27 points. William Scott added 17 for Kansas State.

"I don't think we beat ourselves," Mitchell said. "We got some key defensive rebounds that helped us stay in the race. We ran our offense the way we wanted to, the shots just didn't fall."

Stephens had a team-high 20 points for Purdue, which finishes 29-4 while setting a school-record for single-season victories. Lewis had 19 points, and Melvin McCants and Mitchell added 13 points apiece.

"My hat's off to Kansas State," Keady said. "Their coaching staff did a tremendous job.

"The situation was, we had a great season, but Kansas State played a better game tonight."

The Boilermakers closed the first 20 minutes with an 8-2 run, giving them a 43-34 lead at half-time.

Purdue started the game with two near-perfect minutes, hitting 4 of 4 shots and holding Kansas State to 0 of 5.

McCants hit a baseline jumper on the first possession, and Stephens followed with back-to-back three pointers. A short jumper by Mitchell made it 10-0 and forced the Wildcats to use a timeout with 2:01 gone.

"We wanted to put them away," Keady said. "We wanted to get 15 up if we could and not rush things. It just wasn't to be."

But Kansas State wasn't about to fold. There's too much pride. Too much tradition.

Richmond sandwiched a short jumper between two Scott three-pointers. At the 14:58 mark, the Wildcats were within 14-10.

They later pulled within one point twice — at 22-21 and 24-23. But the Boilermakers kept answering K-State rallies with three-pointers. Lewis and Stephens each had three in the first half.

Richmond, who had 15 first-half points, completed a three-point play to pull the Wildcats within 33-30 with 5:17 left in the half. Lewis hit two free throws, and then Kansas State's Mark Dobbins got inside for a layup.

Then Purdue dominated the final 4 1/2 minutes.

After a Wildcat turnover, Stephens hit another three-point shot to put the Boilermakers ahead 38-32. Richmond got called for a charge, and McCants came back with a turnaround jumper. Following a K-State miss, Stephens fired up an airball, but Mitchell rebounded and dunked it in for the largest lead of the half at 42-32.

Richmond hit a short jumper, and Lewis finished the first-half scoring by hitting 1 of 2 free throws.

Lewis had 12 points in the first half for Purdue. Stephens scored 11, McCants nine and Mitchell eight.

The Boilermakers were outrebounded 20-19 in the first half but committed just two turnovers. Kansas State had five first-half turnovers but only two in the last 20 minutes.

"I told my seniors (Lewis, Mitchell and Stephens) that I was very proud of them and that I hope they have great futures in whatever they do," Keady said.

Purdue's dream ends

March 26, 1988 - By now, perhaps the sting has lessened a bit, but the truth - that Purdue isn't going to win the NCAA basketball tournament - is just as bitter for Boilermaker players and fans.

Kansas State 73, Purdue 70.

It wasn't supposed to happen. The second-ranked Boilermakers were favored to win Friday night's Midwest semifinal: they'd trounced Kansas State in December, were seeded first, had impressive fan support and, most importantly, were playing well.

It certainly wasn't supposed to happen

as it did. A 10-0 lead became a 9-point deficit. There were two last-minute turnovers by sure-handed Everette Stephens — whose two three-pointers twice pulled Purdue within two points, at 69-67 and 72-70. Television cameras found his mother somewhere in the Silverdome in Pontiac, Mich. "She looks very disconsolate," CBS announcer Tommy Heinsohn said.

And while Purdue was becoming the first No. 1 seed to fall, Iowa was being trounced by Arizona. A few hours earlier, Michigan had lost to North Carolina. A bad day for the Big Ten Conference.

"My favorite to win it all is no longer Purdue," CBS analyst Billy Packer said.

PURDUE BIG 2 ATOP BIG TEN

Men Move into First After Winning 95-94 Thriller at Michigan

by Tom Perrin

March 7, 1994 — ANN ARBOR, MICH. — Glenn Robinson speaks of himself as an unselfish player, one who measures his performances by whether the Purdue basketball team wins or loses.

Sunday afternoon in Crisler Arena, Robinson took control of the situation to be certain he could give himself a positive self-evaluation.

In what will be one of the most memorable moments of a memorable season, Robinson hit a 10-footer off a spin move with 6.5 seconds left to give the ninth-ranked Boilermakers a 95-94 victory over No. 3 Michigan.

The win gave Purdue (25-4, 13-4 Big Ten) a half-game lead over the Wolverines in the conference race.

"I was taking the shot regardless. I wasn't passing. I was going to take all the blame," said Robinson, who scored 37 points. "If somebody else would have been open, I'm sorry, but I felt this is my time."

It was, and Robinson affirmed it by driving straight toward the basket and swishing the shot in the face of Michigan's Jalen Rose.

After three timeouts (Michigan called the first one and the third) and three changed plays in the Purdue huddle, Robinson caught a midcourt in-bounds pass from Cuonzo Martin inside the center circle.

He wasted no time going to work on Rose, who had done a respectable job defending him for most of the second half, but had four fouls.

"The whole time during the timeouts and all, I knew that I was going to be right there when he shot the ball," Rose said. "It was just a matter of whether I should try to slap it out of his hand on the way up. I knew he was going to get right in my face.

"If I had it to do all over again, I would have gone with my first instinct, which was to try to slap it out of his hand."

Purdue had trailed 92-84 with 2:31 left and Robinson's shot capped off an improbable comeback, but Michigan still had time to pull out a victory.

Unlike Purdue, though, Michigan wasn't able to get the ball to its best player to attempt the game winner. Dugan Fife's deep 3-pointer with two seconds left rimmed off and so did Rose's followup off the rebound.

Purdue's celebration at midcourt was reminiscent of the Wolverines' celebration at Mackey Arena earlier in the season after coming from behind to beat the Boilermakers, 63-62.

"It was a game that with a minute and a half to go, we all thought we had it won," Michigan coach Steve Fisher said. "Then when there was no time on the clock, Purdue is celebrating at midcourt. I'm sure they're saying justice prevailed, but that doesn't make it any easier."

Juwan Howard led Michigan with a career-high 27 points, and Ray Jackson also had a career high with 21. The Wolverines shot 54.4 percent from the field and Purdue shot 53.3 percent.

Purdue outrebounded Michigan, 35-30, led by Ian Stanback's season-high 10.

By winning its two remaining games this week (Penn State at home and Northwestern on the road), Michigan (20-6, 12-4) can clinch at least a share of the Big Ten championship.

Purdue can do the same with a victory over Illinois next Sunday at 12:30 p.m. in Mackey Arena.

"We feel very good about it, but the (NCAA Tournament) seed is what we're interested in more than anything else," Boilermaker coach Gene Keady said. "I've won three Big Ten titles at Purdue and ended up apologizing at the banquet because we didn't do well in the NCAA."

Even in all the postgame elation, the talk was of unfinished business. Illinois, which has beaten Purdue six consecutive times, isn't likely to be an easy opponent.

"I like to be a winner, and winning the Big Ten means you're the best and you're the champs," Robinson said. "But we don't have the Big Ten title, yet. We still have one more game and our mission is not completed."

Hot-shooting Purdue led by as many as 15 points midway through the first half before Michigan used a pair of scoring runs to get back into the game.

The Wolverines tied the score at 47 with 1:04 left, but Martin's fast-break basket with 32.8 seconds left gave the Boilermakers a 49-47 halftime lead.

"I myself, I thought we were in trouble. We've had a tendency all year long when we get those leads like that, we let them slip," Martin said. "We get lackadaisical and stop running our offense and stop doing what got us there."

Michigan began the second half with a 10-2 scoring run to lead 57-51. Robinson's first basket of the half, a 3-pointer with 13:20 left, tied the score at 61.

Robinson, who scored 22 points in the first half, didn't score again for almost eight minutes. That put the burden on Martin, who responded with 11 points during the time Robinson was struggling to get open shots against Rose.

"I didn't look at it like it was pressure on me," said Martin, who finished with 21 points. "I just played within our offense and the shots were falling."

Michigan took its biggest lead at 86-76 with 5:29 left before Herb Dove's three-point play and a 3-point shot by Robinson cut the gap to 86-82 with 4:38 left.

After Robinson made a pair of free throws with 3:50 left, Dove drew a technical foul for a retaliatory shove against Howard in front of the Purdue bench and referee Phil Bova.

The impact on the Boilermakers ended up being just one point, a made free throw by Rose to give Michigan an 89-84 lead.

Purdue got a pair of clutch 3-pointers from Matt Waddell to close within 94-90 at 1:20. Waddell finished with 15 points.

Jimmy King attempted an ill-advised 3-pointer for Michigan with 1:03 left and Purdue rebounded. With 49.2 seconds left, Robinson took King to the basket and converted on a three point play to narrow the gap to 94-93.

With 10.5 seconds left, Rose made a bad pass against double coverage at the top of the key that King lost out of bounds at midcourt.

That set the stage for Robinson's game-winner and Purdue's first lead since halftime.

"After they threw the ball away, I said I wanted the ball and I was going to make the shot," Robinson said. "That was all in my mind. All I wanted to do is get the ball."

PURDUE HAS LAST LAUGH

by Tom Perrin

March 7, 1994 — ANN ARBOR, MICH. — Contrary to popular opinion among Michigan players, Sunday's game against Purdue wasn't over when Ray Jackson hit a free throw to put the Wolverines ahead by eight points with 2:31 left.

The Boilermakers knew better.

"Jackson, when he was on the free throw line, he was smiling and giggling and talking trash with his teammates," Purdue forward Glenn Robinson said. "And Juwan (Howard) told me that we (choked) up again, I guess because we had a 15-point lead in the first half."

The fact that Purdue had prepared all week to deal with the situation it faced in the final minutes of a 95-94 comeback victory made it all the more satisfying.

"Coach has done a good job drilling on us on last-minute situations," Boilermaker guard Matt Waddell said. "It was just the exact thing you saw today, making hard cuts and getting the ball in the hands of the person we wanted, obviously Glenn."

In the final 4:38, Robinson scored 10 of his 37 points. And unlike the 82-80 loss at Indiana on Feb. 19, Robinson got his hands on the ball to attempt a game-winning shot, a 10-footer which he made.

Last week, Keady and his staff used a video presentation of the Boilermakers' closest Big Ten games to illustrate a list of do's and don'ts in the final minutes.

The No. 1 'do,' of course, is get the ball to Robinson. But there's more to it than just that. If Robinson hadn't been able to attempt the game-winner, second and third options for Cuonzo Martin and Waddell were in the plan.

"Sure, your nerves are going and you're excited. But when you practice it and practice it, it relieves a lot of anxiety," Waddell said. "We've watched a lot of film and it helped a lot."

There were three timeouts before Martin inbounded the ball to Robinson to drive for the final shot, and the play was changed each time. Not liking what he saw in the Michigan defense, Martin called the second timeout.

"They had every angle covered," Martin said.

Robinson's scoring effort after finally catching the ball made Keady seem even smarter.

"It's like the guy in the crowd said someplace this year: 'It makes it look like you can coach, Keady,'" Keady joked.

Of Purdue's final 10 shots, nine were attempted by Robinson, Martin and Waddell — the team's three designated shooters. Waddell's consecutive 3-pointers with 2:16 and 1:20 remaining brought the Boilermakers within 94-90.

While Michigan was throwing up an ill-advised 3-pointer and committing a stupid foul and a key turnover in the final minutes, Purdue was maintaining poise.

The scenario was a reversal of what happened in the Wolverines' 63-62 victory over Purdue on Feb. 1.

Both times, the team that played smarter was rewarded with a victory.

"We didn't execute in late-game situations right to the very end. When that happens, you give a crack," Michigan coach Steve Fisher said. "And when you have a great player like Glenn Robinson, what happened can happen."

ROBINSON GIVES BOILERS NO. 1 CLAIM

by Jim Lefko

March 14, 1994 - College basketball's best player just might be playing for college basketball's best team.

Glenn Robinson displayed his brilliance yet again Sunday in Purdue's Big Ten clinching 87-77 victory over Illinois, erupting for a career-high 49 points.

Then the Boilermakers grabbed a No. 1 NCAA Tournament seed, gaining the top berth in the Southeast to match the Purdue women, who also drew a 1 in the West.

What a remarkable day.

Voters in the AP poll have a chance to verify today what Big Ten fans have seen all year. Purdue is not only the outright champion of the nation's premier league, but arguably the top squad in the country.

With victories in nine of their last 10 games, including five in a row, the Boilers are the hottest team among the elite schools.

The only team ranked higher than Purdue that didn't lose over the weekend was North Carolina. The Tar Heels, though, have two more losses than the Boilers.

"I'm going to vote us No. 1," Purdue coach Gene Keady said. "It wouldn't be unjustifiable."

Robinson, who showed the type of all-around excellence against the Fighting Illini that will make him an instant NBA superstar, said he might give the nod to North Carolina, since it won the ACC

tournament title. "They deserve to be No. 1," he said.

Unlike football, there is a post-season tournament to determine the best basketball team. So the polls don't matter anyway.

What does count is the incredible streak Robinson has going. He's scored 30 or more points in six straight games, winding up with the NCAA's top average, 30.3.

"We've never had a player impact the Big Ten like he did," marveled Illinois coach Lou Henson. "He's great."

Consider the variety of plays Robinson made Sunday. He hit five 3-point shots. He had five steals and five rebounds. He was 18 of 26 from the floor and 8 of 10 from the line.

Beyond the numbers, he had his usual assortment of magical plays. Another alley-oop slam off a Porter Roberts feed. A string of 10 straight points for Purdue. Another streak of 13 in a row after Illinois had closed to within two.

On one move, a play that left strangers high-fiving, Robinson beat a double team, hung in the air, drew a foul from Deon Thomas, then somehow hit a 5-footer on his way down.

Finally, Robinson's 3 at the 2:00 mark ended the drama, putting Purdue ahead by 10.

The only question was if Robinson would reach 50. After missing the front end of a 1-on-1 and then losing the ball on a fast break, he was forced to settle with 49.

"Glenn was unbelievable. I had no idea he could have that many points," Keady said.

Robinson scored 32 of Purdue's 47 second-half points.

"It was a great time to get into the zone," said Robinson about the mystical level players sometime reach where they can do no wrong. "I've been waiting on one of these kind of games since I first started my career at Purdue."

Dodging questions about whether Sunday was his last home game, Robinson instead talked about the joy of winning the Big Ten outright. A tie, he said, would have been like "going to a party and somebody's got on the same outfit as you do."

Not to worry. There could be 100 guys wearing No. 13 and it would take a nanosecond to find the Big Dog. He's the one who has caught the scent of a championship.

Glenn Robinson's ability to block shots was overlooked during his career at Purdue. In two years, he rejected 65 shots, seventh most in school history.

Glenn Robinson battles for a rebound, one of the 602 he grabbed for Purdue.

SWEET SUCCESS

by Tom Perrin

March 25, 1994 — KNOXVILLE, TENN. — It was Cuonzo Martin from the outside and Glenn Robinson from absolutely everywhere.

With Robinson scoring 44 points Thursday night and Martin adding a season-high 29, Purdue advanced to the championship game of the Southeast Regional with an 83-78 victory over Kansas in Thompson-Boling Arena.

Martin broke a Purdue school record with eight 3-pointers, five in the second half.

Robinson broke the Purdue record for points in an NCAA Tournament game he shared with Rick Mount and Joe Barry Carroll. Robinson scored 36 last year in a first-round loss to Rhode Island.

"We're not a one-man team, so when you come at me, you leave Cuonzo open for eight 3-pointers," Robinson said with obvious relish in his voice about the success of his roommate and close friend.

The Boilermakers (29-4) will play Duke (26-5) at 6 p.m. Saturday, in the championship game. The Blue Devils advanced Thursday with a 59-49 victory over Marquette.

Purdue advances to the NCAA's Elite Eight for the first time since the 1979-80 team made it to the Final Four.

It was a milestone victory for 14th-year Boilermaker coach Gene Keady, who dedicated it to Lafayette-area photographer Chuck Young, who is recovering from having both legs amputated.

Martin, 0 of 7 from 3-point range for his career prior to this season, hit 8 of 13 against the Jayhawks (27-8). He scored 20 points in the second half to Robinson's 14.

By paying special defensive attention to Robinson, Kansas challenged the Boilermakers to beat them from the perimeter. Martin did the job by himself, moving well without the ball and looking for his favorite shot, the 3 from either corner.

"I always do that in every game," Martin said. "I try to flatten the defense and get to the corner to lose my man."

Martin didn't get his first field goal until 10:46 remained in the first half. But once Martin got going, he never cooled off.

"Everyone expected Glenn to get his points, but Cuonzo gave them a lift with 29 points," said Kansas forward Richard Scott, who scored 15 points. "He was on fire like Glenn was."

Robinson was 15 of 33 from the field and 6 of 10 from 3-point range.

"I have no fault for the way we guarded Glenn Robinson," said Kansas coach Roy Williams, who could only offer his admiration for the performances of both Robinson and Martin in pressure situations.

Purdue shot 27 of 65 from the field for 41.5 percent, but the Boilermakers' 15 3-pointers broke a school record. Kansas was 30 of 62 from the field.

The Boilermakers tied a school record for victories established by the 1988 team, which finished 29-4.

Glenn Robinson was unstoppable with the ball in 1993-94 when he won the John Wooden Award as the top player in the nation.

Purdue led 78-73 with 1:52 left but wasn't able to extend the lead after consecutive turnovers by Martin and Robinson and a missed one-and-one opportunity by Matt Waddell with 42.8 seconds left.

Sean Pearson, who led Kansas with 20 points, hit a 3-pointer with 33.5 seconds left to narrow the margin to 78-76.

Martin hit two free throws with 23.8 seconds left to put Purdue ahead 80-76.

Pearson missed a 3-pointer from the right wing with 12 seconds left. Porter Roberts rebounded for Purdue and was fouled with 11.2 seconds left. He made two free throws to give the Boilermakers an 82-76 lead and seal the outcome.

"We beat a great coach and a great basketball program," Keady said. "Now we'll try to finish the job of getting to the Final Four on Saturday. I have felt all along that this team will take care of business as it has to."

Robinson wasted no time getting started in the second half, scoring Purdue's first two field goals to put the Boilermakers ahead, 48-44, with 17:59 left.

Consecutive 3-pointers by Martin gave the Boilermakers a 55-46 lead with 16:25 left.

Ian Stanback's tip with 15:43 left — the first Purdue field goal or points by someone other than Robinson, Martin or Waddell — put Purdue ahead, 57-47.

With 13:48 left, Robinson's slam dunk on the fast break off a wraparound pass from Waddell put Purdue ahead 62-52. Robinson was fouled on the play and made the bonus free throw.

Martin made a 3-pointer from the deep right side with 12:41 left as he was fouled by Scott. Martin made the free throw and Purdue led, 66-54. A steal and coast-to-coast layup by Martin with 11:58 left gave the Boilermakers a 68-54 lead.

But Kansas dashed any notions of a blowout by scoring the next 13 points as Purdue's shooting went cold.

Center Greg Ostertag scored inside to pull the Jayhawks within 68-67 with 6:40 left.

"Give credit to Kansas. They fought hard for 40 minutes," Waddell said. "We'd get them down and they'd come back on us."

Martin ended the Boilermaker drought with 6:21 left, hitting a 3-pointer from the top of the key to put Purdue ahead, 71-67.

Martin broke the school record with 5:30 left, hitting a 3 from the right wing to give the Boiler-

makers a 74-67 lead.

Kansas pulled to 76-73 with 2:45 left on Patrick Richey's uncontested layup that followed a Purdue turnover.

Robinson launched a 3-point airball with 2:19 left, but Roberts came up with the rebound. Robinson got the ball right back and made a 9-foot jumper with 1:52 left to give the Boilermakers a 78-73 lead.

Robinson scored 30 points in the first half, two fewer than he did in the second half of the March 13 Illinois game, when he finished with 49.

Robinson, Martin (nine points) and Waddell (five) accounted for all of the Boilermakers' first-half points and all but three field goal attempts.

By contrast, eight Kansas players scored in the first half, led by Steve Woodberry's 14. Woodberry scored just two points in the second half.

A tip by Scott for Kansas with two seconds left narrowed the Purdue lead to 44-42 at half-time.

Glenn Robinson scored 44 points against Kansas, a school record for an NCAA tournament game.

LITTLE TIME TO CELEBRATE WITH DUKE NEXT

by Jim Lefko

March 25, 1994 — KNOXVILLE, TENN. — Halfway home.

That's the position Purdue finds itself in after dispatching Kansas in dramatic fashion Thursday, 83-78.

Three postseason games down. Maybe three to go.

A 6-0 tournament means an NCAA Championship.

But before visions of Final Four grandeur creep through the Boilers' minds, there is the matter of Duke on Saturday.

"If I were just a fan," said Kansas coach Roy Williams, "I would pay the scalpers' price to come in and see that game."

The Blue Devils (26-5) waylaid Marquette 59-49 in the early game Thursday and looked pretty good.

Purdue didn't look shabby either, maybe not as impressive as the rout-minded Boilermaker women, but solid nonetheless.

With Glenn Robinson going bonkers during a mystical 30-point first half and Cuonzo Martin setting a school record with eight 3s, the Boilers won their eighth consecutive game.

Continuing to elevate his game, Robinson proved he is not only the Player of the Year, but one of the game's all-time greats.

Robinson finished with 44 rugged points, a school tournament record, while Martin sizzled with 29.

For one night anyway, Purdue was a two-man team.

"I like the one-man team better," Martin joked.

He then told a reporter that he does not want to be known as Little Dog, either. "I like Zo better," he said.

As enjoyable as Thursday was, Saturday promises more of the same, starting with the matchup of the coaching K's, Purdue's Gene Keady and Duke's Mike Krzyzewski.

Both men have been at their respective schools for 14 years. Keady has yet to reach the Final Four. Krzyzewski has been there six times, winning it all twice.

"Every coach in Division I wants to go to the Final Four," Keady said. "But you can't just get there and focus on that. You want to finish the job."

Purdue is looking a lot like a team that can go as far as it pleases, although it is not looking past Duke.

The intrigue Saturday will start with the Robinson-Grant Hill showdown.

The son of former NFL running back Calvin, Grant is not only the Blue Devils' go-to guy, but he also leads No. 2 seed Duke in assists.

Hill glided for 22 points Thursday, half of Robinson's total.

Robinson scored Purdue's first 10 points and 16 of the initial 19. He started 5 of 5 from the field with four 3s in the opening nine minutes.

Kansas opened with 6-foot-6 Richard Scott on the Big Dog, then switched 6-4 Steve Woodberry onto Robinson. The Jayhawks also used a 1-3-1 zone, but Martin shot them out of it.

"I have no fault with the way we defended Glenn Robinson," Williams said as he choked back tears after the game. "They tried to do the best they could and in fact did a pretty good job.

"If you'd have asked me before the game if I'd have taken Glenn going 15 of 33 (from the field), I'd have said, 'Yes.'"

Robinson, as is his norm, played all but two minutes of the emotional game.

"I try to get most of my rest in the first half. I don't think about being tired or exhausted, especially not at this time. I have all summer to rest," he said.

Robinson's best play of a remarkable first half was a slam over 7-foot-2 Greg Ostertag. Yapping at the KU center, Robinson then turned to the crowd and encouraged the Purdue faithful to salute his exploits.

Purdue built a 14-point lead midway through the second half, only to see it evaporate as quickly as another double-digit margin had in the first half.

But Martin's outside shooting ultimately kept Kansas at bay. He finished with 20 in the second half, wearing out the net with all of his long-range swishes.

"Glenn hit a lot of big baskets for them down the stretch but Cuonzo was really the key for their team," Scott said. "He really gave them a lift."

All the way to the Elite Eight.

After a quick celebration comes a not-so-blind date with perennial favorite Duke.

College basketball doesn't get any better than this.

Brandon Brantley battles for a rebound against the Jayhawks.

DREAM DIES HARD

Duke Halts Purdue's Final Four Bid, 69-60

by Tom Perrin

March 27, 1994 — KNOXVILLE, TENN — A day after Purdue superstar Glenn Robinson said the championship of the NCAA Southeast Regional would be decided by "supporting casts," his prophecy came true.

In a game Robinson and Grant Hill of Duke were supposed to dominate, the two All-Americans combined for just 24 points.

The outcome was determined by the rest of the Blue Devils, who played outstanding defense and never lost poise in a 69-60 victory over the Boilermakers in Thompson-Boling Arena.

Duke (27-5) advances to the Final Four for the sixth time in seven years, while Big Ten champion Purdue finishes 29-5 following its most lopsided loss of the season.

The Boilermakers lost their other four games by a total of 12 points.

"Nobody thought we would get this far, so I'm proud of our guys," said Boilermaker coach Gene Keady, who took Purdue farther than it has gone since 1980, but fell short of his first Final Four.

Robinson scored a season-low 13 points on 6 of 22 field goal shooting. The 6-foot-8 junior forward was held to just five points in the second half and went 0 of 6 from 3-point range.

"Everyone has a bad game. I was just hoping I wouldn't have a bad game in the tournament," said

Robinson, who averaged 37.1 points in Purdue's previous nine games. "I think they did a great job scouting us."

More than that, Duke played tough man-to-man defense, getting help when necessary, denying Robinson the ball and making it difficult on him after he caught it.

The primary defender on Robinson was the 6-foot-8 Hill, who scored just 11 points but was still named the Regional's Most Outstanding Player.

"I guess I'd say this was the best (defensive job on Robinson), because it was the biggest game of the year," Keady said. "Wisconsin did the same kind of job on him when they beat us at their place."

Robinson scored 15 points on 5 of 26 shooting in the Jan. 15 loss to the Badgers.

With Hill and Antonio Lang in Robinson's face and 6-11 center Cherokee Parks lurking in the middle, the "Big Dog" never got on a roll.

Neither did No. 2 scorer Cuonzo Martin, who was held to 12 points on 5 of 14 shooting and made two of seven 3-point attempts.

"Cherokee did a great job inside," Lang said. "We tried to make them take tough shots."

Hill, who entered the game a 46.3 percent field goal shooter, made only 4 of 12 shots.

However, with Lang and freshman point guard Jeff Capel scoring 19 points each and Parks adding 15, it didn't matter.

"Usually, when two guys like that face each other on the court, neither one plays well,"

Guard Matt Waddell scored a team-high 16 points in the 69-60 loss to Duke in the NCAA Elite Eight. It was the first time all season for Waddell to emerge as Purdue's top scorer.

Robinson said in Friday's press conference when he was asked about the matchup with Hill. "The thing that will decide this game is both of our supporting casts."

Purdue's only consistent offense was provided by junior guard Matt Waddell, who scored 16 points to lead the Boilermakers in scoring for the first time all season.

"I got some good shots and the guys did a good job setting screens," Waddell said. "I felt like I was in a good flow that I haven't found in the last couple of games."

Midway through the first half, it looked like the Boilermakers would be continuing their season in Charlotte.

No more than four points separated the teams until the Boilermakers broke loose for a 13-2 scoring run to lead 25-16 with 8:41 left on a drive to the basket by Porter Roberts.

That prompted a timeout by Duke coach Mike Krzyzewski, whose team responded with a 12-2 scoring run. An 18-footer by Hill with 4:54 left put the Blue Devils ahead 28-27.

During the run, Purdue was called for six consecutive personal fouls and a technical on assistant coach Frank Kendrick. "I don't know what you can do about that situation except try to keep your composure and nobody lost their composure, really," Keady said. "It was just one of those things where, bang, it happened."

Waddell came back with a running layup to put the Boilermakers back in front, and the teams played evenly the rest of the way.

One game after hitting a school record eight three-pointers, Cuonzo Martin hit just two of seven long bombs against Duke.

The score was tied 32-32 at halftime. On television during halftime, Wisconsin coach Stu Jackson and Kentucky coach Rick Pitino were asked who they thought would win. Jackson picked Duke and Pitino picked Purdue.

It was just that close.

But as happens so often in tight games, the first few possessions of the second half made the difference.

Capel hit a long 3-pointer and an 18-footer to put Duke ahead, 37-32 with 17:59 left, prompting a Keady timeout. Lang's 12-footer put the Blue Devils ahead, 39-32.

Purdue missed its first five field goal attempts and didn't score until Roberts' drive with 17:02 remaining made it 39-34.

Duke maintained control the rest of the way, though, staying calm even after Hill picked up his fourth personal foul with 9:54 left.

Robinson's 8-foot jumper brought Purdue within 46-43 with 9:45 left, but Duke went on an 8-3 scoring run with Hill on the bench to lead 54-46 with 7:06 left on Lang's 6-footer.

The Boilermakers were never closer than six points the rest of the way.

Instead of talking about reaching their goal of a national championship, Purdue was left to credit Duke and look ahead to next season.

"We weren't expected to win the Big Ten and we did that. We weren't expected to get this far in the tournament and we did that," Waddell said. "We're not satisfied, but we can accept it."

STATS FAIL TO CAPTURE BIG DOG'S GREATNESS

by Jim Lefko

March 27, 1994 — KNOXVILLE, TENN. — The magic was missing for Glenn Robinson Saturday.

After a month of Michael Jordan-like performances, he returned to mortal status against Duke.

In what may have been his final game in a Purdue uniform, Robinson was just 6 of 22 from the field in a bitter, season-ending 69-60 defeat.

After a month-long stretch of superstar scoring efforts, he finished with just 13 points, a season low.

He scored only five second-half points when Purdue needed him the most.

"Everybody's going to have a bad game," Robinson said. "I'm not ashamed at all."

Whether he will be back is uncertain. All Robinson would say Saturday was, "When I'm ready, I'll leave. I'm not ready.

"My thought process is to go back to the gym and work on my jump shot."

What Robinson is ready to do is remind everyone of the sensational season Purdue had, the Big Ten title, and three NCAA Tournament wins, unprecedented in the 14-year Gene Keady era.

"We had a helluva season," Robinson said. "I felt we could have won it all. Maybe there are some other teams better than us. But we went far enough. Some people said we wouldn't beat Kansas."

The Jayhawk game in the regional semifinals turned out to be the finale of a nine-game sequence where Robinson scored 30 or more points each time out.

While his shot was consistently short most of the night Saturday, he did lead Purdue with 13 rebounds and played a solid defensive game.

"They did a great job defensively on him," Matt Waddell said. "Just because he does it 90 percent of the time, when he has that one bad game, everybody's surprised."

Inconsistent officiating played a role in Robinson's off night, too.

"I got frustrated by some of the calls," Robinson said. "That took me out of sync."

Actually, the frustration started early. Robinson's first shot was blocked by Duke's Cherokee Parks. The Blue Devils' center swatted away another Robinson jumper later.

Among the other Robinson lowlights were a rare second-half airball, six misses on as many tries from 3-point land and half a dozen unsettling turnovers.

"You'd have to say this was the best (defensive) job on Robinson since it was the biggest game of the year," Keady said.

The man primarily responsible for Duke's defensive heroics was Grant Hill. Assigned to guard Robinson one-on-one most of the night, Hill stayed on top of Robinson all game.

On the few occasions when Robinson got a screen to free himself from Hill, Antonio Lang made the defensive switch and blanketed the Big Dog. And when Robinson went inside, there was Parks, waiting with arms outstretched.

"Everybody has a bad game," Porter Roberts said. "But he didn't have a bad game. He just didn't score the 33 points he usually does.

"That's the best defense I've seen anybody play on us this year."

Once the pain of the season-ending loss subsides, Robinson will be able to reflect on a stellar season, unmatched in Purdue annals.

The national awards will start rolling in, with Robinson a cinch to claim most — if not all — of the player of the year trophies.

What a wonderful ride he took Purdue on. That it wound up one win shy of the Final Four doesn't diminish a thing.

We saw grandeur all season long. The Robinson legacy is one of greatness.

If Saturday was his last game, my final memory will be of Robinson's exit after he fouled out with 39 seconds left.

First he exchanged congratulations with a couple of Duke players, including his future NBA buddy Hill.

Then came the true emotion. Robinson hugged Keady. It was a telling gesture between two men who hold each other in the highest regard.

Finally, it was assistant coach Frank Kendrick's turn. Kendrick recruited Robinson to Purdue. Their relationship is close to father-son.

The Robinson-Kendrick hug lasted awhile, a private moment in front of 23,370 people.

It was a lot like Robinson's two years at Purdue. He showed us all something extraordinary, but never really let us into his head or his heart.

Somehow though, the on-court moments were more than enough.

What he allowed us to witness was golden.

Glenn Robinson had no luck penetrating the defense of Duke's Grant Hill. Robinson had a season-low 13 points in the final game of his college career, missing 16 of 22 shots.

NEXT STOP MILWAUKEE

Robinson's Pro Career Starts Close to Home

by Jeff Washburn

June 30, 1994 — INDIANAPOLIS, IND. — Beer. Brats. Badgers. Brewers. Bucks. Boating.

Needless to say, those who work and play within Wisconsin's boundaries are fond of words and activities which begin with the letter "B."

A Boilermaker whose nickname is "Big Dog" will be a more-than-welcomed addition to Milwaukee's professional basketball franchise — the Bucks.

The Bucks quickly ended what little NBA Draft suspense existed Wednesday night by making Glenn Robinson the No. 1 selection.

The 6-foot-8 forward, who averaged 30.3 points and 10.1 rebounds for Purdue University last season, sported a bright gold suit and a broad smile as he walked to the podium after NBA commissioner David Stern made the announcement that Milwaukee had indeed picked the "Big Dog."

"Everybody told me to keep my composure and not to be nervous," Robinson said of the moments leading up to his selection. "I was still nervous. I can't believe this is happening.

"It means a lot to me to be here, knowing that I played as much as I did and for as long as I did. It's sure helping me right now. There are a lot of great players out there, and I look forward to meeting them. All I wanted was an opportunity to play. That's all you can ask for."

Robinson and Milwaukee appear to be a good match. The Gary native noted that his parents, relatives and friends will have a relatively easy two-hour drive to the Bucks' Bradley Center.

"I feel I have to improve on everything," he said. "I'm only 21 years old, so I feel I still have room to improve on every aspect of my game.

"Everybody wants to be like Mike (Michael Jordan), but I'm just going to go out and give it my best shot."

Depending on the outcome of the collective-bargaining agreement between the NBA and the league's players' association, Robinson could sign a multi-year contract worth as much as $150 million, according to agent Dr. Charles Tucker.

The Bucks recently increased the price of each ticket for the 1994-95 season by $2 despite posting a 20-62 mark during 1993-94.

BUCKS CALM G-ROB'S NERVES

by Jeff Washburn

June 30, 1994 — INDIANAPOLIS, IND. — The sign — *The Big Dog now is the Big Buck* — said it all.

Much to the pleasure of the Milwaukee fan who designed the sign, Purdue All-American Glenn Robinson now is a member of the Milwaukee Bucks.

The Bucks used the 1994 NBA Draft's No. 1 pick Wednesday night in the Hoosier Dome to select the 6-foot-8 forward who affectionately is known among Boilermaker fans as the "Big Dog."

It certainly came as no surprise even though Robinson, who could sign a long-term contract worth as much as $150 million, said he was nervous until NBA commissioner David Stern made it official at 6:37 p.m.

"The hardest part was the waiting," said Robinson, who shopped for a new hat Wednesday afternoon in Indianapolis in an effort to take his mind off the draft. "I woke up early this morning — earlier than I usually do.

"Then, I just kind of hung out in the lobby and waited to come over here."

Dallas used the second pick to select California point guard Jason Kidd. At No. 3, Detroit selected guard/forward Grant Hill, and Minnesota acquired Connecticut forward Donyell Marshall with the No. 4 choice.

Michigan center/forward Juwan Howard was taken at No. 5 by the Washington Bullets.

Indianapolis native Eric Montross, a center, was taken at No. 9 by the Boston Celtics, and the Indiana Pacers used the No. 15 pick to acquire Nebraska's forward/guard Eric Piatkowski.

Three times louder than the boos for Piatkowksi's selection was the roar when the Pacers selected Damon Bailey with the 44th pick in the second round. Three picks earlier, Indiana selected 6-9 forward William Njoku of Canada.

But this was Robinson's night — an evening for which the ex-Boilermaker anxiously had waited.

"There have been a lot of distractions, even when I was trying to focus on the NCAA Tournament," Robinson said. "It just feels good to have this part of it over with."

Robinson says comparisons to the dominance of Orlando's Shaquille O'Neal and Golden State's Chris Webber are flattering, but also premature.

"It feels great to be a player who is coming into the league like that," Robinson said. "In one respect, it's bad, because people are going to expect for me to come in and want me to do more than what I can do.

"I'm not going to let that worry me, but it worries a lot of people on the outside."

Frank Kendrick, a former NBA player and the Purdue assistant coach who recruited Robinson out of Gary Roosevelt High School, says the comparisons are fair.

Kendrick was among Robinson's friends and family who attended Wednesday's draft in the Hoosier Dome.

"There was never a doubt in my mind that this would happen," Kendrick said. "You could see right away that he was special. He just had everything it took to be a superstar.

"It's just getting started. He's just special. He's one of those kids that can just go up to another level."

Kendrick is convinced that Robinson has all the tools to be an NBA All-Star.

"He has every one and then some," Kendrick said. "The hardest part for him will be that people will want his time.

"I'm extremely happy for him."

Dr. Charles Tucker, Robinson's Lansing, Mich.-based agent, is anxious to begin negotiations with Milwaukee.

Tucker and Mike Dunleavy, the Bucks' coach and general manager, have known each other for several years.

"I hope there aren't any problems, because Glenn wants to be in Milwaukee," Tucker said.

"Mike and those guys are professionals, and I think Glenn will be there.

"I'm not going to focus on $100 million or $150 million. I'm just hoping we can get a fair deal and that they get the collective bargaining agreement solved. If that doesn't get solved, then it might become a bidding war. But I want Glenn to be happy. If it means less money to play where he wants to play, that's more important."

MARTIN ZONES IN ON RECORD

Lewis' 3-Point Mark May Fall Tonight

By Jeff Washburn

February 18, 1995 — Troy Lewis knew it would only be a matter of time.

In fact, Purdue's No. 4 career scorer is surprised that his school-record 151 field goals from 3-point range have topped the Boilermaker charts for seven seasons.

Now, senior forward Cuonzo Martin, who came to Purdue as a defensive specialist and did not make a single 3-pointer until his junior year, is poised to pass Indiana's 1984 co-Mr. Basketball.

Martin needs one 3-pointer during tonight's Big Ten Conference game against Northwestern in Mackey Arena to tie Lewis' record and two to break it.

Lewis, a sales representative for Victory Wholesale Groceries in Dayton, Ohio, said Friday he will be cheering for Martin.

"I'm happy for him because of his work ethic and how he presents himself as a person," Lewis said. "He's a quality guy. I know him off the court, and I couldn't ask for a better person to break it.

"He's had very good success as far as winning in the program, and that's all you want as an ex-player—to see guys excel in the program."

Lewis, an Anderson native who was a prolific perimeter shooter in high school, played two sea-

sons at Purdue before the 3-point shot was incorporated into the college game.

He made 51 shots from 3-point range during his junior year and added 100 during the 1987-88 season, when the Boilermakers posted a 29-4 record, winning the Big Ten championship with a 16-2 mark.

"You can always say, 'What if Rick Mount had a 3-point shot?'" Lewis said. "You can go on and on. I had my two years, I made what I had to make and I'm satisfied with it. There's nothing I can really do to change it.

"But it would have been interesting to see how many I would have hit if I would have had the 3-point shot for four years."

When Lewis completed his Purdue career, he was convinced that Woody Austin would break his 3-point record. But Austin was declared academically ineligible for the 1990-91 season's second semester and finished with 199 3-pointers.

Martin, according to Lewis, is a surprise 3-point derby winner.

"Obviously, if you looked at it, you wouldn't think he would break it, just because he didn't make a 3-point basket until his junior year," Lewis

Not all of Cuonzo Martin's field goal attempts came from long distance.

said. "That's just a credit to him—how much he improved his jump shot and how much he worked on it during the summer and after practice.

"I got a chance to work out with those guys a couple of years ago, and I could see how hard he worked. This is the reward that you get."

Martin, who also is Purdue's career 3-point shooting percentage leader, made four 3-pointers during Wednesday night's 71-51 victory against Penn State.

"I was aware Wednesday night, but I didn't want to tie it," Martin said. "I wanted to break it. I was looking at it as two 3-pointers, and I couldn't get them to go. Hopefully, I'll be able to make them (against Northwestern)."

The record, according to Martin, is one he'll appreciate later in life.

"I don't know right now how much it will mean, because I'm still playing," he said. "But maybe five or 10 years down the road, it will mean a lot. Somebody probably will have broken it by then. Right now, I'm just playing and trying to compete.

"We're going down the stretch, and it's tough to play down the stretch. The last four games are going to be tough, so I'm just competing right now."

Penn State coach Bruce Parkhill, who is 1-5 against Martin-led Purdue teams, said the Boilermaker leader is most deserving.

"I've always loved him," Parkhill said of Martin. "I just love the way he plays hard. He defends well, he's a competitor and obviously shoots the ball well. I've always been a big fan of his."

And while Purdue coach Gene Keady is happy for Martin, he's much more concerned about the task at hand—beating last-place Northwestern, which upset the Boilermakers 62-59 in Mackey Arena during the 1992-93 season.

Cuonzo Martin plays it cool during a practice in the midst of his standout senior season.

"I can remember a couple of years ago, they came in here and beat us," Keady said. "I hope we'll be ready."

Chances are, his leading scorer will be.

TAKING CARE OF BUSINESS

Purdue Creeps Closer to MSU; Martin Breaks 3-Point Record

By Jeff Washburn

February 19, 1995 — There are good days in athletics, and then there are *really* good days.

Purdue's basketball program experienced one of those *really* good days Saturday.

The Boilermakers, who got some much-needed assistance Saturday afternoon from Minnesota, took care of their own business Saturday night in Mackey Arena.

The results are as follows:

• Senior forward Cuonzo Martin is the school's new 3-point field goal king, surpassing Troy Lewis with three long-range baskets during 25th-ranked Purdue's 94-57 Big Ten Conference mauling of Northwestern.

Martin, who scored a game-best 25 points, now has 153 field goals from 3-point range. Lewis finished his Purdue career with 151.

The Boilermakers' leading scorer tied Lewis' 3-point record with 11:34 remaining before intermission and broke it with 2:59 showing on the first-half clock.

"Glenn (Robinson) made it a lot easier for me," Martin said of breaking the 3-point record. "He helped me in developing my confidence. When guys would double up on him, I had to knock those (3-point) shots down for us to be successful as a team.

"It's just one of those things where hard work and constant practice paid off."

Martin said he began serious work on his 3-point shot after his freshman year, although he did not make one until his junior season, when he and Robinson led Purdue to the Big Ten championship.

"My sophomore year, I missed my first six (3-point shots), and I stopped shooting it," he said. "My junior year, I made the first couple (3-pointers) and just stuck with it. It was just a confidence thing."

• Coupled with Minnesota's 66-57 Saturday victory against league-leading and eighth-ranked Michigan State, Purdue now is 1/2 game behind the Spartans and is tied in the all-important loss column.

Purdue is 18-6, 9-3 in the Big Ten. Michigan State is 18-4, 10-3.

Northwestern, which shares last place with Ohio State, slipped to 5-17, 1-12. Purdue now has beaten the Wildcats 23 times in the past 24 meetings.

• The Boilermakers now have successfully completed 40 percent of a five-game, must-win Big Ten sequence.

Cuonzo Martin breaks the Purdue three-point shooting record, formerly held by Troy Lewis.

Martin scored 15 first-half points, and senior guard Matt Waddell added 11, hitting 5 of 6 floor shots.

Purdue made 19 of 33 first-half field goal attempts (57.6 percent), while Northwestern hit only 9 of 26 (34.6 percent), including only 3 of its final 15 during the opening 20 minutes.

The Boilermakers used a 16-3 second-half spurt, during which Martin scored seven points and Waddell five, to take an 81-44 lead with 8:03 remaining.

Keady's non-starters played the rest of the way, finishing Purdue's ninth victory in 10 Mackey Arena starts.

Waddell finished with 16 points, junior forward Roy Hairston added 14 and freshman center Brad Miller had 10 points and nine rebounds.

Freshman guard Joe Branch led Northwestern with 16 points.

Keady, who is battling a cold, felt better after Saturday's game, especially after Martin broke the 3-point record.

"He wasn't very confident," Keady said of Martin's freshman- and sophomore-year 3-point attempts. "It's just the fact that he went to work. He's a great example for young people—what you can do if you put a lot of extra time in, whether it's hitting a baseball, pole vaulting or playing golf.

"If you put the practice time in, you're going to get better. He did, and he had the heart to do it. He's just shown so much courage with that knee. He's an amazing story and doesn't get enough credit for it."

Martin, who has hit 65 of 135 shots from 3-point range (48.1 percent) this season, had arthroscopic left knee surgery in late November.

Northwestern coach Ricky Byrdsong claims that Martin is among the nation's best 3-point shooters.

I thought Cuonzo played an outstanding game," Byrdsong said. "He had 25 points, no turnovers and five assists, so I don't think you can ask for much better leadership than that.

"He's an outstanding player. It's difficult to compare individuals, but I'd take him and be happy. Just knowing his history, I know that he's made himself a player, and I have a great deal of respect for him."

Purdue defeated Penn State 71-51 this past Wednesday and will play at Ohio State Wednesday night.

The Boilermakers then have consecutive home games against Wisconsin and Iowa.

If coach Gene Keady's team defeats the Buckeyes, Badgers and Hawkeyes, it will have a 12-3 Big Ten record entering a season-ending sequence that will include games at Illinois and Minnesota and a home contest against Michigan.

Northwestern actually led this game 8-2 and 12-8, but during the first half's final 15:09, the Boilermakers outscored the Wildcats 38-10, taking a commanding 46-22 advantage into the dressing room.

BOILERMAKER'S "BIGGEST" MOMENT ALSO SCARIEST

Dove Prevents Evans' Game-Winning Basket

by Jeff Washburn

February 26, 1996 — BLOOMINGTON, IND. — When the ballots are counted, Indiana senior forward Brian Evans will be selected the Big Ten Conference's 1996 Player of the Year.

The 6-foot-8 forward from Terre Haute is the league's leading scorer with a 22-point average, and he's made a habit of hitting clutch shots.

With 13.7 seconds remaining in Sunday's game in Assembly Hall and Purdue leading 74-72, Boilermaker senior forward Herb Dove knew who would take the Hoosiers' final shot.

"It's probably the biggest defending moment that I've had," Dove said. "I've sacrificed (offense) to give as much defense as I can. I enjoy doing it because we're winning."

When Evans caught the ball on the left side with less than five seconds to play, Dove's heart began to pound.

"That final play was probably the most scary play of my life," Dove said. "If Evans would have hit that shot, I would have been remembered as the guy who let Evans hit the final bucket in a big Purdue-Indiana game."

But Evans' 3-pointer bounced off the front of the rim, and Purdue point guard Porter Roberts rebounded, sealing the Boilermakers' first Assembly Hall victory since 1990 and their ninth consecutive Big Ten triumph.

"I was just trying to be up on him," Dove said. "I think he was trying to draw a foul, because he jumped into me, because his shot was short. Maybe if he had stepped back and squared up, he might have hit it."

Roberts, who led Purdue with seven rebounds, won't soon forget No. 7.

"We knew they were going to try to get either Evans or Neil Reed open for a 3-pointer," Roberts said. "(Evans') shot came off the rim kind of funny.

"It bounced through a couple of my teammates, and I looked around and the ball was in my hands."

He dribbled away from the basket as time expired and then punted the ball high above the Assembly Hall floor.

"Last summer in pickup games, we would lose a little bit, and I'd get frustrated," Roberts said when asked about his kicking skills. "I used to be a soccer player, but this (kick) was just out of emotion.

"I didn't try to hurt anybody, and I hope I didn't hurt anybody."

He didn't.

Dove claims that a change in Purdue's practice routine for the IU game was a key to breaking the Hoosiers' five-game winning streak against the Boilermakers in Assembly Hall.

During the time Dove has been at Purdue, the Boilermakers have not practiced in Assembly Hall the day before the game.

This time, they practiced Saturday in Assembly Hall and made 10 of 20 shots from 3-point range on Sunday.

"I don't know why we don't come down here and practice like we do everywhere else," Dove said. "Why change up for Indiana? We'd always go to Indianapolis and stay the night and have to get up early and drive here for a shootaround.

"I mentioned a long time ago that we should just come here and practice like we do normally and not change any routine. We did it and we got a win with it."

But there were distractions.

Play was stopped with 15:50 remaining in the first half when a breakaway basket would not slide back into place after three IU dunks.

Assembly Hall employees replaced the basket and play resumed.

Purdue players claim the basketballs provided for pregame warmups were not properly inflated, and Dove said there were no towels in the dressing room after the Boilermakers showered.

"But that's fine, because we won the game," he said.

PURDUE RULES

Triumph at IU puts Third Straight Title in Sight

by Amy Higgins

February 26, 1996 — Victorious Purdue University basketball players stepped off the team bus to a calm, quiet Sunday evening. No crowd, no cheers, no fight songs.

True, several hundred raving fans in gold and black had gathered — but on the other side of Mackey Arena.

The fans sprinted around the building and loudly greeted the team, fresh from its 74-72 victory at rival Indiana University.

Members of the crowd carried signs reading "3-Pete" in hopes of the third consecutive Big Ten title — one more win clinches a tie — and brooms to signify seventh-ranked Purdue's sweep of Indiana this season.

They chanted players' names and gathered around them getting autographs.

"This is what you work for," Purdue coach Gene Keady said as members of the crowd shook his hand in congratulations.

Purdue fans agreed.

"It was a great game," said Gerald Thomas, who played for the Boilermakers from 1973-1977 and gathered with other fans to welcome the heroes home. "It's been a while since they've beaten IU at home...and that's not easy to do."

Purdue senior Todd Julian knows it has been hard — Purdue hadn't beaten IU in Bloomington since 1990, when Julian was in high school in Carmel. He wanted to celebrate with the team one last time before graduation in May.

"It's a great accomplishment for the team," Julian said. "I wanted to be part of it. I've been a strong supporter all my life."

David and Pam Powers, Purdue graduates of the 1970s, traveled from Frankfort to be part of the festivities Sunday evening. They brought their two sons, who already know they're going to grow up to be Boilermakers.

"I don't think they have a choice," Pam joked.

Diane and Trent Johnson also have started training their children for future Boilerhood. Megan, 5 and decked out in a Purdue cheerleader's dress, said she's going to be a cheerleader when she grows up.

And Cody, 2, has learned all he needs to know: "IU stinks."

SWEEP FOR PURDUE

Austin's Shot Toppled Indiana Again, 74-72; Threepeat Just One Win Away

by Jeff Washburn

February 26, 1996— BLOOMINGTON, IND. — Late in Purdue's Friday afternoon practice in Mackey Arena, assistant coach Jay Price directed a segment during which the nation's seventh-ranked team worked against a zone defense.

"I think they'll play some zone," Price said of Indiana, which plays a zone defense almost as often as Hoosier coach Bob Knight invites referees to his home for dinner.

But Price, who does the Boilermakers' scouting, was right, and Purdue used his hunch to secure a 74-72 Big Ten Conference victory against its archrival Sunday afternoon in sold-out Assembly Hall.

Sophomore guard Chad Austin's dramatic 3-pointer from the right corner against IU's 2-3 zone with 13.7 seconds remaining gave Purdue (23-4, 13-2 Big Ten) its first Assembly Hall victory since 1990 and a sweep of the season series.

Coach Gene Keady's Boilermakers have a 2 1/2-game Big Ten lead on 14th-ranked Penn State with three league contests remaining.

Purdue would clinch no worse than a share of the conference title with a Thursday night victory against Minnesota in Mackey Arena.

Keady's team would nail down a third consecutive outright Big Ten championship with a victory against the Golden Gophers and a Saturday night triumph against Northwestern in Mackey.

Indiana (15-11, 8-6) battled foul trouble throughout the second half and switched from man-to-man to a zone with 5:27 remaining and the score tied at 64.

Purdue, which made 10 of 20 shots from 3-point range against IU, made three during the final 3:33, including Austin's game-winner.

Austin, who led the Boilermakers with 18 points, took a pass from guard Todd Foster and was wide open when he released the shot.

"I wasn't going to hesitate," Austin said. "I was going to shoot it. If it went in, it went in. If I miss, I miss.

"If you get nervous, that's when you miss the shot, so I wasn't nervous at all. You've got to keep calm and just shoot."

Indiana had one more chance to win or force overtime, but senior forward Brian Evans' 3-pointer with three seconds remaining bounced off the front of the rim, and Purdue guard Porter Roberts rebounded as time expired.

Roberts kicked the ball high into the air and joined a wild celebration at center court.

Once order was restored, Price smiled as he discussed the obvious ramifications of Purdue's Friday practice against a zone.

"I don't know if it makes coaching fun, but it's

what helps us keep our jobs," Price said. "If we had been wrong, I might have gotten fired. It's nice to go ahead and pull plays up and show them what the other team is going to do.

"That's what's so rewarding — when you know what they're going to do, and you do something to counter-act it."

Austin is a clutch 3-point shot veteran. The Richmond High School graduate's 3-pointer with 10 seconds remaining in the 1992 Indiana state championship game against Lafayette Jeff forced overtime and helped the Red Devils win the title.

He claims the state finals' basket was the most important he's ever made, but Sunday's isn't far behind.

"It felt good," Austin said. "After it left my hand, I knew it was going in. It's a player's dream, but we've still got a couple of games to take care of."

Foster, who made 5 of 8 attempts from beyond the arc for 15 points, almost took the shot with Indiana leading 72-71 and less than 20 seconds to play.

"We just tried to get a good shot," Foster said. "When I got it, I thought about shooting it, but then I saw that Chad was wide open right down in that corner.

"He'd missed a couple right before that, but I have faith in Chad, and he's a great shooter. It was a great shot."

Austin missed his first three second-half 3-point attempts but made the one Purdue needed most in winning its seventh Big Ten road game in eight attempts.

"Chad had attempted a couple right before that one, and he'd shot kind of flat," Roberts said. "I went up to him and was like, 'Hey, that's your shot. You've got to hit that. We need you.'

"I think he really responded well by knocking that shot down from the corner. It took a lot of courage to shoot that shot in the clutch."

There were many clutch shots in Sunday's thriller, during which Purdue built a 52-41 lead with 17:18 remaining before Indiana charged back.

The Hoosiers used a 19-3 run from the 17:06 mark until 9:59 remained to take a 60-55 advantage.

But Purdue countered with a 9-2 spurt, including five Roy Hairston points, and the stage was set for yet another dramatic ending in what may be college basketball's finest rivalry.

Senior center Todd Lindeman led Indiana with a game-best 21 points and 10 rebounds, and sophomore guard Charlie Miller added 18. Evans finished with 17.

The Boilermakers' non-starters outscored IU's reserves 32-2, getting 14 from center Brad Miller and the aforementioned 15 from Foster.

Now, Purdue is poised to join Ohio State (1960, '61, and '62) as the only teams to win three consecutive outright Big Ten championships.

"We thought we could be a good ballclub, but with six seniors, you can't worry about who is going to start and who is going to play the most minutes," Foster said when asked to explain why this team has won 23 of 27.

"That's where the team concept comes into play."

DESPITE MIXED REVIEWS FROM MEDIA, BOILERMAKERS' THIRD ACT A HIT

by Tom Kubat

February 26, 1996 — BLOOMINGTON, IND. —
It was the exclamation point to another incredible season for the Purdue men's basketball team.

Sunday's thrilling 74-72 victory over rival Indiana was not only a rare Boilermaker win in Assembly Hall, it all but assured Purdue of its third consecutive outright Big Ten Conference championship, something that hasn't been done in more than 30 years.

At 13-2, the Boilermakers have a 2 $1/2$-game lead over Penn State (10-4), with only three games to play. It would take a total Purdue collapse in home games against Minnesota and Northwestern and the regular season finale at Iowa for this title to slip away.

It ain't gonna happen.

After Chad Austin hit a 3-point jumper from the corner with 13.7 seconds left, and Indiana's Brian Evans missed an off-balance shot from the left of the key with four seconds remaining, the Boilermaker seniors were relishing their first victory in Assembly Hall.

Gene Keady-coached Purdue teams have won only four of 16 games in Assembly Hall, and the Boilermakers' last victory here was an 81-79 overtime decision in 1990.

"It doesn't get any better than this," said Purdue senior Herb Dove, who was guarding Evans

on his final shot. "We finally did it. We want to use this momentum and hopefully go pretty far in the tournament."

The Boilermakers, as usual, already have gone further than most people expected.

Every season, the Rodney Dangerfields of college basketball get no respect. They just keep winning championships.

"It's a motivating factor for us," senior Justin Jennings said. "We don't get upset. Coach tells us if you read the news clippings, you should read them for motivation and not for inspiration. It's real rewarding."

This year, the Boilermakers have won with a veteran team featuring six seniors. And with a lineup that doesn't have a go-to guy, but a bunch of players that take turns stepping up.

And above all, with defense. In your face, belly-to-belly team defense.

While Indiana scored 72 points Sunday, well above the 55.5 average of Purdue opponents in the last eight games, it was two key defensive stops when the game was on the line that helped win it for the Boilermakers.

After Indiana had erased a nine-point Purdue halftime lead and taken a 70-68 lead, the Boilermakers went to a full court press and got a 10-second call against Indiana.

Todd Foster, who had hit 4 of 5 shots from 3-point range in the first half, responded with another one to give Purdue a 71-70 lead.

And then there was Dove sticking to Evans like glue on the final shot.

For the day, the Boilermakers were 10 of 20 from 3-point range, including 5 of 8 for Foster and 3 of 7 for Austin, including the game-winner.

"It was a play we set up to get him open and it worked and he knocked it down," Keady said. "Sometimes those plays don't work, sometimes they do. We set it up and it worked, that's all I can tell you."

It seems a lot of things Keady and the Boilermakers have tried in recent years have worked.

Even the little things.

Like practicing in Assembly Hall on Saturday.

"The kids wanted to come here and practice yesterday," Keady said. "A lot of years they didn't want to come over here at all. But they wanted to come practice on this floor because they felt like last year we didn't get enough shooting time on it."

Whatever. Purdue shot 48 percent overall and 50 percent from 3-point range.

Even with his third consecutive Big Ten title all but in the bank, Keady followed up on the no-respect theme by doing a little campaigning with the media for senior point guard Porter Roberts.

Roberts scored eight points Sunday, and he had six assists with just one turnover.

For the season, his numbers aren't spectacular, with an 8.1 scoring average. But he nearly has a 2-to-1 assist (142) to turnover (73) ratio.

Keady is concerned Roberts will be overlooked in the voting for the All-Big Ten teams.

"If Porter is not the best point guard in this league, then I don't know much about basketball," Keady said. "What other point guard in the nation has won three championships in a tough league?

"C'mon you guys, vote for him. The man deserves to be first-team All-Big Ten. Now, if you're going to give it on stats, which you guys usually do, instead of how people win, then he won't get it."

And when reminded that there's a good chance the league's coaches won't vote Roberts to their first team either, Keady said, "You know what they'll vote, they're like you guys. Maybe that's why we're winning, some of them don't understand the game."

Obviously most not as well as Keady.

CHAMPS, CHAMPS, CHAMPS

Boilers Savor 3-Peat

by Jeff Washburn

March 3, 1996 — They danced, they sang and most of all, they celebrated.

Purdue's overachieving men's basketball team officially completed its three-peat Saturday night.

The fifth-ranked Boilermakers, who crushed Northwestern 79-56, are the first Big Ten team to win three consecutive outright titles since Ohio State in 1960-62.

The feat became reality 2 1/2 hours before the game, when Minnesota upset second-place Penn State 65-60.

But Purdue did not disappoint the 14,123 fans who filled Mackey Arena to see Senior Night, during which coach Gene Keady's six seniors were honored.

At game's end, players received hats marking their triple triumph, and Big Ten commissioner Jim Delaney presented the league trophy.

"During the past two months, you have accomplished something that hasn't been accomplished in almost two generations," Delaney told the Boilermakers and their fans after the players danced and sang to rap music.

"Purdue put a man on the moon since."

Spirits were almost that high after the trophy presentation.

"This is a special night for Boilermakers around the world," Keady said.

But Purdue's six seniors opted not to address the crowd. They told Keady they want to wait to speak until after this year's Final Four, a place they hope to reach.

Center Brad Miller zeroes in on a rebound.

MACKEY ARENA LOVEFEST LAUNCHES BOILER SENIORS INTO HISTORY

by Jim Lefko

March 3, 1996 — They bowed out in grand fashion Saturday night.

Purdue's special six, the seniors who played their final game at Mackey Arena, said goodbye with an emphatic 79-56 triumph over Northwestern.

Hugging their parents in a special pregame ceremony and toasting the local faithful in a stirring postgame lovefest, Roy Hairston, Brandon Brantley, Todd Foster, Porter Roberts, Justin Jennings and Herb Dove made Saturday a night to remember.

With the outright three-peat already assured prior to game time thanks to Penn State's loss at Minnesota, Saturday was an evening-long appreciation.

Northwestern did its part, keeping things interesting for about 15 minutes, then playing the role of designated loser before clearing out for the victory party.

The atmosphere was electric all night. Signs scattered throughout the arena attested to the Boilermakers' prowess.

"It's a great feat to 3-Pete," read the posters given out at the door, enhancing the local flavor. And the seniors — that motley crew of misfits that everyone else regarded with scorn just a few months ago — didn't let anyone down.

Human highlight film Jennings had a trio of spectacular dunks to get the crowd on its feet.

Foster drew one of his trademark charging fouls against an unsuspecting Wildcat big man to draw a huge ovation. Then it got heated when he was shoved out of bounds directly in front of a referee, but didn't get a whistle.

Gene Keady added to the festivities by drawing a rare first-half technical, protesting another mistake by the officials.

Basketball though, was little more than a sidelight Saturday. What came after the game was truly unforgettable.

Following an impromptu circle dance by the players, the obligatory championship hats came out. Then the T-shirts were presented, and of course, the trophy.

An elaborate multi-media production, featuring the two previous year's trophies, culminated with Big Ten commissioner Jim Delany handing off the newest piece of hardware.

With "We are the Champions" playing in the background and fireworks exploding overhead, the players promenaded around the court in joyous celebration.

Putting an exclamation point on the evening, Keady brought the house down with a series of one-liners about his exiting seniors.

Thanking Foster for his MVP-level effort, Keady quipped, "He doesn't really hate Mackey, he just can't shoot worth a damn here."

Foster was 0-for-9 from the field Saturday. Luckily for him, the remainder of his college career will unfold in gyms with more Foster-friendly rims.

Keady summed up out-going Jennings this way: "He's going to run for president."

Hairston drew this comment from Keady: "We call him Happy now. He didn't smile for a year. I think he was just trying to copy me."

Keady also had kind words for Brantley ("He's been tremendous"), Roberts ("the best point guard in the Big Ten") and Dove ("the best defensive player in the league").

As popular as the players are to the local faithful, it was Keady who drew the biggest applause all night long. Every time it had a chance to salute the beloved team leader, the crowd went nuts.

Clearly Keady is the heart and soul of this team, the man many in Greater Lafayette, the state of Indiana and the nation think of first when the word "Purdue" is mentioned.

A memorable evening, which also happened to include win No. 25 of the season, represented one of the all-time high points in Purdue's illustrious basketball history.

The nation's premier coach, the conference's premier team and a crowd Keady called the "greatest in the Big Ten." It's truly an unbeatable combination.

Energetic point guard Porter Roberts dribbles between a pair of Northwestern defenders.

BOILERS SENIORS GO OUT-RIGHT

Boilermakers Beat Up Wildcats 79-56, join OSU in Big Ten History Books

by Jeff Washburn

March 3, 1996 — Purdue's "three-peat" party began earlier than anticipated Saturday.

And it carried deep into the night.

The fifth-ranked Boilermakers clinched a third consecutive outright Big Ten Conference championship at 5:31 p.m. Saturday, when Minnesota upset 12th-ranked Penn State, 65-60.

With a place in Big Ten history secured, Purdue (25-4, 15-2 Big Ten) finished the home portion of its schedule with a rousing "Senior Night" drubbing of last-place Northwestern, 79-56.

The Boilermakers are the first team since Ohio State (1960, '61 and '62) to win three consecutive out-right Big Ten titles, and they achieved the "three-peat" with a hounding defense and collection of role players.

With a March 9 game at Iowa remaining, only two of Purdue's 17 Big Ten opponents have shot at least 50 percent against the Boilermakers, who also have had six different leading scorers in league play.

Northwestern made only 33.3 percent (20 of 60) of its field goal attempts Saturday night in Mackey Arena.

"Most definitely, it was our defense," senior point guard Porter Roberts said when asked about the key to Saturday's victory. "On a night like this when a team comes out during a real emotional time, it can be flat on offense.

"In times like that, we always rely on our defense, because you can always play defense, regardless of how your shots are falling. We held them to 56 points and that worked out pretty well for us."

An opponent has scored no more than 61 points against Purdue in eight of the Boilermakers' past 11 games.

Purdue clinched its 13th Mackey Arena victory in 14 starts this season with a 26-5, first-half-closing run.

Northwestern (7-19, 2-15) led 26-20 on an Evan Eschmeyer layup with 6:43 remaining in the opening half.

But from the 6:35 mark until the half's end, the Boilermakers exhibited the skills with which they won the Big Ten championship.

Sophomore guard Chad Austin's 13 points highlighted Purdue's 26-5 run, and senior forward Justin Jennings added six of his 10 first-half points during the victory-sealing spurt.

Jennings and Austin shared game scoring honors with 17 each. Guard Geno Carlisle led the Wildcats with 14, but he made only 5 of 17 floor shots.

"Our starters came out kind of slow, and I just wanted to come in and get some easy buckets, and then everybody will feed off me," Jennings said of his strong first half.

"I kind of had to get on Chad for a second, because he really wouldn't shoot. That was really hurting us because Northwestern started backing off him when he wouldn't shoot. Then, he really came through for us at the end of that stretch and in the second half."

Austin made three 3-pointers during the half's final 5:37, helping Purdue finish the opening 20 minutes with 15 field goals in 27 attempts (55.6 percent).

The Boilermakers finished 26 of 58 from the field (44.8 percent) on a night when the school's 21st Big Ten men's basketball championship was realized.

Jennings had a 12-point first half, making each of his five field goal tries and a pair of free throws.

After playing well for more than 13 minutes, Northwestern made only one field goal and three free throws during the half's final 6 1/2 minutes.

The Wildcats closed to within 11 twice during the final 20 minutes, but an 18-6 Purdue run from the 5:59 mark until the final horn gave the Boilermakers their most lopsided victory since a 75-42 romp on February 7 at Wisconsin.

Purdue extended its winning streak to a season's best 11 games. The Boilermakers have won 21 of 23 since a December 9 loss to Villanova in Anaheim, Calif.

"This really hasn't hit me yet," Jennings said. "Right now, I'm more focused on getting ready for the NCAA Tournament and doing great there.

"Later on, this night will be something that I can look back at and really appreciate. Right now, the train has stopped at the Big Ten, and that's good for us."

The Boilermakers' 25th victory gives Keady five seasons of at least 25 triumphs.

During this "three-peat," Purdue is 79-16, including 20-6 in Big Ten road games.

Despite having his jersey grabbed, center Brad Miller rebounds against Northwestern in Purdue's three-peat clinching win.

KEADY RULES

Miller Dominates to Give Legendary Boilermaker Coach Record Win No. 372

by Jeff Washburn

December 7, 1997 — LOUISVILLE, KY — The week from Hell had a Heavenly ending.

When the Purdue basketball team looked at its 1997-98 schedule, an eight-day stretch stood out like a neon beacon.

- North Carolina or UCLA on November 29 in Alaska.
- Kentucky on December 3 in Chicago.
- And Louisville on Saturday night in tradition-rich Freedom Hall.

Add Gene Keady's quest for school-record-setting victory No. 372 to this scenario, and it's no wonder there's been lots of tension among the sixth-ranked Boilermakers.

But even Keady was smiling and poking fun at himself after an 87-69 victory against Louisville in front of 19,976 fans, many of whom have watched Denny Crum's Cardinals win national championships in 1980 and '86.

Purdue (6-2) recovered from a brutal beginning — it made only 2 of 12 shots and turned the ball over nine times in the first 7:57 — to place an exclamation point after No. 372.

The Boilermakers spotted the Cardinals a 13-5 lead, then outscored their more than gracious hosts 36-11 during the opening half's final 11:44.

Keady had an extra skip in his step as he led his team to its locker room at halftime.

He had a 40-24 advantage, and Ward "Piggy" Lambert's 51-year-old record was 20 minutes from being broken.

The Boilermakers didn't let him down, breaking their modest two-game losing streak with an eye-opening 18-point victory.

Senior center Brad Miller had 27 points and 14 rebounds, and senior guard Chad Austin added 20 points, five rebounds, six assists and four steals.

Austin played without a protective mask for the first time since breaking his nose during a November 19 practice.

The Boilermakers also made 10 of 20 shots from 3-point range, pulling away from Louisville (2-3) with six treys in a 7:29 span midway through the second half.

There were lots of important numbers on this night for the Boilermakers, but none more important than 372.

It's in the books, and there's now a sense of accomplishment and ease among Keady's players, who were disappointed when they fell short against third-ranked North Carolina and again against seventh-ranked Kentucky.

Gene Keady is honored as the winningest coach in Purdue basketball history.

"Now, we all can say we were a part of the team on the night coach Keady broke the record," said Miller, who had 16 first-half points.

But when Purdue started so slowly, Miller wondered if he'd ever help Keady attain No. 372.

"We played really, really, really, really bad at the start," Miller said. "It wasn't hard to play much better than we played the first couple minutes of the game.

"Turning the ball over every time and going 2 of 12 shooting isn't Purdue basketball."

Fighting back and refusing to lose is.

A Miller free throw with 11:44 to go in the first half began an 11-0 Boilermaker run, and Keady urged his team on to even better things.

"We came out of the timeout at the 12-minute mark and just told ourselves that we were going to play better," the center said.

And they did.

"We wanted to get this one for coach Keady against North Carolina, but we just had to put the last two games behind us," said Jaraan Cornell, who broke out of a mini-slump with three key 3-pointers. "Finally, we started playing well and stayed in command."

That's what Keady liked.

"It was an unusual game for us, and I really don't know what changed it for us," Keady said of turning an 8-point deficit into a 16-point halftime lead. "I'm happy with the way we came back after being on the road — the way we've traveled."

Those early traveling calls against Purdue became sharp cuts to the basket, and missed shots began finding the bottom of the net.

"Coach got on us at one of the timeouts and just told us to get cut in," sophomore forward Brian Cardinal said. "We did. Everybody started doing their own little thing and playing their own role — hustling and doing all the little things to put us up by 16 at the half.

"Getting this victory here is special for Coach Keady, because Coach (Denny) Crum is a great coach, and it's always great to come into Louisville and come out with a victory. We wanted this for coach. He was awfully happy and proud."

So were his players.

Gene Keady shows the type of sideline demeanor that has become his trademark.

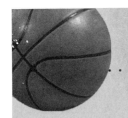

PURDUE AVENGES LOSS TO MICHIGAN STATE

Miller's 30 lift Boilermakers in Big Ten finale

by Jeff Washburn

March 2, 1998 — EAST LANSING, MI — If the men's Big Ten Tournament championship game is this good, conference officials will be patting themselves on the backs.

Eleventh-ranked Purdue and 10th-ranked Michigan State walked off the Breslin Center court late Sunday afternoon patting each other on the back, as well they should.

Showing why they were heavy preseason favorites to win the Big Ten championship, the Boilermakers got the game of his life from inconsistent center Brad Miller and rallied for a 99-96 overtime victory against the Big Ten Tournament's No. 1 seed.

Miller's 30 points and 12 rebounds helped Purdue (24-6, 12-4 in the Big Ten) deny Michigan State (20-6, 13-3) an outright league championship and handed the Spartans their first Breslin Center conference defeat this season. The Boilermakers' victory give Illinois a share of the crown.

This Purdue victory appeared improbable when Michigan State freshman forward Andre Hutson completed a three-point play with 17:34 remaining, extending the Spartans' lead to 57-45.

It was at approximately that point in the teams' December 30 meeting in Mackey Arena that Michigan State pulled away for a 74-57 victory.

But on this day Purdue displayed the intestinal fortitude for which Gene Keady-coached teams are famous.

They outscored MSU 15-3 in the next 5:35, during which Alan Eldridge and Tony Mafield combined for three 3-pointers.

It was tied at 60 with 12:19 remaining in regulation.

Michigan State countered with another mini-run to lead 80-75 at the 5:53 mark, but Purdue refused to go away.

Miller scored 13 points during regulation's final 8:15, including a basket with 18.4 seconds to go that gave the Boilermakers a 92-90 lead.

Could it end that way? Would it end that way? No way.

MSU's Jason Klein missed a jumper with four seconds on the clock, but Hutson's acrobatic rebound and subsequent tip back into play landed in the hands of teammate Morris Peterson, whose layup with 2.1 seconds to go forced overtime.

Keady shook his head, and a sellout crowd of 15,138 braced for a five-minute overtime.

Miller scored the extra session's first basket, but a Klein field goal with 45 seconds to play gave Michigan State a 96-95 advantage.

Again, Purdue went to Miller, but his short shot rimmed out, and teammate Mike Robinson grabbed one of 23 Boilermaker offensive rebounds and was fouled.

He calmly made two free throws with 30.7 seconds remaining, and Purdue led 97-96.

That set the stage for probable Big Ten MVP Mateen Cleaves, the gifted MSU point guard who wanted the ball in his hands, where it had been all day.

He drove the lane and launched a running jumper with four seconds to play. It bounced off the rim, and Robinson snatched the rebound, passing to Eldridge who was fouled at 0.8. The left-hander's free throws appeared to ice it.

But a game this good needed one final twist in its plot. Cleaves caught an inbounds pass 50 feet from the basket and let fly as the horn sounded.

The 3-point shot was on line, but somehow, it rimmed out, and Purdue proved that it can win a big game without injured starter Jaraan Cornell, whose badly-sprained left ankle isn't improving.

"I was proud of this game," said Miller, who played 41 minutes without a turnover. "Lately, it seems teams have been double- or triple-teaming me, and they weren't doing that today. I had to take advantage of that."

He did, and on those rare occasions when he missed, Robinson, Brian Cardinal or Gary McQuay were there to gather in the rebound.

Purdue's primary interior players combined for 74 points, 30 rebounds, seven assists and five blocks.

Cardinal finished with 19 points and four rebounds, Robinson added 17 points and nine boards and McQuay had eight points and five rebounds.

"I had a decent last home game against Minnesota, and I just wanted to finish strong," Miller said of his inspired play.

Miller claims the game's key was Purdue's rebounding — a 42-31 advantage. Michigan State had 17 more rebounds than Purdue in the first meeting and won by 17.

"We knew coming in that that would be the key," Miller said. "When we came back and made that run after halftime, rebounding was the reason."

The center hopes Purdue is re-energized for the Big Ten Tournament.

"We won the Minnesota game, but we could have won that game by a lot more," Miller said. "Now, I think the team has adjusted to life without Jaraan. Now, we have to count on him not playing."

Cardinal, who kept Purdue within striking distance with 15 first-half points, said Sunday's participants probably enjoyed this game more than the fans.

"That was a great game," Cardinal said. "You can't ask for anything more than that. We wanted to do this for ourselves, because we played terrible when Michigan State came to our place."

Purdue shot 52.2 percent from the field and won a game in which Michigan State scored more first-half points (49) than it had all season.

"Brad played great," Cardinal said when asked to analyze the victory. "We got the ball inside, and he was our go-to guy. Chad (Austin) wasn't shooting very well (2 of 11), and Brad is a great player who stepped up."

The Cardinal family had an additional reason to enjoy this victory. Brian's father Rod is Illinois' athletic trainer and will now receive an additional Big Ten championship ring — thanks in part to his son's play.

"I talked to my dad Friday, and he said he's not sure if he's ever seen more Illinois fans turn into Purdue fans," Cardinal said. "I wanted to go out there and get a victory for them, too, because I know they had a great season and wanted to get a Big Ten ring, too."

Keady said he also enjoyed this thriller — when it was over.

"That was a great college basketball game," Keady said. "I don't think you could ask for a harder-fought game. That's what intercollegiate sports are all about, trying to be at your best. It's too bad anybody had to lose this one, because it was a dandy."

PURDUE ROLLS IN FIRST ROUND

Balanced Attack Fatal to Overmatched Blue Hens

by Jeff Washburn

March 14, 1998 — CHICAGO, ILL — The Purdue basketball team's Sheraton Towers Hotel room TV sets have been tuned almost exclusively to CBS during the past two days.

They watched Richmond stun South Carolina. Then, they saw Western Michigan upset Clemson.

And when Bryce Drew and Valparaiso shocked Mississippi late Friday afternoon, the 11th-ranked Boilermakers had seen enough NCAA tournament drama.

There would be no upset — not even a challenge — from No. 15 seed Delaware on Friday night in the United Center.

Purdue scored the game's first 18 points, led 53-17 at halftime and coasted to a 95-56 Midwest Regional first-round victory against the Blue Hens. The Boilermakers will face Detroit on Sunday. Detroit held off St. John's 66-64.

The Boilermakers' 39-point margin is the school's most in NCAA tournament competition, erasing a 31-point, opening-round victory against Central Florida in 1994.

Playing their fifth game this season in the United Center, the Boilermakers (27-7) made 60.5 percent of their first-half field goal attempts in establishing the fourth-highest Midwest Regional victory margin ever.

Sophomore forward Mike Robinson's 19-point, nine-rebound performance led five Boilermakers in double figures.

"Our team sat back in the hotel and watched all the upsets," Robinson said. "We didn't want to be one of those teams to be upset. We talked about

Brad Miller helped Purdue keep its focus early as the Boilermakers blew out Delaware. Their 39-point margin of victory was a new school record.

Forward Michael Robinson dunks vs. the Blue Hens. He had 19 points to lead the Boilermakers.

coming out and being ready to play in the first five minutes."

Known throughout this season for digging itself into early double-digit deficits, Purdue was more than ready to play this completely out-manned opponent.

When Miller and Austin were freshmen, Wisconsin-Green Bay missed a last-second shot that would have handed Purdue a first-round defeat.

Ditto in 1996, when No. 16 seed Western Carolina had No. 1 seed Purdue praying in the final seconds. A 3-pointer rolled off the rim, salvaging a Boilermaker victory.

Last year, a Cardinal 3-pointer forced overtime against Rhode Island, and Purdue advanced into the second round.

Coach Gene Keady is accustomed to first-round nail-biters, so when the Boilermakers mauled Delaware, he almost didn't know how to react.

"If you've watched the scores the last couple of days, we were really leery of this game," Keady said. "I guess you might say it's the understatement of the year that they were focused."

With Cardinal at 100 percent after battling the flu during last weekend's Big Ten Tournament, and with Jaraan Cornell back in action for the first time since spraining his left ankle on February 10, Purdue hit on all cylinders.

"We shot the ball extremely well and were able to take their post feeds away," Keady said. "That was a big part of taking their offense out of its rhythm, and the kids did a great job in our fastbreak. It's very unusual for something like this to happen."

Delaware (20-10) got 17 points from forward Mike Pegues but was never close to being in this game.

Purdue needed less than five minutes to build its 18-0 lead and less than 10 to build a 29-9 advantage.

"When we got the 18-0 lead, we talked at the first timeout about keeping our heads in the game," Austin said. "We wanted to play good basketball for 40 minutes, and we did."

They all agreed the start was the key.

"This is the most focused we've been at the start of a game in a long time," Miller said. "Delaware just happened to be the team that we were playing tonight. We had our whole team back, and they got the first glimpse of it."

Austin said the Big Ten Tournament may have set the stage for this Purdue blowout.

"I think it helped us a lot, playing three games in three days," Austin said. "We played it here, so that helped us, too. Just getting that tournament experience helped a lot."

"FINALLY, WE'VE BEATEN OSU"

Pure Joy For Holmes as Jinx Ends

by Jim D. Stafford

January 4, 1991 — Joy Holmes and Rhonda Mateen wanted Purdue's first victory against Ohio State to be memorable.

Thursday's 105-45 decision over the Buckeyes in the Big Ten Conference opener for both schools before a crowd of 3,889 at Mackey Arena likely will be one they won't soon forget. Consider:

• The third-ranked Boilermakers improved to 10-0, the best start in the program's history, and also ended Ohio State's string of 20 consecutive victories since the series began.

• The 60-point margin of victory was Purdue's largest ever and also was Ohio State's worst loss in its history.

• Purdue shot better than 50 percent (38 of 70) for the seventh consecutive game and scored more than 100 points for the fourth time this season.

• Holmes registered six steals to become Purdue's all-time leader with 261.

"I didn't even realize I was close to the career record in steals," said Holmes, who finished with 15 points. "That is great, and this win...I'm speechless. It's a great win. I've been here all these years and finally, we've beaten Ohio State.

"It's something I've always wanted to do and hopefully we can do the same thing when we go play them again."

The victory was especially sweet for Holmes and Mateen, who led the Boilermakers with 24 points. Both are from Ohio, Holmes from Mansfield and Mateen from Akron. The players couldn't help but show their emotion after the game.

Joy Holmes helped Purdue obliterate Ohio State by 60, the most decisive win ever for the Boilermakers. Holmes scored 15 points in the triumph.

Joy Holmes is the second leading scorer in Purdue history with 1,747 points.

"I only have one thing to say," Mateen said. "It was so much fun to beat them."

Mateen and Donna Gill hit jumpers followed by a 3-pointer from MaChelle Joseph, who finished with 22 points, eight rebounds and nine assists, to put Purdue up 7-0. After the Buckeyes scored, Mateen had a layup and Joseph added a basket to increase the margin to 11-2.

"The first six or eight minutes I think the tempo of the game was in our favor," OSU coach Nancy Darsch said. "But once Purdue got some steals, some layups and some offensive rebounds, it was like a runaway train. It started with turnovers and then they were able to turn those into transition baskets."

Stacy Kraiza came off the bench and hit a jumper to ignite a 21-0 Purdue run which held Ohio State scoreless for more than six minutes and increased the lead to 38-10.

"Early on we were experimenting with two or three defenses, trying to decide which one would cause them the most problems," Purdue coach Lin Dunn said. "Once we went with our half-court traps and our matchup defenses, I think that's when we really took control of the game. That's when we spurted ahead. We created some problems for them with our pressure and I think we were able to dictate the tempo throughout the game."

That pressure forced Ohio State into committing a season-high 32 turnovers and resulted in numerous transition baskets for Purdue.

"Any time you're turning the ball over at the rate that they were turning it over, and we're getting steals and going in and scoring layups, that's a major factor."

The Boilermakers ended the first half with a 15-4 spurt to pad their lead to 55-18. Tina Eddie came off the bench to score five of her career-high 11 points during that run. The sophomore forward also finished with six rebounds. Staci Carney also came off the bench to notch a career-high 15 points. And for the third consecutive time, the sophomore guard had the basket to put Purdue over 100 points.

"We were outmatched physically," Darsch said. "I fully expected Purdue to come out and come at us and they did. Obviously, it was a game that Purdue dominated and had an opportunity to show their strengths and personnel and why they are ranked third in the country."

Darsch limited the playing time of three starters, including Averrill Roberts, the team's leading scorer (18.0) for not complying with team rules.

All of Purdue's players played at least 10 minutes with the exception of senior forward Erika Brooks, who has two hyper-extended fingers.

The Boilermakers travel to Iowa City, Iowa, to play seventh-ranked Auburn (10-2) in Saturday's inaugural Big Ten/Southeastern Conference Challenge. Both games are to be nationally televised by CBS (Ch. 29 in Indianapolis) at 1:30 p.m. The host Hawkeyes play Georgia in the second game.

NEXT STOP: RICHMOND

Purdue Rolls into Final Four

by Mike Carmin

March 28, 1994 — Palo Alto, Cal — It was not until six seconds remained that Jennifer Jacoby released her emotions.

Her scream of enjoyment was heard throughout Maples Pavilion late Saturday night because the sellout crowd of 7,500 was stunned into silence.

They had just seen Purdue dismantle host Stanford 82-65 to capture the West Regional championship of the NCAA women's basketball tournament.

The victory places the eighth-ranked Boilermakers into the Final Four for the first time. Eighth-ranked Purdue (29-4) plays fourth-ranked North Carolina (31-2) at 2:30 Saturday afternoon at Richmond, VA.

Stacey Lovelace realized the Boilermakers were heading to the Final Four earlier than Jacoby. "With about 1:30 left, I turned to (assistant coach) MaChelle (Joseph) and said, 'We are going to the Final Four,'" she recalled.

At that point, Purdue held a 72-60 lead and was hot from the foul line. The Boilermakers connected on 18 of 20 in the final 2:28 to seal the victory. They also hit 16 straight to close the game.

It was the worst home loss for 11th-ranked Stanford (25-6) in nine years.

"We hit our free throws," said Jacoby, who made 10 of 12, including 8 in the last 2:28. "They started fouling with about three minutes to go and we knew if we were going to win it, we would have to hit our free throws."

Jacoby led the top-seeded Boilermakers with 20 points, hitting all four shots from the field, including two 3-pointers. Leslie Johnson, who was named the regional's most outstanding player, added 14 points.

Lovelace contributed 12 points and seven rebounds while Tonya Kirk had 11 points and four steals for the Boilermakers, winners of 17 of their last 18 games.

Purdue never trailed after taking a 11-10 lead with 14:34 left in the first half on Cindy Lamping's short jumper.

Johnson picked up her second personal foul two minutes later. But the Boilermakers did not panic and went right to their bench.

Sparked by the play of Shannon Lindsey and Danielle McCulley, Purdue went on a 15-6 run to grab a 28-17 advantage with 5:35 left in the half.

Lindsey and McCulley combined for four points and eight rebounds during the first 20 minutes. The pair helped defend Anita Kaplan and Rachel Hemmer, Stanford's top post players.

"When you get right down to it, we had four post players and they had two," Purdue coach Lin Dunn said. "We were able to get them in foul trouble and create some problems for their inside game."

Although Hemmer finished with 17 points and Kaplan had 12, they struggled all night to shoot without getting contact.

"Purdue played well defensively," Kaplan said. "They executed what they wanted to do. Purdue had a lot of people coming off the bench and they stepped up."

The second-seeded Cardinal, who had their 14-game winning streak snapped, used a 9-0 run early in the second half to tie the game at 36 with 14:33 to play.

But on Purdue's next possession, Kirk delivered a 3-pointer to quiet the crowd which had reached a frenzied level.

"I wanted to calm the crowd down and to let our team know we were still in it and not to get down," Kirk said.

Said Jacoby: "If T.K. is open she is going to shoot. We needed that because they were starting to collapse down on Leslie and our post players."

Dunn said as long as the Boilermakers maintained their lead, the crowd would not be a big factor.

"We told the kids, the crowd was going to go through spurts," she said. "There were going to be times when the crowd is just going to go crazy and if we would just relax and keep our composure, then they would calm down."

The Cardinal pulled to within 56-54 on Hemmer's layup, but Purdue used a 9-2 run to increase its lead to 10 with 2:28 to play.

Stanford coach Tara VanDerveer said Purdue's defense caused the Cardinal problems all night.

They finished shooting 37 percent from the field, including 29 percent in the first half, and committed 18 turnovers — 11 more than their tournament average.

What impressed VanDerveer was the Boilermakers' composure throughout the game.

"There were a couple of spurts where we didn't distract them," she said. "With their size, we were not getting into the passing lanes and getting deflections. One of our team goals is to get 20 deflections a game, and we only had four at half-time. We were not able to disrupt them."

Stanford's quickness forced Dunn to shift from her 1-3-1 halfcourt trapping defense. Instead, the Boilermakers played a matchup zone most of the game.

"They were getting the ball down the floor awfully fast," Dunn said. "It was hard to get back and get the trap set as much as we usually do."

To beat Stanford on its home floor is quite a feat. The Cardinal had lost there only three times in eight seasons and had won all 10 of their NCAA games at home prior to Saturday.

Dunn was not ready to discuss North Carolina immediately after the game.

"I'm just going to cherish this moment with this team and be excited about what we accomplished," Dunn said. "It's just a wonderful feeling."

POINT GUARD'S PLAY HAS CALMING INFLUENCE

by Mike Carmin

March 28, 1994 — Shannon Lindsey heard all week that it was time for Jennifer Jacoby to have a good game.

Lindsey received her information from a reliable source — Jacoby.

The pair were roommates during the week as the Purdue women's basketball team competed for the West Regional championship.

The Boilermakers took the title with an 82-65 victory against Stanford late Saturday night to advance to their First Final Four at Richmond, Virginia.

When Jacoby hit her first shot — a 3-pointer — it put the Boilermakers at ease. It also quieted the boisterous crowd of 7,500 that assembled at Maples Pavilion to root on the Cardinal.

The junior point guard finished with a team-high 20 points and was 4 of 4 from the field. Jacoby hit both of her 3-pointers and was 10 of 12 from the free throw line, including 8 of 10 in the final 2:28.

"Jennifer Jacoby did a great job for them, in terms of their scoring and their passing," Cardinal coach Tara VanDerveer said. "She is an excellent shooter and a floor leader."

For the third time this season, Jacoby played 40 minutes and did not appear tired. It was her second-best offensive performance of the season after her 23 points at Minnesota.

Jacoby is now averaging 10.3 points and shooting 63 percent from the field in Purdue's four tournament games.

Saturday, she was asked to handle Stanford's press and its changing halfcourt defenses.

"She was the coach on the floor," Purdue coach Lin Dunn said. "Jennifer was the catalyst as far as her setting an example with her poise and her composure.

"When she stepped up and hit her free throws, that was a real calming factor for the rest of our team. She had a tremendous game."

Twice during Saturday's game, Jacoby gave the Boilermakers some breathing room:

- Her 19-foot jumper gave Purdue a 47-44 lead with 9:15 to play.

- Her driving layup with 4:30 left started a 9-2 run, which led to a 65-55 advantage.

"That is something we have been working on all year," Lovelace said of Jacoby's performance. "When the other team gets all excited, we just have to calm down and play our game. Jennifer did that very well."

Jacoby also settled the Boilermakers down after three straight turnovers helped the Cardinal during a 9-0 run that tied the game at 36.

"I was mad at myself because two of those were my turnovers," Jacoby said. "I knew if I turned the ball over, everyone else would turn to ball over. Coach called me over and said I would have to calm down."

UNBELIEVABLE

Purdue Women
Big Ten Champs

by Jim Lefko

February 24, 1997 — CHAMPAIGN, ILL. — An amazing story played itself out here Sunday. And by the time the tale was finished, a most unlikely group of players earned the right to be called champions.

The Purdue women's basketball team found a way to silence the largest crowd in Big Ten history — 16,050 — by playing a near-perfect second half to whip Illinois 80-75.

Technically, the Boilermakers, Fighting Illini and Michigan State tied for the league title at 12-4.

But with a 2-0 record against Illinois and a split with MSU, Purdue wins the tiebreaker and gets the No. 1 seed in the postseason conference tournament.

Even if Purdue wins the national championship, the scene won't be any more joyous than what transpired after the final buzzer Sunday.

First the players gathered together on the court and did a group jump that depicted the pure joy of the moment.

Then came a tribute to head coach Nell Fortner. She endured a 20-yard ride on her players' shoulders. The affection the athletes feel toward their coach was evident, even if Fortner was sheepish about the touching gesture.

Next came the hugs. Players hugged players. Coaches hugged players. Coaches hugged coaches. Fans, several hundred of whom made the trip from the Greater Lafayette area, hugged anyone whose arms looked welcoming. One player even found a jaded sportswriter to squeeze.

It was pure happiness, the kind that comes from the realization that a seemingly impossible goal had been met.

"Who says you can't win it the first year?" rookie coach Fortner said, marveling at what her players produced. "I'm just overwhelmed."

She wasn't alone.

"All we wanted was the opportunity. We took advantage of it," said Corissa Yasen, the player responsible for the unpardonable sin of hugging a journalist. "We didn't give up. We're fighters. We just wouldn't break."

If anyone personifies the rags to riches story of this team, it's Yasen. A year ago, track was her life. The greatest female athlete in Purdue's history had never played a minute of college basketball.

Then came the purge. When Lin Dunn exited, so did most of the team.

It fell on Fortner to pick up the pieces. Initially, it looked like the season would be a foundation builder for next year when a strong freshman class arrives.

Walk-on Corissa Yasen switched from track, where she enjoyed an All-American career, to basketball, where she helped first-year coach Nell Fortner and the Boilermakers engineer a shocking Big Ten title.

With only three players back from 1996 — Stephanie White, Ukari Figgs and Jannon Roland — Yasen was enticed to come out and play. She quickly became a starter. So did freshman Mackenzie Curless.

Two other first-year players, Michelle Duhart and Tiffany Young, became the bench. All of it.

And that's what Fortner had to work with, in a league as potent as the Big Ten.

But an amazing thing happened. This unusual conglomeration of talent meshed.

Roland turned in a Player of the Year season, capped by her 32-point explosion Sunday.

White became the player she used to be at Seeger.

Figgs developed into a long-distance bomber, with her 16-point effort Sunday marked by a stunning 4 of 5 showing from 3-point land.

With Duhart playing the game of her life in place of foul-plagued Curless, it added up to a totally unexpected triumph.

"This overrides everything," said Roland, the only Boiler who was around the last time Purdue won a league title. "My freshman year it was really special after everyone picked us to finish fifth. But this is better because we have a team of inexperienced players."

They aren't inexperienced anymore. Not after what they engineered Sunday.

It's almost a shame Purdue has to play more games. Because unless they win it all, the feeling the team shared in such a hostile setting Sunday was one that may never be repeated.

Unexpected success tends to be the most delicious to savor.

BIG TEN CHAMPIONS

Purdue Defies Experts, Defeats Illinois 80-75

by Mike Carmin

February 24, 1997 — Nell Fortner bent down toward the end of the Purdue bench and began soaking in the excitement of a championship.

Ukari Figgs and Stephanie White embraced, while Jannon Roland flashed a big smile.

A Big Ten Conference championship was starting to settle into the Boilermakers' hearts and minds. It is a feeling that each member of this surprising team will savor for a long time.

Sunday's 80-75 victory over 17th-ranked Illinois at Assembly Hall gave Purdue a piece of the conference championship — an unexpected title at that. Picked eighth in the preseason coaches poll, the Boilermakers beat the odds and came out on top.

Purdue shares the championship with the Fighting Illini and Michigan State with a 12-4 record in league play.

The Boilermakers thanked their first-year coach by hoisting her up on their shoulders. They picked up Fortner, dressed in her superstitious road outfit — black turtle neck and gray pants — and carried the 37-year-old over to a large group of Purdue supporters.

Most of the 16,050 — a Big Ten record — booed when Fortner was being paraded around, but none of the Boilermakers seemed to mind.

In turn, Fortner thanked her team for an unbelievable season to this point.

"These kids worked very hard and have earned everything," said Fortner, who started to enjoy the moment with five seconds on the clock.

It was an emotion that ran rampant through each player.

"This is a great feeling," said walk-on Corissa Yasen, who wasn't even thinking about playing basketball at this time last year.

Yasen was one hero in this title-clinching game. There were several others.

Jannon Roland, the leading candidate for conference player of the year, carried the Boilermakers with her determination, leadership and all-around play. The senior scored 20 second-half points and finished with 32 along with 10 rebounds.

"We fed off Jannon," White said. "She's been playing great all year. She's scored and rebounded all year. If she wasn't having a good night on offense, she played great defense. She is the one that has held us together."

Figg's shooting in the first half gave Purdue a cushion to work with. The sophomore point guard hit three 3-pointers and gave the Boilermakers a six-point lead before the Illini took a 35-34 halftime advantage and part of the momentum.

The late spurt didn't bother Fortner's team.

"We played pretty loose in the second half," Figgs said. "We knew we had 20 minutes left, and we were going to leave everything out on the floor."

The unrecognized player of the game was Michelle Duhart. Not only was the freshman brilliant on defense, but she provided some unexpected offense. Two free throws by Duhart with less than five minutes to play kept Purdue's lead comfortable.

Yasen's offensive output in the second half prevented the Illini from focusing their attention on Roland. Yasen had 11 of her 13 points in the final 20 minutes.

Yasen began to assert herself after Illinois had obtained its biggest lead, 57-50, midway through the second half.

The senior scored seven points during a 13-2 run that gave the Boilermakers a lead they wouldn't relinquish at 63-59 with 7:18 to play.

From that point, Purdue's excellent free throw shooting took over. The Boilermakers hit 12 of their last 13 free throws to keep the Illini from winning the championship outright.

Although Ashley Berggren paced Illinois with 25 points, no other starter reached double figures for coach Theresa Grentz's team.

"They played a great game," Grentz said of Purdue. "Jannon Roland strapped them on her back and carried them. She is a terrific player that's had a terrific year."

And that year continues to get better.

Sunday's victory places the Boilermakers as the top seed in the upcoming Big Ten postseason tournament. It also should drum up more national attention, a place in the top 25 and a berth in the NCAA Tournament.

"It is nice to win," said Roland, who collected her third conference championship in four years. "This is great. You can't ask for more than that."

NBA FIRST ROUNDERS

By Jeff Washburn

A friendly athletic department janitor took one look at the freshman from Gary, Indiana, and a nickname known to all who follow Purdue basketball was created.

"Big Dog."

Glenn Robinson, a quiet, street-smart kid whose passion for basketball and fierce competitive spirit are at the heart of his success, is one of two former Boilermakers selected first in a National Basketball Association draft.

"Big Dog" Robinson's 10-year, $68-million contract—signed in 1994 with the Milwaukee Bucks—places him at the top of the list of Purdue players selected in a draft's first round.

While he played only two seasons at Purdue, the 6-foot-8 forward's numbers are unforgettable.

After failing to qualify academically for freshman season eligibility, Robinson averaged 24.1 points and 9.2 rebounds during the 1992-93 season.

"Big Dog" was even better in 1993-94, when he earned the John Wooden Award, given annually to college basketball's finest player. Robinson averaged 30.3 points and 10.1 rebounds as a Purdue junior, leading Gene Keady's team to an NCAA Tournament Elite Eight berth.

A month later, Robinson announced he would forego his senior year, making himself eligible for the NBA draft.

"I knew he was special when I saw him at the Purdue Basketball Camp when he was just a kid," said Frank Kendrick, a Boilermaker assistant coach who was a member of Golden State's 1975 NBA championship team.

A unique blend of inside and outside skills, Robinson easily stepped beyond the arc for a 3-point attempt on one possession and then posted up on the next.

Robinson smoothly made the transition from collegian to pro, averaging 21.9 points in his rookie season (1994-95) in Milwaukee. Only Kareem Abdul-Jabbar scored more points as a Bucks' rookie.

In 1997-98, "Big Dog" appeared in 65 games, averaging 41 minutes and a career-best 23.4 points. He shot 47 percent from the floor and averaged 5.5 rebounds. During his four-year NBA career, Robinson has started 293 of 298 games.

Joe Barry Carroll, a 7-foot center who led Purdue to its most recent Final Four appearance in 1980, also was a No. 1 pick in the NBA draft.

The Golden State Warriors used the No. 1 selection in the 1980 draft to take the articulate big man who grew up in Denver.

Carroll is Purdue's No. 2 career scorer with 2,175 points, becoming a dominant point producer after his sophomore season.

He averaged 22.8 points during Purdue's 1978-79 season, when the Boilermakers were second at the National Invitation Tournament. Carroll averaged 22.3 points as a senior, when Lee Rose's team made only the second Final Four appearance in school history.

Joe Barry Carroll

nis balls into used coffee cans remains Purdue's all-time scoring leader with 2,323 points.

Mount averaged 33.3 points a game in 1968-69, when the Boilermakers advanced to the Final Four in Louisville, falling to Abdul-Jabbar and UCLA in the NCAA Tournament championship game.

His fall-away jumper from the right corner at the final horn gave coach George King's team a two-point victory against Marquette in the regional final.

Coming out of high school, Indiana's 1966 Mr. Basketball verbally committed to Miami (Florida), but then had a change of heart when adoring Lebanon fans—Mount's hometown is 35 miles from the Purdue campus—pleaded for him to stay close to his roots.

Rick Mount

Carroll developed a soft shooting touch and is the only Boilermaker ever to amass more than 1,000 rebounds. He finished with 1,148.

"We knew Joe was the kind of player who had the skills to take a team to the Final Four," Rose said. "We were confident going into that season that if we utilized his skills, we would have an opportunity to win every game."

UCLA defeated Purdue in the Final Four semifinals, and the Boilermakers secured third place with a consolation game victory against Iowa.

Another former Boilermaker who literally shot his team into the NCAA Tournament's Final Four was Rick "The Rocket" Mount, who the Indiana Pacers selected in the first round of the American Basketball Association's 1970 draft.

The 6-4 guard from Lebanon who developed an uncanny perimeter jump shot by launching ten-

"Nobody had range like Rick," said former Purdue assistant coach Bob King, who recruited "The Rocket." "Rick made it look so easy."

Although Purdue failed to qualify for the NCAA Tournament in Mount's senior season in 1969-70, he averaged a career-best 35.4 points, including a school-record 61 in a loss to Iowa in Mackey Arena.

With the help of technology, an imaginary 3-point line was superimposed on the game film from the Iowa contest, and it was determined that Mount would have had 78 points—including 17 3-pointers—had the rule been in effect then.

Herman Gilliam, a slashing, athletic forward from Winston-Salem, North Carolina, played in Mount's shadow but managed to make enough of an impression to be selected in the first round of the 1969 NBA draft by the Cincinnati Royals.

Gilliam averaged 16.4 points as a Purdue sophomore, but when Mount joined the team for the '67-68 season, Gilliam's averaged dipped to 15.7. He also averaged 15.7 in 1968-69, when the Boilermakers came within the loss to UCLA of winning the national championship.

He went on to play several NBA seasons, enjoying success with the Atlanta Hawks.

"Herman could do it all," King said. "He could run, shoot, rebound, pass and play defense. A lot of people recall that Mount and Billy Keller were the dominant players of the Final Four team, but we wouldn't have gone as far as we did without Herman."

While Dave Schellhase-led Purdue teams were stuck in an era when Michigan and Ohio State dominated the Big Ten Conference, the 6-foot-6 forward from Evansville was a scoring machine who was selected in the first round of the 1966 NBA draft by the Chicago Bulls.

Seven times Schellhase scored at least 40 points in a Purdue game, including 57 in a 1966 loss at Michigan. That was the school's single-game record for four years—until Mount scored 61 against Iowa.

Like Robinson, Schellhase was a combination inside-outside player. He could use his wide hips and strength to post up a small forward, or he could step outside away from a larger defender and hit a perimeter jumper.

Schellhase averaged 32.5 points a game as a Purdue senior.

Herman Gilliam

One of the most improved players in Boilermaker history was shooting guard Keith Edmonson, who played two seasons for Rose and two for Keady.

Edmonson's improvement caught the attention of the Atlanta Hawks, who used their 1982 first-round pick—the 10th overall—to select the San Antonio native.

He averaged only 1.3 points as a Purdue freshman, but in 1981-82 Edmonson averaged 21.2 points for Keady, shooting 54.5 percent from the floor and 78.4 percent from the free throw line.

By comparison, Edmonson was a 38.8 percent field goal shooter as a freshman and a 53.8 free throw shooter.

In 1983, Purdue had another player—center/forward Russell Cross—selected in the first round. Golden State used its first-round pick—the sixth overall—to grab the 6-9 Cross, whose professional career was hampered by injuries and weight problems.

Glenn Robinson left an indelible mark on Purdue basketball.

In 1970-71, Franklin, George Faerber and Bob Ford formed a burly Boilermaker front line affectionately nicknamed "F-Troop."

Franklin had a soft shooting touch and was a powerful rebounder, but academics were not a priority, and he left school suddenly, deciding to try his hand at pro ball rather than face the difficult task of remaining academically eligible for another season.

He was somewhat successful for a year with the Squires but eventually was cut.

In 1974, Paul Hoffman and Eddie Ehlers were first-round picks by Baltimore and Boston respectively.

Purdue's basketball program can claim one other first-round draft choice, but this trivia question is a tricky one.

Bob Griese, a splendid high school basketball player in Evansville, was the Boilermakers' starting point guard for part of the 1964 season, and was an accurate shooter when used as a scoring option.

But Griese also was the Purdue football team's celebrated quarterback, and he decided after his sophomore season that it was just too much to try to play football and basketball—and go to school.

Griese led the 1966 football Boilermakers to a 9-2 record, including a 14-13 Rose Bowl victory against Southern California in Purdue's only trip to Pasadena.

In 1967, the Miami Dolphins used their first-round NFL draft pick to select Griese, who would lead them to back-to-back Super Bowl victories in 1972 and '73.

"I always loved basketball, but it was impossible to do justice to both sports," Griese said.

He was inducted into the Pro Football Hall of Fame and now provides color analysis of college football games for ABC.

Cross, whose family needed money, averaged 17.7 points as a Boilermaker senior and broke Keady's heart by announcing he would not return for his senior season.

"I've always thought Russell could have benefitted from one more year of college basketball," Keady said.

Another former Boilermaker who left school early for professional basketball was free-spirited 6-7 center William Franklin, who was picked in the 1971 ABA draft's first round by the Virginia Squires.

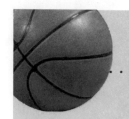

JOHN WOODEN, PURDUE LEGEND

by Jeff Washburn

John Wooden chuckles as he considers the striking contrasts in a wonderful life that began on October 14, 1910.

College basketball's most successful coach is known as "The Wizard of Westwood"— a wealthy, trendy section of Los Angeles in which UCLA's campus is nestled.

Glitter. Tinsel. New wave. Big bucks.

That's where Wooden carved a collegiate coaching dynasty that almost certainly will never be equaled.

From 1964 through 1975, Wooden's Bruins won 10 of 12 NCAA Tournaments. From the 1966-67 season through '72-'73, the Bruins won an astounding 205 of 210 games.

Kareem Abdul-Jabbar, Bill Walton, Gail Goodrich, Sidney Wicks, Curtis Rowe, Keith Wilkes, Dave Meyers and Marques Johnson listened to the former high school English teacher's every word— and won.

But Wooden has often wondered what might have happened had his father, Hugh, not lost the family's small farm in tiny Centerton, Indiana, in 1916, when "The Wizard" was 6.

"My dad was always interested in sports, but when it came to the farm, it was chores first," Wooden said.

With wife Roxie and three young sons to house and feed, Hugh Wooden needed work, and he needed it quickly.

It was eight miles south on Indiana 37 to Martinsville, where artesian wells were plentiful. In and around World War I, Martinsville was known for its sanitariums—resorts where the wealthy traveled to rest and regain their health by "taking the artesian waters."

Hugh Wooden was a strong, muscular man whose hands were perfect for a job as the masseur at Martinsville's most popular sanitarium.

The Wooden family settled in Martinsville, where John's prolific basketball skills blossomed.

HIGH SCHOOL STAR

He led the Artesians to Indiana's 1927 state championship and to second-place state tournament finishes in 1926 and '28.

Wooden's high school academic proficiency was every bit as impressive as his basketball achievements. While excelling in humanities courses—especially English— Wooden was determined to study civil engineering.

While fatherly Everett Dean had built a highly successful Indiana University basketball program in Bloomington just a few miles south of Wooden's Martinsville home, "The Wizard" selected Purdue, where Ward "Piggy" Lambert was the scholarly coach.

"I wanted to study civil engineering, and everyone knows that Purdue is among the finest engineering schools in the nation," Wooden said. "Today, people think I selected Purdue because I wanted to play for Mr. Lambert.

"They say that because that's the way many basketball players today make their college choice. When I was a student, we selected an area of study and matched it with a university."

Certainly, it would have been easier for the Wooden family to follow John's playing career had he attended Indiana.

But Wooden's hunger to study civil engineering would be best satisfied at Purdue.

There were no athletic scholarships in the late 1920s and early '30s, and Wooden's family was unable to provide much more than a few dollars for their basketball-playing son's college education.

Wooden paid for his meals by serving as a Beta fraternity house bus boy, and he paid for tuition and housing by taping ankles for the football team, painting Ross-Ade Stadium and selling game programs for football games.

FRESHMEN INELIGIBLE

While Wooden certainly would have earned a starting berth for Purdue's 1928-29 season, NCAA rules prohibited freshmen from playing varsity basketball.

So, Wooden had to be content scrimmaging with the freshmen, watching Charles "Stretch" Murphy lead Lambert's team to a 13-4 record.

In retrospect, Wooden claims the rule banning freshmen from varsity competition probably was a good one in his case.

"I was a strong student, but my academic advisors placed me in an upper-level physics class, and I was struggling," Wooden said. "I went to Coach Lambert, and he tutored me. People think of Mr. Lambert as a great coach, but many don't know that he was quite the scholar at Wabash."

Those who loved Purdue basketball anxiously awaited the beginning of the 1929-30 season—when "Mr. Inside" (Murphy) and "Mr. Outside" (Wooden) finally would play in the same starting lineup.

It was obvious during early-season practices that Lambert had something quite special in Wooden and Murphy. Wooden handled the ball, scored, played tenacious defense and fed Murphy.

The 6-foot-7 Murphy controlled almost every "center jump" and triggered Lambert's vaunted fastbreak by rebounding every missed shot.

Purdue doubled the score—38-19—on Washington, Missouri, in the first Wooden-Murphy Show.

Coach John Wooden in 1993.

Predictions of an undefeated season dominated conversations throughout the Greater Lafayette area.

Then, however, a mini-disaster struck.

Wooden and a fraternity brother decided to take the street car from the West Lafayette levee into Lafayette the day before the season's second game—a trip to Indianapolis to face Butler.

"It was snowing quite heavily, and as my friend and I attempted to jump onto the street car, he dropped something, and I bent down to pick it up off the street," Wooden recalled. "A car slid in the snow and struck the back of my leg. A rod from the car penetrated my leg."

Wooden was hospitalized, missed the trip to Butler, and Purdue lost, 36-29.

The day after the loss at Butler, Lambert visited Wooden in the hospital.

"He paced the floor," Wooden said. "He told me, 'Without you, everything was out of sync. Murphy thought he was a forward.'"

Wooden missed the next game—a 43-22 victory against Vanderbilt—but was determined to return for a showdown with talented Montana State in West Lafayette.

"I thought I could go on the leg, but within a few minutes, I realized that I wasn't ready to come back," Wooden said.

Montana State defeated the Boilermakers, 38-35, and Purdue's "Dream Team" was 2-2.

Wooden was close to 100 percent for the season's fifth game, and Purdue didn't lose again, finishing 13-2.

"I certainly don't want people to misinterpret this, but I've often been told that our 1929-30 team would have gone undefeated had I not injured my leg in December," Wooden said.

TEMPTING OFFER

After the splendid guard's sophomore season, a prominent Lafayette physician and an avid basketball fan approached Lambert and offered to pick up the tab for the remainder of Wooden's time at Purdue—tuition, room, board and books.

The doctor also offered to give Wooden several season tickets to sell with the understanding that the player keep the money he received from the sales.

Wooden weighed the offer for several days but opted to continue to go his own way—much to Lambert's approval.

Murphy's collegiate eligibility expired at season's end, and the 1930-31 Boilermakers faced a year of transition. They were only 6-4 through 10 games, losing a pair of frustrating two-point decisions.

But with strong late-season play from Wooden, Purdue was 6-1 in its last seven games, closing with a five-game winning streak and a 12-5 record.

Wooden's senior season—1931-32—is one he never will forget. The nucleus from the 1930-31

team returned, and while the Boilermakers lacked a dominant big man, their fastbreak and tenacious defense wore down almost every opponent.

With the exception of a 28-21 loss at Illinois, Purdue was perfect, finishing 17-1 and winning the Big Ten Conference championship. In Wooden's final three collegiate games, the Boilermakers registered 15-, 14- and 35-point victories.

Wooden earned a third consecutive All-American award, was selected college basketball's Player of the Year, broke the Big Ten scoring record and was awarded the Big Ten Medal for proficiency in scholarship and athletics.

"I will never forget the banquet after my senior season," Wooden said. "Coach Lambert talked briefly about my scoring record, but he went on and on about how I was the best-conditioned athlete he'd ever coached and that I was a splendid defender. That was wonderful."

Soon after graduation in 1932, Wooden married long-time sweeheart Nell, with whom he lived 53 years until her death in 1985.

The Woodens moved to Dayton, Kentucky, where Wooden accepted a high school teaching and coaching position. Two years later, he returned to Indiana, accepting the varsity basketball coaching position at South Bend Central High School, where he also taught English.

In 11 seasons, Wooden's high school basketball teams compiled a 218-42 record—an 83.8 winning percentage.

From 1943-46, Wooden served as a lieutenant in the United States Navy. Upon his discharge, Wooden accepted a job at Indiana State University, serving for two years as the Sycamores' athletic director, basketball coach and baseball coach.

UCLA BECKONS

After the 1947-48 season, UCLA officials decided it was time for a change in their basketball program and asked Wooden to come to sprawling Los Angeles, where movie stars and sunshine were plentiful.

Wooden accepted this new challenge, and in his first season in Westwood, Calif., guided a team that had posted a 12-13 record the year before to a 22-7 mark.

When Wooden traveled to Kansas City for the 1949 NCAA Tournament, he had a meeting with Purdue athletic director Guy "Red" Mackey.

The meeting almost changed the course of college basketball history.

Purdue's 1948-49 team had experienced a strange season for coach Mel Taube, who had replaced the ailing Lambert midway through the 1945-46 season.

Taube's 1948-49 team finished 13-9 but had three three-game losing streaks, including one to end the season.

Mackey made it clear to Wooden that Taube's days at Purdue probably were numbered and he wanted "The Wizard" to come home to West Lafayette.

"Mackey wanted to let Taube coach the 1949-50 team and then replace him with me—regardless of how well that Purdue team did," Wooden said. "I didn't like that method of doing business, and I told Mackey that. I decided that I would remain at UCLA. Did I want the Purdue job? Most definitely, but not under those conditions."

Taube's 1949-50 Purdue team was 9-13, and on March 27, 1950, Taube resigned under pressure. He was replaced, ironically, by Ray Eddy, a former Wooden teammate at Purdue.

While Eddy enjoyed some success, Wooden's career skyrocketed at UCLA. His teams consistently won 20 or more games, and in 1964, he guided the Bruins to a perfect 30-0 record and the first of his 10 NCAA Tournament championships.

Wooden brought his 1968 NCAA champions to West Lafayette for Mackey Arena's dedication game, which the Bruins won 73-71 on a last-second shot, ruining the splendid debut of Boilermaker all-time leading scorer Rick Mount.

"The Wizard" retired after his 1975 team won the NCAA championship. He finished 27 seasons in Westwood with a record of 620-147—80.8 percent.

He has remained active in basketball for the past 23 years, often lecturing about his "Pyramid of Success"—a 15-part formula for building championships—whether in sports, business, education or life.

"People still ask me about the Pyramid, and I find it interesting that several portions of it come directly from Mr. Lambert," Wooden said. "He was especially fond of conditioning and team spirit, and I think anyone must have those attributes to reach their potential."

The brilliant man from humble beginnings in Centerton, Indiana, reached his potential with a relentless pursuit of excellence and a logical, gentle and fair method of dealing with others.

Competitive greatness, poise and confidence are the top three blocks of Wooden's Pyramid.

"The Wizard" continues to attain them all.

WARD "PIGGY" LAMBERT, COACH/TEACHER EXTRAORDINAIRE

By Jeff Washburn

Ward "Piggy" Lambert probably was destined to pursue a career in entertainment.

The legendary Purdue basketball coach—whose school-record 371 victories lasted more than 51 years until Gene Keady broke it on December 6, 1997 at Louisville—was the son of Henry Clay Lambert, the advance booking agent for Ringling Brothers Circus.

Theatrical, antimated and charismatic, Lambert's fondness for uptempo basketball entertained fans while removing an opponent from its comfort zone.

While most collegiate teams from 1916 through 1946 featured a slower, more structured offensive set, Lambert's Purdue teams ran and ran and ran. Then, they ran some more.

From 1921-1940, the Boilermakers won 11 Big Ten Conference championships. In 28 1/2 seasons at Purdue, Lambert compiled 228 Big Ten victories, second only to Indiana's Bob Knight.

He coached 10 consensus All-Americans, including John Wooden, Charles "Stretch" Murphy and Lafayette native Jewell Young.

In many ways, Lambert was a contradiction. He preached discipline and was a conservative by nature. Yet his brand of basketball was considered quite liberal by his peers.

Lambert loved teaching young people—even the legendary Wooden claims his former coach was a basketball teacher and a not a basketball coach—yet he married late in life and never had children of his own.

EARLY HISTORY

The man who put Purdue basketball on the map was born in 1889 in South Dakota, the second of H.C. Lambert's four children.

Ward lived in South Dakota for several years before H.C. Lambert relocated the family to Crawfordsville, Indiana, less than 30 miles from the Purdue campus.

Lambert's father purchased a large home near the Wabash College campus but was rarely there. Soon, H.C. Lambert was working almost exclusively in New York City and essentially abandoned his wife and children, who remained in Crawfordsville.

As the oldest son, Ward became the head of the household and did all he could to help support his mother, two brothers and sister.

Eleanor Lambert, now 94 and still working five days a week at her exclusive New York City public relations firm, remembers Ward as her hero.

He was 14 years older, and he was as dedicated—if not more—than any husband.

"He was like a second father to me," Eleanor said of Ward Lambert. "We were totally dependent on Ward. It made me uneasy that he had to do that."

Any extra money he secured, Lambert gave to his mother and siblings.

He also found time to excel in the classroom and as a basketball and baseball player at Wabash College. He sister recalls he earned the nickname

Lambert's (bottom left) Purdue team from the 1930-31 season. All-American John Wooden is fifth from the left, with bandages on both knees.

"Piggy" because he often hogged the ball as a young basketball player, prompting rivals to comment, "You're a pig."

A LEGEND WAS BORN

Upon graduating from Wabash, Lambert coached high school and college basketball in Montgomery County, accepting an offer in 1916—at the age of 27—to become Purdue's head coach.

When Lambert arrived in West Lafayette, he quickly fell in love with his secretary, Grace, but because of the financial obligations to his mother and siblings, "Piggy" waited 13 years before asking Grace for her hand in marriage.

He was 40 when they were married.

"They would have married earlier, but Ward didn't think it was fair to Grace as long as he was responsible for mother and I," Eleanor Lambert

said. "He was such a generous man. He was a wonderful, caring person."

And a coaching genius well ahead of his time.

Lambert stressed conditioning and explained to his players that if they wanted to run a fastbreak offense and use pressure defense at the same time, they had to be in much better shape than their opponent.

It wasn't uncommon for a Lambert team to practice extremely hard for two hours and then cap the session with a one-hour full court scrimmage.

"It made sense," Young said. "We had to do that for the style we played."

Lambert's best team probably was his 1929-30 squad that featured center Murphy and guard Wooden. The Boilermakers won the Big Ten title and probably would have been perfect instead of 13-2 had Wooden not sustained a leg injury when struck by a car, forcing him to miss losses to Butler and to Montana State.

John DeCamp, who broadcast Purdue basketball games for more than 38 years, remembers that Lambert was an icon on campus.

"There was great excitement about Purdue basketball even then, and a lot of that was because of Lambert," DeMoss said. "He was so entertaining. He would work the officials, and the crowd would really get into the games."

Yet Wooden recalls that as competitive as Lambert was, he had a wonderful knack for leaving the game—along with his complaints about the officiating—on the court.

"When the game was over, it was over," Wooden said.

ACADEMIC EMPHASIS

And when it was over, Lambert expected his players to spend even more time on academics. Those who failed to achieve Lambert's classroom expectations often found themselves seated on the bench next to their coach.

"He loved to stress the little things," said Wooden, who was chastised early in his Purdue career for always driving the basketball to the right. Lambert insisted that Wooden work again and again on driving to his left.

By Wooden's senior season, the All-American was as proficient driving left as he was driving right.

Even at the expense of turnovers, Lambert demanded that his teams run and run. He once told Wooden that a guard that doesn't make turnovers isn't doing his job.

The Boilermakers made turnovers during the Lambert glory years, but they won much more often than they lost. With Wooden in his lineup, Lambert's Purdue teams were 42-8.

Former Illinois high school standout Bill Berberian was among Lambert's final Purdue recruits, but while Berberian noticed that Lambert may have been slipping a bit, he was still the Midwest's most respected coach of that era.

"I had a chance to go to Illinois, but I went to Purdue because of Lambert," Berberian said.

Those who worked with Lambert always knew where he stood on an issue. Former Purdue track coach Dave Rankin remembers Lambert as a

Charles C. "Stretch" Murphy, one of 10 All-Americans Piggy Lambert coached.

man who certainly had a mind of his own and was fiery in almost everything he did.

"But I really liked him," Rankin said. "If his team lost, they might go back out on the court an hour later and practice for an hour or two."

Lambert believed that college basketball was intended to be played on college campuses, and that stubborn philosophy may have cost Purdue the 1940 NCAA Tournament championship.

Purdue won the Big Ten and received the automatic berth to the tourney, which was to be played in New York's Madison Square Garden.

Lambert, however, knew that many gamblers frequented the Garden and didn't want his players associating with or being near those who would dare bet on the outcome of games.

When he declined the tournament bid, Indiana was selected to represent the Big Ten, and the Hoosiers won the NCAA crown.

Nearing 60, Lambert realized during the 1945-46 season that the stress and strain of coaching college basketball was beginning to overwhelm him.

He was contacted by a group of wealthy sportsmen who asked Lambert to serve as the first commissioner of the American Basketball League.

After a victory against Indiana—No. 371— Lambert turned the coaching reigns over to long-time assistant Mel Taube and went on about his business of running the ABL.

Within six months, Lambert quit, telling those who hired him that he missed the spirit and charm of amateur athletics.

His health began to fail in the late 1940s, and Ward "Piggy" Lambert died in the early 1950s. He was buried in Crawfordsville, not far from the home H.C. Lambert purchased for his family more than 50 years before.

"He never cared about money," Eleanor Lambert said. "I doubt he ever had more than a few dollars in his pockets."

But he provided joy that money can't buy to the Boilermaker fans who adored him.

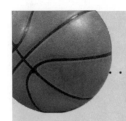

ERNIE HALL, PURDUE BASKETBALL PIONEER

By Ken Thompson

If Ernie Hall had his way, he would have broken the Purdue basketball team's color barrier much sooner than 1951.

After three standout seasons at Lafayette Jefferson High School, where he remains one of the school's all-time scoring leaders, Hall graduated in 1949 and wanted to be a Boilermaker.

Even though 1947 Indiana Mr. Basketball Bill Garrett had broken the Big Ten color barrier at Indiana University two years earlier, then-Purdue coach Mel Taube wasn't interested in the 6-foot-2 Hall.

"I never could understand why I couldn't play for Purdue," Hall said nearly 50 years later from his home in Oxnard, California. "I knew I could play. Sam Lyboult (Jeff assistant coach) taught me every decent play I know about basketball. I just figured black people had to go where they could."

In 1949, that was Ventura (California) Junior College, where Hall enjoyed two successful seasons.

A beloved figure in Hall's life, Lafayette Jeff team doctor L.J. "Doc" Holladay, would become instrumental in Hall's historic return to Lafayette to play for former Boilermaker star Ray Eddy, who replaced Taube in 1950.

"Doc Holladay talked me into coming back to Purdue," Hall said. "He was like a father to me."

Holladay's fatherly advice was soon appreciated by Eddy and Purdue fans, many of whom had cheered for Hall at Lafayette Jeff. Their familiarity with Hall helped avoid many of the problems other

Ernie Hall erupted for 32 points in one of his first games at Purdue in 1951.

African-American sports pioneers endured during this era.

"I was happy there. Everybody treated me great," Hall said. "All the guys were great to me. That whole team, we were all like family."

Another former Lafayette Jeff standout and a teammate on the 1951-52 Boilermakers, Dennis Blind, says nobody cared about the color of Hall's skin.

"Back in those days, we didn't talk about the black-white issues. We just accepted him as a great athlete," Blind said. "We respected him for his ability, and he was one of the guys. It never even dawned on us."

PURDUE DEBUT

On December 1, 1951, Hall became the first African-American and junior college transfer to wear a Purdue uniform. He scored four points in a 67-51 loss at Kansas State. He became a starter for the next game, a 68-56 win over DePauw in which he scored five points.

After the DePauw game, Carl McNulty—the star of the 1951-52 Boilermakers—gave a premonition of things to come over the next 32 days.

"I still think Ernie is going to be one of the most important members of this team," McNulty said. "I look for him to loosen up any night now. Every player is tense and nervous starting into college competition, but Ernie will get over that."

Five days later, Hall loosened up enough to nearly break McNulty's single-game scoring record. Hall recorded 32 points in an 81-68 victory over a Marquette team coached by Tex Winter, who would become famous as the architect of the Chicago Bulls' triangle offense 40 years later. Hall could have tied McNulty's record but missed two free throws in the final two minutes.

Just to prove that performance was no fluke, Hall scored 26 in an 82-65 victory over Louisville on December 15 to set a Purdue record for most points in consecutive games. He then had 12 points in a 60-54 triumph over Bradley on December 18.

Even though Hall was now established as one of Purdue's standouts, his fame didn't entitle him to enter one of Lafayette's restaurants without a white person accompanying him. Usually it was former Lafayette Jeff teammate Dan Casey, with whom Hall remains friends to this day.

Ernie Hall played for Purdue for less than two months before he was dropped from the team. The Boilermakers went 2-11 without him.

"When we wanted to go uptown to a restaurant, they wouldn't let me in without Dan Casey," Hall said. "It's too bad it had to be that way."

Hall struggled during the Christmas-time Hoosier Classic in Indianapolis, scoring just two points in a 55-51 win over Butler and four points in a 64-50 loss to Notre Dame.

BIG TEN DEBUT

Whatever was wrong with Hall's game was corrected in time for the Big Ten opener at Wisconsin on January 5, 1952. His 23 points set a Wisconsin opponent's scoring record and he also pulled down 10 rebounds in a 79-64 win.

"Ernie surely looms as one of the league's most brilliant sopho-mores," *Lafayette Journal and Courier* sports editor Gordon Graham wrote after the game.

On January 14, two days after scoring just six points in an 85-83 loss to Northwestern, Hall was dropped from the team after being arrested on an assault and battery charge, of which he was acquitted a month later.

Eddy didn't explain to the Boil-ermakers why Hall was no longer with them and no mention of Hall's arrest ever appeared on the *Journal and Courier* sports pages. Today, a similar situation involving any ath-lete would make front page headlines.

Ernie Hall drives with the basketball during his brief Purdue career.

"It was kind of quiet. All we knew was the next day we were told he was no longer with the team," said Blind, who didn't learn the reason for Hall's departure until recently.

Ironically, Blind would become one of the beneficiaries of Hall's departure. Eddy revamped his lineup and the freshman guard became a starter. Blind eventually became Purdue's first 1,000-point scorer.

It saddens Blind to think of what might have been with Hall. After his departure, Purdue lost 11 of its next 13 games to finish 8-14.

"He was an outstanding basketball player. He had as much natural talent as anyone I've seen," Blind said. "If he had been able to stay at Purdue, he had the potential to be an All-American."

Hall, who would complete his basketball ca-reer and graduate from Cal-Poly SLO, holds no grudges against Purdue.

"I still follow Purdue everytime they're on TV," Hall said. "I wish I could read more about them out here."

PURDUE'S 1932 TEAM: NATIONAL CHAMPIONS

By Ken Thompson

The sign honoring Purdue's 1932 National Championship team in Mackey Arena blends in with others commemorating 21 Big Ten championships and Final Four appearances.

But other than knowing that Johnny Wooden played for that 1932 team, most Boilermaker fans couldn't tell you anything about one of the greatest squads of its era.

It was a time before polls and preseason magazines. Basketball was still played in a similar style developed by Dr. James Naismith when he invented the game in 1891.

Jump balls after each basket. A deliberate manner of play founded on passing many times before taking a shot. Good shooting in those days was making 40 percent of your attempts.

So, it was no surprise that many opponents weren't prepared for the style of play Ward "Piggy" Lambert's 1931-32 Purdue Boilermakers would unleash—a running game that would feature a future Hall of Famer in Wooden.

BALANCED TEAM

The 1932 Boilermakers are fondly recalled by Wooden 66 years later for a characteristic that would describe many of his championship UCLA teams—balance.

"Our '32 team had great balance," Wooden said. "We were very experienced because we had almost everyone back from the year before. Harry Kellar and Ray Eddy were very good players, but the whole team was very balanced."

The 1931 team, the first in four years to play without All-American center Charles "Stretch" Murphy—whom Wooden calls the dominant big man of his era—still managed to finish second in the Big Ten.

Still, the *Lafayette Journal and Courier* wasn't prepared for the greatness the 1932 team would achieve. Citing only two returning seniors, co-captains Wooden and Kellar, the unnamed writer was cautiously optimistic that Purdue would at least do no worse than its Big Ten runner-up finish of the previous season.

Eddy, one of the new starters in 1932, would prove to be a pivotal player in Purdue basketball history. Eddy would win an Indiana high school state basketball championship at Madison in 1950 before coaching the Boilermakers from 1951-65.

Wooden already was one of the nation's most celebrated players, having earned All-American honors in his sophomore and junior seasons. So it was expected that he would star in the season opener, a 52-23 humiliation of Washington University in St. Louis. He scored just seven points but his "brilliant passing and defensive work" according to the *Journal and Courier* set up 12-point games by Kellar and junior center Charles Stewart.

An injured hip limited Wooden to four points, but Purdue's defense engulfed Notre Dame in a 32-24 victory in South Bend. The Boilermakers held the Irish to seven first-half points and 9 of 58 shooting overall. Keller and Eddy led Purdue with eight and seven points, respectively, as the Boilermakers shot just 24 percent (12 of 50).

Wooden soon regained his health, much to Pittsburgh's regret. In "one of the worst lickings of a Pitt team in 10 years," *Journal and Courier* sports editor Gordon Graham wrote, Purdue routed the Panthers 41-23 in the home opener.

Wooden used his speed advantage to score a game-high 15 points. Eddy added 11 points in an "unusually rough" game, according to Graham. His idea of unusually rough would seem tame in today's Big Ten game, 14 fouls called on each team.

The victories over Notre Dame and Pitt convinced a *Journal and Courier* columnist who used the byline "W.H.R." that Purdue would have a big year and that Wooden "is elusive as quicksilver. A guard that depends more on speed and cleverness than physical power."

Wooden wasn't the only local figure making national news over the Christmas holidays. Purdue's first successful football coach, Knowlton L. Ames, committed suicide in Chicago on December 23. And former area resident Winnie Ruth Judd began her 40-year stay on the nation's front pages as the convicted Phoenix trunk murderess.

Purdue's first two games after Christmas were disappointing to Lambert despite the ease of victory, 51-21 over Montana State and 51-26 over Monmouth. Wooden had 17 points and Kellar 10 against Montana State as the *Journal and Courier* noted that Purdue scored almost at will. But Lambert was upset with the Boilermakers' poor passing. That element of the game improved slightly against Monmouth with Wooden and Eddy scoring 12 points apiece.

FINDING THE SPOTLIGHT

Purdue first received national attention with a 49-30 rout of Indiana on January 4. Associated Press writer John W. Stahr called Purdue's style of play "fire department basketball" after having witnessed years of methodical play.

Wooden believes that must have been the first time Stahr witnessed a Purdue game because "Lambert teams were always fast-breaking teams.

"I think he adjusted to his personnel but to the best of my knowledge, his teams always ran," Wooden said.

The Boilermakers sped to a 44-17 lead before Lambert called off the dogs with 10 minutes to

play. Wooden left to a great ovation after scoring 14 points, sharing game-high honors with Stewart. Kellar added 10 points and impressed Graham in the process.

"Wooden and Kellar made Indiana look foolish on numerous occasions," Graham wrote.

CURSE OF 13

It may seem silly today, but in a story previewing the January 9 game at Illinois, a *Journal and Courier* writer wondered if Wooden's uniform number, 13, had anything to do with his numerous injuries during his career. At that time, Wooden was suffering from a sprained thumb and a charley horse. As a sophomore, he was hit by a truck while rushing to catch the train for a game and sent to the hospital. His junior season was hampered by a badly infected floor burn on a hip.

A superstitious person might believe that story foretold Purdue's only loss of the season, 28-21 to the Illini. To this day, the loss is an unpleasant memory for Wooden.

When asked what he remembered about that game, Wooden politely replied, "I would just as soon not discuss that game."

What is known is he scored a team-high 10 points but couldn't rally Purdue from a deficit of 19-5 at halftime.

Two days later, the retirement of legendary Supreme Court justice Oliver Wendell Holmes stole the headlines from one of the fiercest rivalries of the 1930s. Lambert reportedly disliked Wisconsin coach "Doc" Meanwell and took great delight in the 38-22 victory in which he put away his fastbreaking attack in favor of a delay game. Still, Eddy had 13 points and Wooden contributed 10.

A three-week break for final exams followed, and Purdue struggled in its first post-exam game, a 26-23 victory over Marquette. It didn't help that Eddy missed the game with a bad cold. The game was tied 22-22 with three minutes to play when Kellar rebounded his own miss to score the go-ahead basket. Wooden led Purdue with nine points.

Purdue still hadn't recovered its pre-exam form when it traveled to Ohio State, but Wooden's heroics allowed Purdue to pull out a 38-33 overtime victory. Two minutes into overtime, Wooden stole a pass and threw the ball to Eddy for the go-ahead basket. Wooden followed with a basket and a late free throw to seal the victory. For one of the few times all season, neither Wooden nor Eddy led Purdue in scoring. Junior guard Ralph Parmenter stepped up with 11 points, followed by Eddy with nine and Wooden seven.

The next four games saw Purdue's offense in high gear. Eddy scored 11 of his 17 points in the first half of a 40-27 win at Chicago. Wooden contributed 11.

With fresh memories of their struggle at Ohio State, the Boilermakers gave the Buckeyes no chance for revenge, jumping out to a 27-10 lead en route to a 43-26 triumph. Seeing that it had no chance for victory, Ohio State resorted to very physical play in the second half that offended the *Journal and Courier's* Graham.

"Ribs, knees, elbows and other parts of the human anatomy took an awful thumping and most of the time, somebody ... was standing at the free throw line," Graham wrote.

This game would back up Wooden's statement about Purdue's balance as he, William "Dutch" Fehring and Parmenter each had nine points, and Kellar and Eddy contributed six apiece.

Purdue assumed the Big Ten lead with its 48-33 victory over Northwestern before 4,000 fans who wedged themselves into Memorial Gymnasium. Graham wrote that Purdue's quickness was too much for the Wildcats.

WOODEN ACCOLADES

Wooden not only led Purdue with 15 points but he also held the Big Ten's top scorer entering the game, Joe Reiff, to six points. Kellar added 13 points.

Wooden assumed the Big Ten scoring lead with 17 points and rallied Purdue to a 42-29 victory at Indiana. Illinois coach Craig Ruby, who was scouting the game, told Graham that "Wooden is the greatest basketball player I ever saw."

Also impressed was the *Bloomington Herald-Telephone*, which wrote "In listing the all-time greats of Indiana basketball, it would be sacrilege to omit the name of Johnny Wooden."

The *Bloomington World* went further: "It is a pretty risky thing to pick All-Americans in basketball for the game is too uncertain. But this man Wooden is so far above anything we have seen for so long that he is a real, for sure All-American in our estimation."

Lambert once again frustrated old rival "Doc" Meanwell, using the delay game to preserve a 28-21 victory at Wisconsin. Wooden scored five of his team-high 12 points in the final minutes after the Boilermakers went into the delay.

Wooden and the Boilermakers avenged the loss at Illinois with an easy 34-19 triumph. Wooden penetrated the Illini defense at will, and virtually all of Purdue's points came from the inside. He led a balanced scoring attack with 13 points, followed by Eddy with eight, Kellar with seven and Parmenter six.

LEAGUE CHAMPS

A sellout crowd of 6,000 Northwestern fans went home disappointed after Purdue's 31-17 victory clinched the Big Ten championship. Wooden once again got the best of Wildcats star Joe Reiff with 15 points. Reiff scored many of his 11 after Wooden's departure.

Entering the final game at Chicago, Wooden's teammates knew he needed 15 points to break Branch McCracken's Big Ten single-season scoring record of 147 set in 1930. And despite Wooden's reluctance to put himself ahead of the team, they intended to make sure he got the record.

"From the tipoff, it was evident that Kellar had only one idea in mind—to help John set a new mark," Graham wrote. "John was not so willing to take all the honors and the boys had to urge him to shoot unless he was absolutely open near the basket."

Wooden broke the record, scoring 21 points to finish with 154 and Purdue set a Big Ten single-game scoring record with its 53-18 romp. But true to his humble ways, Wooden then ensured Kellar scored eight of his 12 points in the final minutes of his friend's collegiate career.

"I think my teammates were more proud of the scoring record than I was," Wooden said. "What meant more to me was at our banquet, when coach Lambert talked about me, he discussed my defense and my leadership at great length."

Wooden and Kellar, according to Graham, put on a ballhandling show.

"Those two lads did everything that ever has been done with a basketball except hurl it out the front door and since that kind of play would result in exactly no points, they didn't even try it," Graham wrote.

Lambert knew the victory meant his team would be crowned national champions by the media, and he let his emotions show.

"Piggy Lambert, king of all basketball coaches, was one of the happiest men on Earth after the game," Graham wrote.

In an irony Wooden would appreciate, next to the game story on the *Journal and Courier* sports page was the news of his distinguished student rating by Purdue after earning a 6.08 grade-point average on a 6.5 scale. He was ranked 19th out of 4,675 students at the university. The last line of the story proved to be prophetic:

"He is a senior in the school of physical education and intends to take up coaching as a career following graduation this spring."

That career resulted in 10 national championships at UCLA and a second Naismith Hall of Fame enshrinement as a coach.

In addition to the national championship, individual honors were plentiful for the Boilermakers. Wooden was named National Player of the Year and was a unanimous All-Big Ten selection for the third consecutive year. Kellar also was voted first-team All-Big Ten, with Eddy and Parmenter earning second-team honors. Stewart and Fehring received honorable mention.

FAN FAVORITES

By Ken Thompson

The moment an athlete dons a Purdue basketball uniform, he becomes the object of affection for thousands of Boilermaker fans.

But a few earn a special place in fans' hearts. They're usually not the stars of the team, but Purdue fans—many of whom come from blue-collar backgrounds—have always appreciated hard-working, hustling players who also possess an outgoing personality.

Of the thousands to wear a Purdue uniform, four will be remembered for accomplishments that can't be found on a statistics sheet.

BRIAN CARDINAL

It was love at first sight for Boilermaker basketball fans and forward Brian Cardinal.

The Tolono, Illinois native literally crashed into the spotlight in the winter of 1996 with his knack for coming up with loose balls and sacrificing his body to help Purdue win. It was a good day for Cardinal if he left the training room with a bag of ice on each knee and elbow.

"I've always played hard," Cardinal said. "I probably didn't dive on the floor as many times in high school as I do in college, but I didn't have to."

Less than three months into his Boilermaker career, the *Lafayette Journal and Courier* sponsored a contest to give Cardinal a nickname.

Appropriately, "Citizen Pain" was the winner from among more than 260 entries the newspaper received. The nickname became so popular that

ESPN and Big Ten network announcers almost immediately began using it.

"I love it that he's always diving on the floor," said Zac Laugheed, the 13-year-old who submitted the winning nickname. "I also like his leadership and teamwork."

Cardinal, while preferring the nickname "Redbird," was flattered by the attention.

"I appreciate all the support everybody gives me," he said. "It's always nice to know that you're supported by your fans. I just enjoy going out there and playing hard, and whether or not I have a nickname, you'll see the same effort."

Some have called that effort "dirty." The accusation by a couple of Big Ten coaches, reported by CBS announcer Sean McDonough during a 1998 Purdue-Indiana game in Bloomington, outraged Purdue fans, coach Gene Keady and Cardinal.

"If it's a dirty player to dive after a ball and go through somebody for that ball, then I guess I'm the dirtiest player ever," Cardinal said.

"Cardinal does not play dirty because I won't let him. Brian does not play dirty. He plays hard," said Keady, who only a few weeks earlier had rewarded Cardinal with a rare sophomore captaincy.

Cardinal's aggressive playing style is matched only by his sense of humor, which made for several lighthearted moments on Purdue's 1997 European trip.

During the Boilermakers' stay in London, Cardinal goaded one of the solemn, nonspeaking

Buckingham Palace guards into smiling. He wasn't as persuasive once inside the palace, having his request for sitting on Queen Elizabeth II's throne denied. His gift for gab also cost him a chance to witness the return of the Queen and Queen Mother to the palace and the changing of the guard at Windsor Castle.

He was left nearly speechless, however, by his selection—along with teammates Brad Miller and Chad Austin—to the USA Men's 22 and Under basketball team later that summer. He would earn a starting forward position under Rick Majerus, who would coach Utah to the 1998 NCAA championship game.

"Honestly, it's amazing," Cardinal said. "All I tried to do was the things I do well."

LAMAR LUNDY

Lamar Lundy is known to NFL fans as one of the members of the "Fearsome Foursome," the Los Angeles Rams' defensive line that put fear into quarterbacks' hearts in the 1960s.

But few remember that he was one of the Big Ten's best centers in the mid-1950s and an African-American basketball pioneer at Purdue.

"Lundy is the finest defensive man, big or little, the Big Ten has seen in years," legendary *Journal and Courier* sports editor Gordon Graham wrote in February 1957. "Lundy stands out like a lighthouse as a defensive star in a period when all too few players concentrated on this part of the game. Add sharp intelligence and strong leadership and you have quite a ballplayer. Lundy's football and basketball careers rank among the finest ever seen at Purdue."

Lundy, at 6-6, 226 pounds, was the Dennis Rodman of his era, without the earrings, tattoos and multi-hued hair. Unlike Rodman, Lundy could score, too. In his final two seasons as a Boilermaker, he outrebounded and outscored his opponent in every game. As a senior, he averaged 13.4 points and 9.3 rebounds.

When he fouled out of his final game, a 72-63 victory over Iowa on March 4, 1957, more than 8,500 fans in the Purdue Fieldhouse gave Lundy a standing ovation that lasted several minutes.

"We've never seen anything quite like that in basketball," wrote Graham, who began his career with the *Journal and Courier* in the 1920s.

The echoes from that standing ovation linger with Lundy today.

"It was exciting. A final saying that we appreciate you," said Lundy, who is currently president of the Indiana Football Hall of Fame in his hometown of Richmond, Ind. "This was kind of a reward for all the hard work."

Unlike Brian Cardinal, the love affair between Purdue fans and Lundy was slow to blossom. African-American players at Purdue weren't common in the mid-1950s and while Lundy was accepted immediately by his teammates, it took time for fans to realize that Lundy was their kind of player: hard-working and modest.

"I think that now the Rodmans of the world are appreciated by fans but back then that role wasn't," Lundy said. "Those who played the game appreciated it."

He became the only athlete to be named Purdue's Most Valuable Player in football and basketball in the same year. When he picked up his basketball MVP award at the post-season banquet, Lundy was given his second standing ovation and a tribute from another Purdue two-sport star, future PGA player Joe Campbell.

"I know what all of you think of him, but it has been our privilege on this squad to know him as a person as well as an athlete," Campbell said. "Lundy has done a great deal for all of us. I know he has done a great deal for me."

Lundy was elected into the second Purdue Athletic Hall of Fame class in 1995 and was voted by fans as a member of the all-time Purdue football team in 1969.

"It was a good relationship with Purdue, and I'd enjoy doing it again," Lundy said.

MIKE SCEARCE

Mike Scearce got the nickname "Scooby Doo" from childhood friends in Lexington, Kentucky, who said he looked like the Hanna-Barbara cartoon character.

And like his animated namesake, Scearce provided his Purdue teammates with some humorous moments, albeit unintentionally, during his playing career from 1979-82.

For example, there was this legendary tale early in his freshman season. Head coach Lee Rose was discussing an upcoming trip to Hawaii and asked if there were any questions.

"How long will it take to drive there?" Scearce asked a dumbfounded Rose.

Nearly 20 years later, Scearce isn't so sure that story hasn't been exaggerated a bit but admits it was possible he asked a similar question because of his naivete. Before signing with Purdue, Scearce knew little about life outside of Lexington.

"Up until I came to Purdue, I had not traveled and not really done a lot of things that Purdue did on a really nice level: restaurants, hotels, everything first class," Scearce said.

Never was that more evident than on his first road trip with the Boilermakers, when he had dinner with All-American center Joe Barry Carroll.

"Joe Barry said, 'I'll have some filet mignon,'" Scearce recalled. "Then Joe asks me, 'What are you ordering? The filet mignon is good.'

"I told him I didn't want any fish. I look around and everybody was on the floor. The only thing I'd had in my life fileted was fish."

Scearce credits the rest of his education to retired associate athletic director Bob King.

"I probably owe my success to him," said Scearce, assistant manager for the Lexington Housing Authority and owner of Scearce Management, which deals in property and portfolios.

"When I came to Purdue, I'm thinking I'm going to the pros. That's my dream, that's my goal. But when you get in there, the light isn't as bright as you thought, and you have to get serious about other things. Bob King was probably my biggest asset.

"'Coach Bob' would do whatever it would take ... tutoring ... whatever within the rules. I don't know what the ratio is now, but back then on the basketball team the graduation rate was high. Purdue came through for me with shining colors. There was no reason not to get a degree. Every tool was there."

Scearce's friendly nature and all-out style of play made him a fan favorite quickly. Chants of "Scooby, Scooby" greeted Scearce each time he stepped on the court. Their affection still touches Scearce today.

"You wanted to go out and bust your butt for them," he said. "Indiana basketball fans know the game well, and they expect a lot. I appreciated being able to go out and work my hardest for them and do a good job. I enjoyed them and always took time to speak with them. It was a great time in my life."

RALPH TAYLOR

Unlike Brian Cardinal, Lamar Lundy and Mike Scearce, Ralph Taylor wasn't a starter at Purdue. But for some reason that Taylor to this day cannot fathom, Boilermaker fans singled out the Indianapolis native from the 1969 national runner-up team that included Purdue legends Rick Mount, Billy Keller, Herm Gilliam and George Faerber.

"I don't know if it's because fans saw me as someone who had a good work ethic or a player my size (6-2) that was not afraid to mix it up inside," Taylor said. "Fans could always count on me."

Taylor's playing style was similar to Cardinal's, with one exception.

"Brian played a lot more than I did," Taylor said with a laugh. "My playing time was not that much, but when my opportunity came, I gave 100 percent."

Taylor and Keller were the stars of the 1965 Indiana state championship team at Washington High School, where amazingly, Taylor was the center.

That championship experience came into play in 1969, when only the Lew Alcindor-led UCLA Bruins—at the peak of their dynasty—stood between Purdue and a national championship.

"We were a real unique blend of characters and personalities," Taylor said. "My senior year, we had one common goal, win the national championship."

Injuries to Gilliam and 7-foot center Chuck Bavis derailed that dream, but Taylor believes Purdue is on the brink of another shot at a national championship under Gene Keady.

After graduating from Purdue, Taylor passed up a tryout with the Indiana Pacers to begin repaying a debt to those who helped him as a child. He is the director of outreach services at the Indiana Youth Institute in Indianapolis, where he concentrates on youth and health development. Before his current job, Taylor was with the Indianapolis Parks Department, Marion County 4-H and the Marion County Cooperative Extension Service.

His desire to work with youths has been a long-standing one.

"It came from a lot of adult mentors I had when growing up," Taylor said. "Watching them and realizing what they gave to me and others made me realize that's how I want to give back what I have received."

GENE KEADY

By Tom Kubat

He's won six Big Ten championships. He's a five-time national coach of the year.

He's Purdue's all-time winningest coach. And his winning percentage in conference games ranks third on the Big Ten's all-time list.

No doubt, Gene Keady is a winner.

But in today's what-have-you-done-for-me-lately society, there's a chink in his armor.

In 20 years as a major college head coach—two at Western Kentucky and 18 at Purdue—Keady has never led a team to the Final Four.

He's heard the critics and cynics. Those that say Keady is not among the true greats of the day because his resume does not include a Final Four or a national championship.

He knows they're out there.

He knows because Dean Smith faced similar criticism, for not winning more national titles with all his blue chip talent.

And because a coach like Roy Williams is being criticized for Kansas' early NCAA Tournament departures despite its recent phenomenal regular season success.

"If I didn't enjoy my work so much, I'd be worried about it," said the 62-year-old Keady. "The challenge of getting to the Final Four is still there, very much alive. The fire probably is higher and hotter than ever to try to do it."

He knows that by today's standards, if you don't get to the mountain top, in some circles you're not really considered a winner.

The "Can't Win the Big Game" label is hung around your neck.

And Keady's NCAA Tournament record just gives the doubters more ammunition.

TOURNAMENT SHOWING

Not only has he not made it to the Final Four, his tourney record is rather dismal—sub-.500 to be exact, at 13-14.

Only three times has a Keady team survived the first weekend of play and made it to the Sweet Sixteen. And only once have they reached the Elite Eight.

In 1987-88, the Boilermakers, with Troy Lewis, Todd Mitchell and Everette Stephens, lost 73-70 to Kansas State in the Midwest Regional semifinals.

In 1993-94, the Glenn Robinson-led Boilermakers got to within one game of the Final Four before losing 69-60 to Duke and Grant Hill in the Southeast Regional final.

And in '97-98, Purdue lost to Stanford 67-59 in the Midwest Regional semifinals.

"I think 1988 was the biggest disappointment because there were so many expectations," Keady said of that 29-4 team. "As it turns out, we didn't have the best team. K-State had the best team, as far as talent. They had three guys off that team go to the NBA. But we didn't know that at the time. We thought we were just as good, or better. By the ratings we were ranked higher."

In '93-94, Robinson was voted the national player of the year after leading Purdue to a 29-5 record and No. 3 national ranking.

But for Keady, the disappointment of losing to sixth-ranked Duke was tempered by an injury to Robinson.

"He got hurt in the Kansas game (an 83-78 victory in the regional semifinal)," Keady said. "He strained his back and I didn't know if he was going to play against Duke. He couldn't even move the day we practiced between games. But we never built that up so nobody knew it."

Keady's lack of NCAA tournament success has overshadowed his impressive regular season accomplishments.

• He has been named national coach of the year in 1984, '88, '94, '95 and '96.

• He has led Purdue to six Big Ten championships in 18 years, including a "three-peat" from 1994-96, joining Ohio State's Fred Taylor as the only league coaches to win three outright titles in a row.

• With a Big Ten winning percentage of .667, he ranks third all-time, behind Indiana's Bob Knight and former Purdue coach Ward "Piggy" Lambert. He's also third on the all-time victory list, with 215 league wins, behind Knight's 334 and Lambert's 228.

• Now 394-168 at Purdue, Keady is the school's all-time winningest coach, breaking Lambert's previous record of 371 victories with a win over Louisville on December 6, 1987.

In another era, Keady's postseason record might have been different.

Back when there were no at-large bids to the NCAA tournament. Back when only major conference champs and 32 teams qualified for the tourney. Back when a team had to win just four games, instead of six, to capture a national title.

Back before the tourney was known as the Big Dance.

"If I would have won six Big Ten titles in the '60s and '70s, we would have been one of the 32 schools in the NCAA," Keady said. "And all you had to do was win four games to win a national championship. So it might have been a different story then.

"But this is the way it is now, and that's what you live with."

Gene Keady, still seeking first NCAA Final Four trip.

HEATHCOTE PRAISE

Jud Heathcote, the former Michigan State coach who won a national championship with Magic Johnson, is one of Keady's closest friends in the coaching profession.

Heathcote knows of the double-edged sword by which Keady is judged.

"Roy Williams is a good example," he said. "The past two years, he was predicted to win it all. Suddenly the bottom drops out, Kansas gets knocked out early and now the talk shows are calling Roy Williams the Sprewell of coaching, the big choker.

"We have created a situation that puts too much emphasis on the tournament."

Keady's teams, despite their lack of NCAA tournament success, have built a reputation of overachieving.

Even though Robinson is the only NBA player of note to have played for Purdue during the Keady era, the Boilermakers usually have shattered the experts' preseason predictions.

"Gene's personality carries over to the team," Heathcote said. "He's just a great competitor, a tough-minded individual. And he passes that on. Certain coaches have an intangible ability to get their kids to play harder.

"Sometimes I claim that Gene coaches so well his teams just might run out of gas by the end of the season. Robinson was probably the only superstar he's had. His teams usually overachieve all season and then, because of the shorter preparation time and the caliber of the competition, it catches up to them at tournament time."

The lack of blue chippers regularly finding their way to Purdue leads to the other knock against Keady—why can't he recruit better?

Gene Keady, exhorting the Boilermakers on from the sideline.

"Certainly, I can see where people would be upset about it, if I was a fan," Keady said. "I don't think they understand all of our recruiting problems here.

"When basketball was going big in the '50s, '60s and '70s, it was easier to recruit at Purdue because in those days the southern schools didn't all have big arenas. People weren't going to make money in basketball like they are now. Recruiting has been diluted."

Back then the Pacific-10 Conference was the Pac-8, and UCLA was the only school regularly getting top recruits.

Now, prospects usually stay closer to home, and it's more difficult to get the top kids to leave the Pac-10, Atlantic Coast and Big East conference areas.

And then there's what Keady refers to as Purdue's false academic image.

"If you were to ask somebody in the East or West, it's like, oh, man, Purdue is like the Ivy League, it's tough to make it there," Keady said.

"But it's not. You have to understand it's no different than any other college. Once you get them here, and they understand all they have to do is go to class. But the image is that it's really tough here."

RECRUITING STRATEGY

Keady admits that he's at fault for not recruiting enough blue chippers.

And for maybe being too loyal to prep players in the state of Indiana.

"I have a tough time going after a kid I know I'm not going to have more than two years," he said. "It's one of those things, do you want to go after a bunch of blue chippers and not get any of them and miss the Indiana kids? Pretty soon you have no Indiana kids. We've kind of hung in there and stayed with the Indiana kids, and I think it's kept us a little more solid.

"Do you want to be a Top 10 team, which we've been seven out of 18 years, or do you want to go to the Final Four? Naturally, you'd rather have both."

But Keady is running out of time to make it to the Final Four.

He says he has no retirement timetable, although he plans to coach at least three more years, after serving as president of the National Association of Basketball Coaches.

Sportswriters, broadcasters and other experts have speculated that there will be a huge void in Keady's life if he leaves the game without at least getting to the Final Four.

He scoffs at the idea.

"That will not bother me one lick," Keady said. "I've enjoyed coaching too much, at all levels.

"I have hangups about it because I want to do it so bad. But I don't dwell on it, or look back. For three or four years after '88, I did. Finally I shook it. It's motivating to me. I look forward to the challenge each year."

But to be in the twilight of his career and take a team to the Final Four—or win a national title—would be the icing on an outstanding coaching career.

"It'd be a great way to end your career," Keady said. "If I did, I'd quit that year. Oh yeah, that'd be fun.

"Rocky Marciano has always been my idol, because of that. He hung it up at his best. I think that'd be tremendous."

RANKING PURDUE IN THE BIG TEN

By Tom Kubat

Deciding where the Purdue men's basketball program ranks in the Big Ten's overall historical picture depends on which viewfinder you're looking through.

The first one shows a program that has won more conference championships than any other school. It also shows a program that has a winning record against every other team.

But the second one shows a program that has never won an NCAA tournament championship, made only two Final Four appearances, and has a rather so-so 21-17 tourney record.

So, when measured against their Big Ten brethren only, the Boilermakers are top of the line. But when compared on a national level, they probably fall to the second tier.

Even Purdue coach Gene Keady admits that most basketball fans probably think of Indiana, with its five national championships and coach Bob Knight, or Ohio State, because of its early '60s powerhouses led by Jerry Lucas and John Havlicek, as the top Big Ten programs.

Or Michigan with its recent success and Fab Five publicity.

But not Purdue?

"No, because they won most of their Big Ten championships back in the '20s, '30s and '40s," Purdue coach Gene Keady said. "Before I got here, Purdue had only been to the NCAA tournament three times. What's amazing about that is that two of those three times they went to the Final Four."

In fact, 11 of Purdue's 21 league titles were won between 1921 and 1940. The Boilermakers have won six under Keady since 1984.

BIG TEN PROWESS

Purdue's 21 outright or shared conference championships are two more than runner-up Indiana. Purdue is the only Big Ten school to hold a series lead over each of its conference rivals, with an overall 762-522 league record.

The Boilermakers rank first in overall victories and second, behind Indiana, in winning percentage.

"In the '80s and '90s, we should be considered a premier Big Ten program," Keady said. "We've probably had more first- and second-place finishes in the Big Ten with less talent than a lot of teams. We've finished first or second nine out of my 18 years. You do that half the time, that's pretty good."

Purdue finished in the upper division of the Big Ten for a league-record 69th time in 1998.

The program also would be near the top when ranking programs based on star quality.

Ten Boilermakers have been voted consensus All-Americans, for a total of 16 different times.

John Wooden, who went on to a Hall of Fame coaching career at UCLA, was a three-time pick; Charles Murphy, Jewell Young, Terry Dischinger and Rick Mount were two-time picks. The others were Norman Cottom, Robert Kessler, Dave Schellhase, Joe Barry Carroll and Glenn Robinson.

Robinson was the near-unanimous choice for national player of the year in 1994, with six of the seven agencies that make such a selection naming him.

Twenty-six Boilermakers have been named first-team All-Big Ten, second only to Indiana's 31.

Only six schools have had more than one No. 1 pick in the NBA draft, and three are from the Big Ten, including Purdue. Robinson was the top pick in 1994, and Carroll was selected first in 1980.

Indiana (Kent Benson in 1977, Walt Bellamy in 1961) and Michigan (Chris Webber in 1993, Cazzie Russell in 1966) are the other two Big Ten schools with more than one No. 1 pick.

Nine Big Ten schools have produced at least one first-round pick, led by Michigan's 14 and Indiana's 11.

PURDUE MVPS

Surprisingly, only four Boilermakers have received the Big Ten's most valuable player trophy since it was first presented in 1946—Mount in 1969 and 1970, Jim Rowinski in 1984 and Robinson in '94.

"Overall, Purdue ranks at or near the top in the Big Ten," former Michigan State coach Jud Heathcote said. "But, anymore, what is considered competitive? Look at the Fab Five at Michigan. There has never been a group receive more publicity that never won a Big Ten title.

"You ask the average fan which is the top program, and Indiana probably would be mentioned the most, because of Bob Knight and the (five) national championships.

"The purists would have to consider Purdue,

Glenn Robinson punctuates one of the 81 dunks he delivered during his remarkable career with the Boilermakers.

especially in the Gene Keady era, with all his league championships and coach of the year honors."

But, compare the Purdue program with others in the Big Ten on a national level, and the Boilermakers slip a notch or two.

"We're probably not an upper-tier team," Keady said. "We're not like North Carolina, but I think we'd be in the Top 15."

Purdue has been to the NCAA Final Four twice—losing both times to UCLA, 92-72 in the 1969 championship game and 67-62 in the 1980 semifinal game.

By contrast, Indiana has won five national championships and been to the Final Four seven times. Michigan has made six Final Four appearances, with one national title and four runner-up finishes. Ohio State has made it to the Final Four eight times, with one crown and three runner-ups.

Other Big Ten teams that have won a national championship are Michigan State (two Final Four appearances) and Wisconsin.

Illinois has been to four Final Fours, Iowa three (with a second-place finish) and Minnesota one.

"When I think about averaging almost 12 Big Ten wins a year for 18 years, that's difficult to do," Keady said. "And you would think in that time you'd get to the Final Four once, as tough as the Big Ten's been over all those years.

"North Carolina has had NBA players out the gazoo. Kentucky has had NBA players out the gazoo. So who's been the most consistent in the Final Four, in the last few years?"

Purdue is fifth in the Big Ten in terms of NCAA tournament appeareances, with 17. Indiana's 27 appearances leads the way, followed by Michigan's 20, Illinois' 19, Iowa's 18, Purdue, Ohio State's 16 and Michigan State's 12.

"A good example of where Purdue ranks all-time, is that Fred Schaus coached there six years and had teams finish third in the Big Ten three consecutive years," Heathcote said. "That's pretty darn good, but not by Purdue standards."

Except for its continued struggles in the NCAA tournament, the Purdue program certainly has made its mark under Keady.

DOMINANT PROGRAM

In the last two decades, the Boilermakers have won 71 percent of their games. Purdue was 216-86 in the 1980s and so far it is 201-83 in the '90s, for a 417-169 combined record.

"I'd put Gene and his program right there near the top," Heathcote said. "When I look at the players they've had, which haven't always been the best, and the record they've had, Purdue's program has to rank with the best in the Big Ten.

"Winning those three Big Ten championships in a row (1994-95-96) was a tremendous accomplishment. You realize what that would have been 15 years ago? That would have been a crowning achievement, but now it loses its luster because of all the emphasis that's placed on the NCAA tournament."

GREAT PURDUE GUARDS

By Mike Carmin

The first basket in the history of the Purdue women's basketball program was scored by a guard.

Amy Ruley got the Boilermakers going on December 2, 1975 with her memorable hoop as Purdue won an overtime game against Illinois at Mackey Arena.

Guards have continued to shine in the Boilermaker program ever since. Players such as Ruley, Lisa Jahner, Sharon Versyp, Anne Kvachkoff, MaChelle Joseph, Cindy Lamping, Jennifer Jacoby, Ukari Figgs and Stephanie White have helped bring Purdue's program to national status.

Ruley was a three-year starter for the Boilermakers, never averaging more than 9.2 points in one season. But her leadership qualities and her ability to control the offense enabled Purdue to start its program in the right direction.

The 5-foot-4 Ruley took those skills and traits into the coaching ranks. She has enjoyed tremendous success at North Dakota State, leading the school to several Division II national championships and numerous No. 1 rankings.

But Purdue's program didn't begin to flourish until recognizable names ventured to West Lafayette.

PARADE OF MISS BASKETBALLS

The first household name that fans could identify with was Versyp. She was the first Miss

Basketball from Indiana to play at Purdue. And she wouldn't be the last.

Jacoby and White also were selected the top players in Indiana and found their way to Purdue. Jacoby, a native of Rossville, was Indiana's Miss Basketball in 1991 while White, who hails from West Lebanon and attended Seeger High School, grabbed the top honor in 1995.

Even as this century comes to a close, Purdue is still securing the state's top talent. Lake Central High School product Kelly Komara, named Indiana's Miss Basketball in 1998, joined the Boilermakers for the 1998-99 season.

The addition of Komara gave Purdue the opportunity to have three Miss Basketballs on the floor at the same time. Along with White and Komara, Figgs was Kentucky's Miss Basketball her senior season at Georgetown's Scott County High School.

Purdue received its share of Indiana All-Stars as well.

Kvachkoff, Joseph and Lamping were among the best in the state their high school senior seasons, and brought their talents to Purdue. Teri Moren, who was Joseph's backcourt mate, and Indianapolis native Katie Douglas were part of their elite senior classes across the state.

Versyp was a tireless worker, who could play virtually the whole game and not run out of breath. Before the 1996-97 season, Versyp was Purdue's marathon player.

She held school records for minutes played in a season, average minutes played and career minutes on the court. And her overall game never suffered.

The 5-foot-8 native of Mishawaka was a four-year starter for the Boilermakers, playing for three coaches from 1984-88. Her career started under Dr. Ruth Jones, continued with Marsha Reall and finished under Lin Dunn.

Versyp led Purdue in scoring during her first three seasons. She finished her career with 1,565 points in 113 games—a 13.8 average. If Versyp's career had started later in the 1980's, she would have collected more points.

The NCAA didn't adopt the 3-point shot until Versyp's senior season at Purdue. In that season, Versyp nailed 25 of 68 from 3-point range, resulting in 38 percent accuracy. Based on those numbers, Versyp would rank among Purdue's top 3-point shooters of all-time. But since she doesn't qualify (a player must have attempted at least 100 3-pointers), Versyp's talents in this area go unnoticed.

Players after Versyp benefited from the 3-point shot, including Joseph, Jacoby and White.

JOESPH'S HEROICS

Entering the 1998-99 season, Joseph is Purdue's all-time leading scorer. She accumulated 2,405 points while starting all 119 games from 1988-92. Although Joseph was dangerous with her ability to score from any place on the floor, her passing skills were just as good.

Joseph also ranks as Purdue's leader in assists with 628 over her four-year career. Joseph is one of two players in Purdue history to collect more than 1,000 points and 500 assists during her career.

MaChelle Joseph is the leading scorer and assists producer in school history.

Jahner also accomplished that feat, totaling 1,209 points and 517 assists from 1984-88.

As Purdue's record improved so did the quality of players. Not only was Joseph surrounded by talented basketball players, but gifted athletes as well.

Players such as Joy Holmes, who was Purdue's first All-American in 1991, and Donna Gill, who was a multi-sport skilled athlete at Purdue, upgraded the Boilermaker program into the top of the Big Ten Conference and among the nation's best.

Joseph was named a Kodak All-American following the 1992 season. Her career numbers are impressive, averaging 20.2 points, 5.3 assists, 3.6 rebounds and shooting 46 percent from the field. Joseph also was the Big Ten's Player of the Year following her senior season.

Joseph holds 27 records at Purdue, including 10 career marks.

During Joseph's career, the Boilermakers compiled a 96-23 record and advanced to the NCAA tournament each of the four years. Purdue also won its first Big Ten championship in 1991, dominating the rest of the conference with a stellar 17-1 record.

ATTENDANCE SWELLS

The play of Joseph and the rest of the Boilermakers helped Purdue's attendance start to climb. From Joseph's first year wearing the old gold and black until she graduated, the fans began to notice the Boilermakers. Attendance jumped nearly 1,000 per game during Joseph's four years, going from 2,633 to 3,604.

When Jacoby signed to attend Purdue, Mackey Arena became the place to be for women's basketball followers.

The time off allowed Jacoby to come back stronger for her sophomore season, but Purdue struggled through a sub-par season. That set the stage for a remarkable campaign during the 1993-94 season.

JACOBY EXCELS

Jacoby helped Purdue makes its first Final Four appearance in women's basketball. Jacoby was the point guard on a team with no seniors, willing the Boilermakers to new heights throughout the season.

With other scoring threats on the team, Jacoby's no-look passes and ability to see the floor enabled Purdue to excel at a high level. And when called upon to score, Jacoby was always a threat.

Jennifer Jacoby left Purdue with more three-point shots than anyone before her, 157.

MaChelle Joseph had seven 30-point games, no. 1 in Purdue annals.

Jacoby grew up about 15 miles east of West Lafayette in the small town of Rossville. Jacoby was a typical Hoosier, loving the game of basketball. She worked on her skills on the family farm, shooting at a basketball goal hanging on the outside of the barn.

"I've always loved basketball," Jacoby said. "I just enjoy playing it. I would do it all day and all night, if I could."

Jacoby's passion for the game and her talents allowed fans to connect to her, even in high school. She brought those same characteristics to Purdue.

But her first season was not a glorious one. She suffered a season-ending knee injury during the middle of the year, the second time Jacoby had sustained an ACL injury in her career.

Stephanie White has energized Purdue with her multi-faceted game.

White possessed similar talents to Jacoby, but at a higher level. Her 5-foot-11 frame allows White to play inside with little problem and her ability to shoot the 15-foot jumper causes opponents problems on the perimeter. Her passing skills have continued to improve since high school, finding the open player quicker than the speed of light.

White Mania

During her high school days at Seeger, White regularly played in front of sellout crowds. No matter what the distance or the time involved, fans from West Lebanon, Pine Village and Willamsport flocked to catch a glimpse of this talented guard, often compared to Indiana legend Damon Bailey.

White's personality and her character allowed fans to get close to her. She never turned down an autograph, never had a frown on her face and always recognized the faithful fans who followed her career.

She finished her high school career as Indiana's all-time leading scorer with 2,869 points.

"I wanted to go some place where all the Seeger fans could still see me play," White said of her college choice, which was about 45 minutes from her hometown of West Lebanon.

And those fans came to Mackey Arena, as season-ticket and single-game attendance continue to climb. After White's junior season, Purdue was averaging nearly 8,000 fans per game to rank among the top five in the nation.

White was thrust into the starting lineup as a freshman and has never left. The attention and recognition White received in high school, including being selected National Player of the Year by three organizations, unleashed high expectations on the Boilermakers during the 1995-96 season.

They didn't quite live up to those high hopes, failing to win the Big Ten and being eliminated from the NCAA tournament in the first round. But under White's guidance, Purdue is back near the top of the women's college basketball world.

She became Purdue's top 3-point threat. Jacoby was deadly from behind the 3-point line. Three times in her career, Jacoby connected on six 3-point field goals in a single game. Until the 1997-98 season, Jacoby held the single-season record with 54 3-pointers. She totaled 157 in her career, still a Purdue record.

By the time Jacoby left, it was time for another fan favorite to enter Mackey Arena.

Although the interest in Jacoby and the Boilermakers reached an all-time high, it grew to bigger proportions when White put on a Purdue uniform.

PURDUE WOMEN'S COACHING LEGENDS

By Mike Carmin

The cornerstone of any basketball program is its coaches.

They are the leaders, the mentors and the personalities that fans and players connect with. The Purdue women's basketball program is no exception.

Six head coaches have guided the Boilermakers since the program began in 1975. Deb Gebhardt coached the opening season, leading Purdue to an 8-8 record. Dr. Ruth Jones followed for 10 seasons, winning 101 games.

Marsha Reall was hired after Jones died of cancer following the 1985-86 season. Reall stayed one season, putting together a 10-8 record before resigning.

Purdue, though, has enjoyed all of its success since the 1987-88 season. Under Lin Dunn, Nell Fortner and Carolyn Peck, the Boilermakers have amassed a 246-89 record and collected 20 or more victories nine times through the 1997-98 season.

Purdue has won four Big Ten Conference regular season championships, one league tournament title and missed the NCAA tournament only one time during that stretch. The crowning achievement for the program came during the 1993-94 season when the Boilermakers advanced to the Final Four.

LIN DUNN

Dunn came to Purdue from Miami, Florida, where she left as the Hurricanes' winningest women's basketball coach. Dunn's coaching career started in 1970 at Austin Peay State. She also spent one season at Mississippi before heading to Miami.

Dunn felt the potential for success was apparent at Purdue.

"What we had to do was recruit outstanding student-athletes and put in a system that would complement those players and give us the opportunity to be successful," said Dunn, a native of Nashville, Tenn.

Dunn became the program's all-time winningest coach January 5, 1992 with her 102nd victory, passing Jones' total of 101 with a 73-52 victory over Louisville at Mackey Arena.

The 1993-94 season was a special one for Purdue fans.

The Boilermakers didn't have any seniors on their 11-player roster. A Big Ten title and a bid for a national championship seemed to be a year away. But they weren't.

Dunn piloted Purdue to a 20-win season, a conference championship and its first appearance in the Final Four. The Boilermakers were picked fifth in the Big Ten preseason coaches' poll, but finished tied for the top spot with Penn State.

Included in that season was a victory over the No. 1 team in the country. Before an enthusiastic crowd of 9,602 at Mackey Arena, Purdue knocked off the top-ranked Nittany Lions 57-54.

The Boilermakers' trek to the Final Four started with a rout of Radford in the first round and an easy second-round victory over Washington. Purdue, the top seed in the West Regional, beat

Carolyn Peck will leave Purdue for the WNBA after the 1998-99 college season.

Fortner came to West Lafayette following a one-year stint as an assistant coach for the 1995-96 USA National Team. She also was a member of the coaching staff for the 1996 Olympic team, which cruised to the gold medal in Atlanta.

Prior to joining the USA National Team, Fortner was an assistant coach at Louisiana Tech, one of the nation's top women's basketball programs under Leon Barmore. The Lady Techsters compiled a 123-37 record and advanced to the 1994 Final Four during Fortner's stay as an assistant.

Fortner served as an assistant at Stephen F. Austin before arriving at Louisiana Tech. After graduating from the University of Texas, where she was a four-year letterwinner in basketball and volleyball, Fortner was the head girls' basketball coach at Killeen (Texas) High School.

Texas A&M in the semifinals and faced Stanford in the regional final.

The obstacle for the Boilermakers was they were facing the Cardinal on its home floor. Two-time national champion Stanford entered the game 10-0 all-time at home during the NCAA tournament and winners of 108 of its last 111 games.

But Purdue gave the Cardinal an 82-65 loss, its worst home setback since the 1986-87 season. The Boilermakers lost to North Carolina in the national semifinals in Richmond, Virginia.

"I'm just going to cherish this moment with this team and be excited about what we accomplished," Dunn said. "It's just a wonderful feeling."

The next season, the Boilermakers advanced to the Elite Eight, losing to Stanford in the finals of the West Regional. In Dunn's last season, Purdue finished 20-11 and was ousted from the NCAA tournament in the first round by Notre Dame.

One week after that loss, Dunn's contract was not renewed. Dunn's nine-year record at Purdue was 206-68, including a 120-38 mark in Big Ten competition.

Dunn's dismissal had lasting effects on the program. Angry and hurt over her departure, four players transferred, leaving the 1996-97 team depleted of depth and talent, but not heart.

NELL FORTNER

Purdue hired Nell Fortner to take over the program April 25, 1996.

Lin Dunn won 206 games in 9 years at Purdue.

Lin Dunn led Purdue to three Big Ten titles and a Final Four appearance.

The season started with only three players having college playing experience. Jannon Roland, Stephanie White and Ukari Figgs remained after the fallout, giving Fortner and the Boilermakers a solid base.

Fortner's biggest obstacle was to find a way to intertwine the talents of Roland, White and Figgs with the freshman and newcomers. To give Purdue a sense of a bench, Fortner added four walk-ons to the team.

The program received a huge boost when Corissa Yasen joined the team before the season.

Yasen had one year of eligibility after completing a stellar track and field career with the Boilermakers. She was a standout basketball player at Coeur d'Alene (Idaho) High School, leading her team to back-to-back state championships her junior and senior seasons.

Yasen, who went on to play in the WNBA professional league after graduation, gave the Boilermakers some much-needed athletic ability.

Fortner was able to mold the specialties of Roland, White, Figgs and Yasen together with freshmen Mackenzie Curless, Michelle Duhart and Tiffany Young to create a magical season.

Purdue was picked eighth in the preseason Big Ten coaches poll, but finished in a three-way tie for first place along with Illinois and Michigan State.

The Boilermakers earned a share of the championship with a thrilling 80-75 victory at Illinois before a sellout crowd of 16,050 at Assembly Hall on Feb. 23, 1997. At the time, it was the largest crowd ever to see a Big Ten women's basketball game.

Purdue received an at-large bid to the NCAA tournament before losing in the second round to eventual national runner-up Old Dominion.

A lot of Purdue's success during the 1996-97 season can be directly related to Fortner's personality. Her infectious smile and her enthusiasm trickled down through the entire program.

"Life is good, and I love it," Fortner said. "When I wake up in the morning, I'm ready to roll. I love my job, and I really can't wait to get to work everyday. Ninety percent of the time this job is fun. Even the difficult parts are fun because I enjoy challenges."

Fortner's stay with the Boilermakers was short.

She was selected by USA Basketball to coach the 2000 U.S. Olympic Team, opting to leave Purdue after one season. Fortner's replacement came quickly as Purdue athletic director Morgan Burke picked her top assistant, Carolyn Peck, to take over the program.

PECK ARRIVES

Peck spent four years as an assistant coach, including two seasons at national power Tennessee. At first, Peck was apprehensive about taking the job with no previous head coaching experience.

"It's a dream job but only being an assistant coach for four years, I had some anxiety," Peck said. "I told Nell I didn't think I was ready. She told me I would get ready. Having her confidence told me I could do this."

Nell Fortner left quite a legacy in her one year at Purdue, winning a highly improbable Big Ten tri-championship.

Peck's personality is similar to Fortner's. She projects excitement and her smile makes even the most awkward person feel at home. Despite her imposing 6-foot-4 frame, Peck never looks down on anyone. She's cordial, gracious, good-natured and sociable.

Peck inherited a team with no seniors, but plenty of talent.

Big victories over national contenders Stanford, Florida, Arizona, Illinois and Iowa kept the Boilermakers in the spotlight. Although Purdue didn't win the Big Ten regular season, the Boilermakers won the league's post-season tournament with victories over Indiana, Iowa and Penn State.

Purdue advanced to the Elite Eight, losing to Louisiana Tech in the regional finals in Lubbock, Texas.

"To get to the Elite Eight gives this program the type of recognition it had when it went to the Final Four," Peck said. "This is a national contending team. Players want to come to a place where they know they can win."